It Ends Here

Missouri's Last Vigilante

Joe Johnston

T0345235

Missouri History Museum Press

St. Louis

Distributed by University of Chicago Press

On the cover: *The Fatal Fight*. Police officer Joe Burnett in a life-or-death struggle with vigilante Edward O'Kelley.

Unless otherwise noted, the photos in this book are from the author's private collection, and the maps were created by the author.

© 2015 by the Missouri History Museum Press
All rights reserved 19 18 17 16 15 • 1 2 3 4 5
ISBN 978-1-883982-85-0

Library of Congress Cataloging-in-Publication Data is on file with the Library of Congress.

Cover art by Joe Johnston
Distributed by University of Chicago Press
Printed and bound in the United States by Thomson-Shore, Inc.

Contents

Dedicated to the Red Galvins of the world, true journalists, including the 11-Js of Will Rogers High School: our mentor Jan Kizziar, Jan Davies, Steve Hickerson, Don Orchard, Ron Crow, Tom McDonald, Laurel Kelsey, Marsha Slagle, Patty Tingley, Melissa Miller, Karen Karstetter, Laura Pitcock, Dotty Merrill, Judy Carnes, Nita Forrest, Anna Butler, Susie Snyder, Gayle Jacobs, Anne Kilgrew, Phillis Bennett, Susan Talley, Tom Zongker, Pat Barnes, Pam Chibitty, Phil Martin, Diane Maxwell, and Merrily West.

Chapter One
Red and Laura

"There's nothing like getting out of town," James P. "Red" Galvin whispered, watching the world pass by his window.

The train's clatter and sway, the passing fields and farms, and the mix of people in the other seats, traveling to who-knows-where, were a balm to an adventurous newspaper reporter who'd been covering too much big-city politics. Out here, at a steady twenty miles per hour, Red could watch the ever-changing Missouri River, now as wide as the sky, slipping among trees along sandy banks, then narrow and thrashing under sandstone bluffs. And all around, his beloved Missouri, where emerald woods of ash, hickory, and maple danced in ribbons and blankets over a million grassy hills.

Behind were the brick walls of St. Louis, and ahead, the grayest stone walls of all, the Missouri State Penitentiary, dubbed "the Walls." There he would meet Laura Bullion, a member of the Wild West's most infamous band of outlaws, the Wild Bunch. That loose group, led by Butch Cassidy and the Sundance Kid, was collectively to blame for a string of bank robberies, train holdups, and killings that started almost fifteen years earlier, before 1890.

Odd, Red mused, to love this open country so much, and yet his entire career was built in the city, founded on getting along with people, pushing through crowds to win the confidence of this individual

Red Galvin watched the wide Missouri River roll past the windows of the train on his way to meet Laura Bullion. The trip made him one of the few reporters to ever interview a member of the Wild Bunch. Courtesy of Ginger Collins-Justus.

or that one, all to mine the gold of some story buried deep in society's most secret corners. "Not bad for a kid who quit school," Red thought to himself, stretching his feet out to the seat across from him.

As an orphan newsboy he sold newspapers for ten years, learned to be a bootblack, and set up his shoeshine box outside the newspaper offices. One day the *Republic*. Next day the *Post-Dispatch*. Then the *Globe-Democrat*, with its eight-story brick building known as the "Temple of Truth." He worked in the mailrooms and circulation departments of any paper that would hire him. He chatted incessantly with the reporters, found out what they were interested in, and listened to them tell how they got their information. Then from people he met on the street he got his own inside scoops on politics, crime, and even society gossip. He'd pass along the right tip to the right reporter, saving the best tips to whisper to the editors while he polished their two-dollar shoes. Six bits here, a dollar there, and pretty soon he made more on his reporting than his shoe shining. Red became a guerrilla journalist as a teen in the 1880s, at about the age Jesse James became a Civil War guerrilla in the 1860s.

Red heard all about James and men like him while he was growing up in St. Louis. All the new novels romanced the violence with fiction. "Heck, that's current events in Missouri," he laughed. Missouri was a slave state, embroiled in political wrangling and bloody wars along the Kansas border. Then during the war it was an occupied state washed blood-red with guerrilla vengeance. Later, populated with a mix of winners and losers, Yankee veterans and disenfranchised former Confederates, it was common for people to take the law into their own hands. And that mentality still persisted.

Red marveled at the bravery of men who dared to chase and confront dangerous criminals, just like he was sickened by the long series of reprisals that vigilantes always seemed to spawn. Violence only begat violence. Is violence sometimes the only path? he wondered. What are good people to do?

In 1881, after he shined a pair of shoes for a businessman who talked about the Meyers Gang of New Madrid, Missouri, the fourteen-year-old Red started digging for more. He went to the St. Louis library and pored through newspapers. He'd find a fact here, an omission there. He sneaked a pair of scissors into the library and started clipping articles, making notes, and gradually piecing together the story.

Jesse Meyers and five of his inept friends met a slick-talking farmer named Willis Knox at a county fair in New Madrid, made a deal for some livestock, and gave Knox a cash down payment. After weeks went by and Knox didn't deliver the livestock as promised, Meyers gathered the other five suckers. With the help of their own corn liquor they decided they had to not only get their money back, but kill Knox too. Unfortunately for all concerned, they knew only generally where Knox lived. So when they mounted up, armed with every loaded weapon they could lay their hands on, they went to the wrong farm, where Meyers shot Knox's neighbor, George Williams, in the leg. When the first shot didn't kill him, Meyers shot again, missed completely, and wounded a nine-year-old girl playing in the yard. Meyers informed his men, who by that time considered themselves to be the Meyers Gang, that they had to run and they needed cash fast. So they killed and robbed Robert LaForge, a local college student whom the newspaper described as "the perfect picture of young manhood."

The posse that gave chase was half lawmen and half civilians. They cornered the gang at their camp in a swamp, which offered no cover except tree trunks and fallen limbs. In the shootout that followed, one man on each side was killed. The gang then ran to Wayne County and got cornered again in Well Hollow, a gully with steep hills on two sides and an impossible hill on the third. One more of them was killed, one was wounded, and the last three surrendered. The New Madrid County sheriff locked them up, and that night a vigilante lynch mob of three hundred gathered outside the jail. The terrified sheriff knew he couldn't hold them long enough to get to trial, so he wired the governor for help, and the governor promptly answered by sending a steamboat from St. Louis. At dawn the next morning it took the prisoners to the St. Louis jail, and after three weeks they were returned on the same boat and marched straight to the New Madrid courthouse to face attempted murder charges. It was no coincidence that the prosecuting attorney was Charles A. LaForge, cousin of the murdered Robert La-Forge. The jury debated only long enough to smoke a cigarette—they found Meyers and the other two surviving members of the gang guilty. On June 15 the convicts were hanged in full view of an appreciative crowd. It took one month from the livestock deal to the end of the end, and the justice was all home grown.

When Red was satisfied that he had the facts all organized into notes that made sense, he turned them over to Frank O'Neil, who gave him a crisp and colorful one-dollar bill. O'Neil was the premier reporter in St. Louis, and the first to see the potential in Red. He loved the grit of Red's streetwise vernacular, picked up by hanging around the cops, the men they pursued, and the women who loved them, all giving his language vibrant color and a wry smirk that the more polished writers didn't possess.

When Frank began to adopt Red's style, his editor at the *Post-Dispatch*, George Sibley Johns, noticed right away. Johns had grown up in an educated, influential St. Louis family and graduated from Princeton, but he was a self-made journalist. He and his brother started a little community newspaper in their hometown of St. Charles, then sold it. George, sporting a handlebar mustache, freelanced for various papers, fearlessly and tirelessly tracking his stories. In time he joined the *Post-Dispatch* and worked as a crime reporter, special writer, society columnist, arts reviewer, city editor, and managing editor before ascending to the editor's desk. He knew reporters, and he knew style.

"Frank, I love what you've been writing lately." Johns asked through his soaking-wet cigar: "What's happening to your style?" O'Neil had just turned in his Meyers Gang story based on Red's compilation. And when he told Johns about the eager young redhead, the editor's eyes brightened.

During his days as a newspaper co-owner with his brother, as a freelance writer, and as an energetic staff reporter for the Post-Dispatch, *George Johns sported a handlebar mustache. Though he and Red Galvin came from very different backgrounds, as reporters they were cut from the same cloth.*

"It's hard working with him," O'Neil said. "The guy has no education. He really can't string two sentences together, but he gives me the facts, and I make it a story."

"Well, bring him along. If he's good enough to influence you, he might end up being better than you!" Johns joked.

"Already on it, chief," O'Neil retorted. "I gave him a grammar text, and he was so excited he went and picked up a composition book and started filling it up. I've never seen such a newshound. He'll do whatever it takes to be a reporter."

It was in early 1893 that Red, then twenty-seven years old and armed with years of study and filling up composition books, saw a chance to make his mark. A train headed east into St. Louis was held up at Pacific, Missouri. On board was Governor William J. Stone, the state treasurer, and other officials, and they all told the police they'd been robbed by a gang of seven men. All the papers ran the story, and police and sheriffs in surrounding counties were looking for a big gang that could pull off such a job. Missouri hadn't seen such a thing since Jesse James died in 1882, and there was talk that the Wild Bunch, who'd been staging such daring robberies in Utah and Montana, had moved into Missouri.

While the "real" reporters sat in saloons sipping glasses of beer, checking in periodically at the police station, Red left that very day with detectives who took two handcars down the track to look for clues. It was a hot July day, and Red was happy to take his turn at the back-breaking hand pump, just to be there when the story broke. It paid off when they got a little past Pacific and a detective spotted something partly buried near a telegraph pole. Sticking out of the dirt was the handle of a valise, and inside were some clothes, along with an envelope and other notes that all had the name Sam Wilson written on them. Red said, "I know a Sam Wilson . . . young fellow . . . a railroad telegraph operator."

The detectives all looked at Red, and he asked, "What?" They just couldn't believe that he would know an underworld figure that they didn't know. The group pumped their handcars back to St. Louis as fast as they could go. Checking railroad records, the detectives found that Wilson had indeed been a telegraph operator until about a month before. He was from Lebanon, Missouri, and when police alerted the local sheriff, Jasper Jones, he found Wilson at home with his father. Again, while St. Louis detectives and other reporters waited for Sheriff Jones to bring the prisoner to them, Red hopped on a train to Lebanon so he could ride back with the sheriff and the suspect.

Mile after mile clacked away, and the sheriff sat like a rock, his left wrist cuffed to Wilson. Red shook his head. Hard to believe that young man led a train-robbing gang of seven. At twenty, he was much younger than his years, smiling during a train ride that was sure to end in a long jail sentence. He still had plenty of freckles on his face and a shock of yellow hair sticking out from under a skimmer that he bought while he was working the railroad telegraph in St. Louis. Red couldn't help thinking how the citified hat looked out of place with Wilson's plaid shirt, suspenders, and baggy wool pants.

But Red kept his attention on the sheriff. The badge on his coat was the old-style star. He dressed neatly, with a silver watch chain stretched across his vest, and the holster on his hip held a short-barrel Colt .45 Peacemaker. He said not a word, even though Red chatted and asked questions the entire way. Finally, when Red got around to the topic of fried chicken, Jones couldn't resist telling him about his mother's cooking. The quiet lawman opened up like an old book that had never been read. He told about how he'd solved this case and that, about the evil men he'd faced, and about the fishing in Laclede County. By the time they approached the outskirts of St. Louis, Red had sprung a trap that would benefit both of them. "You know, Sheriff, when you get off downtown at Union Station there's going to be a company of railroad detectives, about a hundred cops, and two hundred reporters, not to mention all the thousands of people who've been following this case in the papers."

The lawman's eyes grew wide. The idea of facing that crowd was more terrifying to a small-town country sheriff than any outlaw's gun he'd ever faced. "I've got an idea," Red said.

It was about three in the afternoon when, instead of going all the way to Union Station, the reporter, the sheriff, and the prisoner got off at the Clayton stop and Red rented a rig, then drove them to downtown St. Louis. Editor Johns almost dropped his cigar when they walked into the *Post-Dispatch* building and straight to Johns's office. Johns shook hands and quickly recovered his senses enough to pour glasses of whiskey all around. Red's guests were so impressed with the big-city offices and the editor's hospitality that they didn't have a chance to realize they'd been kidnapped by a man who didn't have a job but wanted to be a reporter.

Wilson still smiled, happy to tell the story of how he pulled off the robbery, while Red typed and the sheriff listened with a judgmental raised eyebrow. With no one to help him, Wilson said he spent the entire day of the holdup dragging heavy timbers onto the tracks to block the train. When the train had to stop, the engineer and fireman looked around for robbers, but they didn't see Wilson quietly slip on board behind the coal tender with his valise. "I climbed up over the coal car with a scarf covering my face, and fired one shot from my pistol," Wilson told Red. "They froze like statues, and I instructed them not to turn around. I said I had six men with me, and we would only be a minute."

Leaving them thinking there was a pistol pointed at their backs, Wilson moved to the first passenger car, pointing his pistols at the passengers. "I told them my gang of six had control of the train and they better hand over the loot," Wilson recalled. "Of course they did. Then I did the same in the other car."

Red shook his head. "Ingenious," he said, encouraging Wilson to keep talking. The sheriff rolled his eyes. "What if somebody pulled out a Colt .45 and started plugging away at you?" Red asked.

"Hooo boy, I was hoping they wouldn't," Wilson said, his eyes growing wide. "You know what I was packing? Two little old H&R .22's. They weren't much."

Red looked at the sheriff, who shook his head.

"I didn't mess with the express car. Don't want the Pinkertons after me! It was quick, just the passengers." Wilson was enjoying his audience. "Then I went back up front, warned the engineer to be still again, and then I changed my coat and hat and covered my nose and mouth with a different scarf, and went through both cars again!" Wilson sat back proudly. "They all thought a big gang did the job."

"Indeed they did," Red complimented him. Wilson went on to say he targeted that train because he handled the telegrams saying the governor and other officials would be on it, and he knew they would have a lot of money on them.

"You know," Red prodded Wilson, "they were all looking for a gang. If you hadn't left that bag sticking out of the dirt they might never have caught you."

"Yes, well, it was dark and I was tired," Wilson said wistfully. "Maybe I should have had six more men to help me." They both laughed. That's what crooks liked about Red. He saw the world from their side when nobody else did.

Red typed as long as Wilson talked, and by that time Sheriff Jones had migrated to Johns's office to talk about beer and St. Louis Cardinals baseball. Red interrupted them long enough for Jones to tell his version of locating Wilson's father and coming face to face with the son to make the arrest, making it all sound far more heroic than it really was.

Red, Wilson, and Jones exited into the St. Louis night and climbed into the rented rig. Red drove them straight to the police station, where they surprised the desk sergeant. "I think somebody here is looking for these two," Red joked. They had avoided the crowds at Union Station, which pleased the sheriff, and avoided the other reporters, which tickled Red. Back at the office, Johns picked up Red's story and leaned back in his chair. "Ha!" He exclaimed to the empty room. "We're the only ones with the story for tomorrow's edition. Hell, the other papers are just finding out that Wilson's in town! Only Red could have pulled that off."

Red's news sources ranged from the saloons of skid row to corporate boardrooms in the business cathedrals of Main Street, and from the shops of riverfront craftsmen to the halls of government. Both sides of the law taught him how to be a detective. Listening to sneak thieves and con men talk about their business, he learned how they made a dirty dollar—and about their unending desperation and eternal optimism. From beat cops, detectives, and judges, he heard about frustration and meticulous investigation, as well as how to ask questions and how to figure the angles. And he learned what it's like for cops to start the day by kissing a wife and children, then going out where uncaring death might wait around the next corner.

Confidence was sacred to Red. He never betrayed a secret nor turned in a story until his sources agreed that it was time to print it. People knew they could trust him. But they also knew he would work like a beaver, gnawing away to get at the truth. That approach might seem like a recipe to let other reporters get the blockbuster headlines first, but on the contrary, it put Red on the front page consistently.

◆——◆——◆

The rise to power of future governor Joseph W. Folk was owed to the same man with the same formula, a young reporter with an accurate and lively news sense. It was a time of widespread epidemic corruption in St. Louis government. Every man who came into government got the carrot and the stick, the bribe and the threat. People from file clerks to councilmen had an opportunity to join in with the schemes, so of course few of them were willing to pass up a share of the ill-gotten wealth. And they all knew there was so much money at stake, men would kill to keep the system working. Even if a person refused to participate, revealing what he knew might have meant his life or the life of a wife or child.

A group of conspirators known as the Combine had developed a system among contractors, banks, loan companies, and real-estate firms. Time after time the Combine made deals with various officials in city and county government who received a payoff for awarding projects or overlooking violations of ordinances. It was usually a building permit, a tax advantage, or a contract awarded, matters of commerce that most people wouldn't notice. After all, working men didn't care which rich man got richer, as long as the working men kept working.

The company or individual who benefited had to make a cash deposit in a specific safe deposit vault. The Combine created a system of duplicate keys, which assured everyone involved that the money was indeed in a certain vault, and when the favor was granted, the money was released to the right government officials with the right keys.

The depth and breadth of the scandal meant no one would talk, until "Holy Joe" Folk, the St. Louis County district attorney, met Red Galvin, the self-taught freelance writer, and they somehow knew instinctively that they could trust each other. In January 1902, Red caught wind that there were some government officials who'd delivered favors, but their payoff had not been released. They were very unhappy. The knot in the criminals' fabric might have been worked out in time, and nobody would have known there was ever any trouble. The crooks and the crooked politicians might have gone on doing business as usual. But Red smelled a chance to bust it up, and he went to Folk, the one man he was sure was clean. It was brave beyond measure, because if Folk had turned out to be as dirty as the rest, Red could have become food for the Mississippi River catfish, and he would hardly have been missed.

Folk was exactly the man Red thought he was, and meeting late at night in a little café in Creve Coeur, they pieced together what had happened with an application for a streetcar line extension. The Combine usually set up its arrangements through "Colonel" Ed Butler, a deal-making political boss. But Red's connections told him the streetcar extension deal was worked through a different man, Phillip Stock, a lobbyist and secretary of the St. Louis Brewing Association. The Municipal Assembly approved the streetcar line extension, but it was later struck down by a court because the project was not let out for bids, as required by city law. Of course the Combine never intended for it to be let out for bids. The problem was that Stock had paid off the assemblymen, never expecting the extension to be contested in court, and judges were out of his reach. The deal was ruined, and that's why the money wasn't being paid out.

Folk called lobbyist Stock and the president of the streetcar line to the empty grand jury room, and in a meeting with just the three of them, told them how the cow ate the cabbage. He knew what happened, and the story was going to run in the *Post-Dispatch*. He told them to report back to that very room when the grand jury convened in three days, and tell everything they knew. At the same time, Red worked with Folk to develop an embellished, yet vague, story, complete with quotes from Folk saying he already knew who was in the mess, and that he intended to clean it up. The public figures who confessed would be treated gently, and the ones who tried to hide would be treated like common criminals. Editor Johns printed copies of the news story as an "advance," distributed them throughout St. Louis government, and the floodgates opened. Key players in the Combine were as eager as the dirty politicians to spill the beans. Nobody wanted to be left out of Prosecutor Folk's good graces when the walls came tumbling down.

Folk followed through as promised. He helped those who helped him, and as for the others, plenty of politicians, public servants, loan sharks, bank officers, and clerks went to jail, along with the criminals, contractors, thugs, and con men. Red had dangled the bait, and Folk brought indictments that toppled an entire era of abuse by public officeholders. The campaign even solidified George Johns's reputation as a fighting editor who wouldn't stand for corruption.

Through the train car window, Red watched a steamer slosh through the Missouri River's waves and remembered the conversation a couple of days earlier, when Johns summoned him to his office. "Red," he'd said, "if you've had enough of politicians' cigar smoke for a while, I have a criminal for you to interview."

Red raised an eyebrow. "Criminals don't always like to be interviewed," he cracked, "except to repeat how innocent they are."

"I think this one will confess to both guilt and innocence," Johns said.

"Now that's intriguing," said the reporter. "Who is he and where do I find him?"

"He is a she," replied Johns. "And she'll be easy to find. She'll be at the Walls for at least a few more months. She may not be the most dangerous of the Wild Bunch, but she may be the prettiest: Laura Bullion, the Desert Rose."

So there was Red, on his way to interview Laura Bullion. Red did his research, looking back through arrest records, court documents, and newspaper archives, and talking to his friends on the police force. He knew Laura was also known as Clare Hayes, Clara Hayes, Laura Casey, Louisa Coxey, Clara Casey, Nellie Rose, Della Rose, Desert Rose, Thorny Rose, and Wild Bunch Rose. She'd been arrested in the lobby

"The Walls," aka the Missouri State Penitentiary.

of the Laclede Hotel at Broadway and Chestnut Street in St. Louis. The police found that she had once been a small-town Texas prostitute, but she had come to really enjoy first-class hotels like the Laclede.

The police found her because they arrested her boyfriend Ben "the Tall Texan" Kilpatrick, a quiet man who stood six feet, two inches, at a rooming house downtown. Kilpatrick had gone to a pawnshop owned by Max Barnett and bought a beautiful $75 watch, paying with four $20 banknotes. Later Barnett walked down the street to Merchants Commerce Bank to make a deposit, which included the twenties. He was greeted by his favorite teller, Victor Jaquemin. Banknotes were federal currency issued to a specific bank and had to be activated with the signature of an officer of that bank. The $20 notes Barnett gave Jaquemin were part of the take in one of the West's most sensational robberies, when the Wild Bunch held up the Great Northern Express on July 3, 1901, near Wagner, Montana. They got over $80,000, most of it in unsigned banknotes bound for the Montana National Bank at Helena.

Ben Kilpatrick, sporting his mustache. Library of Congress Prints and Photographs.

Laura Bullion is shown in front and side views of her Bertillon photos. Library of Congress Prints and Photographs.

The Pinkerton Detective Agency had been hired by the railroad to work on the case, and they sent alerts to every bank in the country warning them to be on the lookout for anyone forging signatures and trying to pass the banknotes. Teller Jaquemin was a studious sort who took the alerts very seriously, and the feminine handwriting on the notes, which had been signed by Laura Bullion, just didn't look right to him.

Jaquemin was no vigilante, but in his own modest way he knew how to become a hero with his picture in the paper. He took the notes to his boss, who showed them to the police, who then had their hands full locating Kilpatrick. He had been in town for a few nights, and people in the saloons had noticed him. He was hard to miss, a tall, handsome, well-dressed stranger spending lots of money. But that man was blond. People told Kilpatrick the cops were asking about him, so he decided it was time to disappear: He dyed his hair and mustache black. So by the time detectives were after him, they believed they were looking for two different men, the blond throwing his money around, and the brunet who bought the watch at the pawnshop with stolen banknotes from the train robbery. They were pretty sure the blond one was Wild Bunch leader Butch Cassidy, and the dark-haired one was Harry Longbaugh, known as the Sundance Kid.

After four days of searching, detectives found the one with the black hair, looking sharp in a neatly pressed gray suit with a colorful striped necktie, and followed him to his rooms at a boardinghouse. The next night, November 6, 1901, two of them, Alphonse Guion and John Shevlin, acted like they were happy drunks, stumbling in the front door of the rooming house, and then right behind Kilpatrick into his rooms. The Tall Texan was surprised to see them in his living room, but glad to help a couple of boys who'd had so much to drink that they didn't know where they were. Guion grabbed Kilpatrick's right arm, making him laugh, but then Shevlin grabbed his left, and they suddenly grabbed both his hip gun and his shoulder gun from their holsters. At that instant, their fellow officers—James Burke, George Williams, William P. Brady, and John McGrath—rushed in and got him in cuffs. A search of the rooms turned up a stash of the stolen banknotes, both signed and unsigned.

In his pocket they found a hotel key, but the tag with the hotel's name and the room number had been torn off. It took a canvass of the area's hotels to track it to the Laclede Hotel, and then an inventory of the Laclede keys to figure out that they had the key to room 100, where Laura was registered as Mrs. John Albert. That just happened to be the day she was to check out and meet Ben downstairs to leave St. Louis, so when they went to her room they found it empty. At the very moment they were riding one elevator up, she was riding the other one down. Catching her at the desk, the cops discovered thousands of dollars' worth of the blank banknotes in her bags, and all she could say was, "I ain't done nothing."

Of course every cop in St. Louis wanted credit for arresting one of the notorious Wild Bunch, and that started a flurry of protests and accusations over who did what. Detectives Williams and McGrath protested to the chief of police Mathew Kiely that detective Guion had been featured in a *Republic* story, describing how he personally managed the arrest. He talked about the suspect as "my man," and Guion was even hailed in the *Republic* by the assistant chief of detectives, Major E. J. Lally. Six patrolmen were at the arrest, with six different versions of how the investigation and arrests happened, and they all wanted to be known for bringing down one of the Wild Bunch and the woman, whoever she was. They also each hoped for the railroad's reward money. When the controversy boiled over into the press, Kiely called

Ben "the Tall Texan" Kilpatrick is front and center in this classic Wild Bunch photo. Left front is Harry Longbaugh, the Sundance Kid, and right front is Butch Cassidy. Left rear is Laura's first boyfriend, Will Carver. Right rear is the diminutive Harvey "Kid Curry" Logan.

all six men into his office and berated them for their childish behavior. But their point had been made, and from that time forward, every news story about the case mentioned all six men, and they all received silver medals from the department.

So whom did they have in custody? The Pinkertons were sure the train robbery was a Wild Bunch job. Nobody else in the West could have pulled off such a big job with such bravado. But the Wild Bunch had been known to include a kaleidoscope of characters, and that sent the St. Louis police and Pinkertons into a whirlwind of confusion about who was in jail. As the days passed, Laura revealed nothing about the case, giving different versions of her own name and refusing to tell Kilpatrick's name. As far as she was concerned, he was Mr. Rose, adding demurely, "I knew he had money 'cause I seen it. I don't know if he was crooked, but he was always good to me." Once she understood that the lawmen honestly didn't know who they were, she had some fun with the detectives, mentioning that she once found a dictionary in his pocket, and written inside was, "Harry Longbaugh, Helena, Mont."

Through repeated interrogation, which the police called "sweating," Kilpatrick was coolly polite, but stoic. Chief of Detectives William Desmond asked him if he'd been in Montana.

"No."

"Where were you before you came to St. Louis?"

"I came from Memphis."

"Where were you on July 3?"

No answer.

"Where were you on July 4?"

No answer.

He wouldn't give his name or anything else. The more the police looked at photos of the Wild Bunch, the more convinced they became that Kilpatrick was Harry Longbaugh. But Longbaugh also looked a lot like fellow Wild Buncher Harvey Logan, known as Kid Curry. Every newspaper in the country fanned the excitement, which had after all been started by the police themselves, saying they had arrested one of the big names in the Wild Bunch, and then calling him Harry, Harvey, and Henry, and giving his last name as Logan or Longbaugh, which they sometimes pronounced with an *a* in the middle, "Longabaugh." And all of that was because in pictures of the outlaw gang, the sandy-haired Kilpatrick had always been clean shaven. Longbaugh and Logan both had black hair and mustaches. So when Kilpatrick was arrested with black hair, lawmen were sure they had Longbaugh or Logan. Of course, the Tall Texan was the tallest in the Wild Bunch, so the police ruled out a couple of the shorter members of the gang. But nobody had figured out the hair dye; did Kilpatrick newly dye his hair, or had one of the others always dyed it? And the whole time, rumors persisted that the blond man who'd been seen was not Kilpatrick, but Butch Cassidy. That led to rumors that Cassidy was still in town, which led to more rumors, newspaper stories, and police worries, that he and the rest of the gang were planning to bust the unidentified Kilpatrick out of jail.

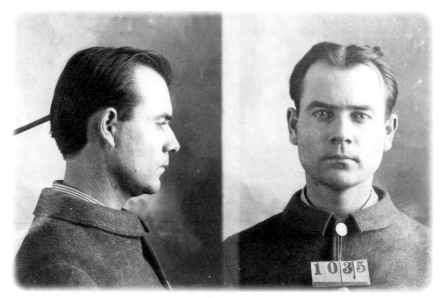

Ben Kilpatrick is shown in his Bertillon photos—clean shaven—following his arrest in St. Louis. Library of Congress Prints and Photographs.

But the Pinkertons had long known the benefit of compiling files of notes, photographs, and legal documents about people, sometimes not even sure of who they were or how they might be connected to their cases. Laura, who still hadn't given her name, was one of those. The agency had been building files on every possible member of the Wild Bunch because they were identified or suspected in a five-year string of train robberies across five states. Agents knew from photos that Laura wasn't Longbaugh's girlfriend, Etta Place; and not Della Moore, Logan's girl; and probably not Josie Bassett, who had consorted with the gang for years but rarely left her giant cattle ranching and rustling operation. No, the Pinkertons were pretty sure the woman in custody was "the other woman" they knew little about, except that her name was Laura. In their files was the name of George Postel, a former San Antonio storekeeper who knew Laura there. But George had since sold his store and moved, so the Pinkertons had to track him from Texas to Mascoutah, Illinois, before they could bring him to St. Louis. It was a lot of work and an amazing bit of investigation, and it resulted in Postel identifying Laura.

One person who was tiring of the cops' inability to figure out the identity of Laura's boyfriend was St. Louis police chief Kiely, who was a pioneer of forensic evidence. He studied science of all kinds, always looking for how it might help the police. When he was assistant chief, he brought to St. Louis the Bertillon system, a new method of prisoner identification developed in France. At the time, it was a rare, progressive police department that took a photo of every prisoner, and Kiely saw the wisdom in Bertillon's requirement of photographing both a front and side view. The prisoner also had to undergo a series of aggravating measurements like the length of his or her arm, foot, and head. A detective counted teeth and noted every little scar, mole, and birthmark. It worked miracles for police all over the world until the advent of fingerprint science in 1903. Thanks to Kiely, St. Louis police were using the Bertillon system when they had Laura and Kilpatrick in custody.

Right: Police and Pinkertons looked at this photo of the Wild Bunch's Harry Longbaugh and his girlfriend, Etta Place, and knew that Laura wasn't Etta, but they were convinced Ben was Harry. Below: When St. Louis detectives arrested Ben, they first thought he might be Harvey Logan. But they determined that Logan was too short, and after studying this photo of Logan with his some-times girlfriend, Della Moore, they knew this wasn't the woman they had arrested, who turned out to be Laura. Both images Library of Congress Prints and Photographs.

Laura and Ben were arraigned at the Four Courts in St. Louis, the home of city and county justice. This photograph was taken shortly after it was built in 1871, and by the time Laura and Ben were there, the streets were paved. Stereograph by Boehl and Koenig, 1870s. Courtesy of Missouri Historical Society.

Kiely expressed photographs of Kilpatrick to Chouteau County (Montana) prosecutor Charles Pray, asking if the man in the picture was one of their train robbers and if they wanted him. Then two days later, St. Louis detective chief Desmond walked into the interrogation room with a telegram and laid it on the table in front of Kilpatrick. It said Chouteau County's Sheriff Crawford claimed it was Harry Longbaugh in the photograph, and he would leave for St. Louis "with papers of extradition" so the prisoner could face a Montana trial for train robbery, which carried a death sentence. Desmond hoped that threat might get his prisoner to start talking. What Desmond didn't know was that his prisoner couldn't read, so he didn't know the telegram said the extradition papers were not for him, but for Longbaugh. Ironically, when Kilpatrick didn't say that wasn't his name in the telegram, it made Desmond even surer that Kilpatrick was Longbaugh.

On the Montana train to St. Louis with Sheriff Crawford was D. S. Elliott, general manager of Great Northern, and Michael F. O'Neill and Channing Smith, who had been fireman and express manager on the train that was robbed. Chief Desmond took them to the Four Courts, St. Louis's magnificent hall of justice serving the city and county. It was an imposing building in the Renaissance style, and though it had only three courts, one of the judges who was born in Ireland said it reminded him of the Four Courts in Dublin, and the name stuck.

The basement housed the armory and big rooms for police duty watches and training. There, out of public view, both train crew men immediately identified Kilpatrick as the one who started the holdup. The prisoner just smirked and was led away to his cell. O'Neill and Smith then described to prosecutors how Kilpatrick boarded the engine as it was creeping out of the station at Malta, Montana, surprising the engineer and fireman, and pointing a pair of Colt Peacemakers, one nickel plated, at them. He told them to just do their job until he said to stop, then he sat down in the jump seat and calmly watched the scenery. After about eight miles he told the engineer to stop at a high trestle bridge near Wagner, and when he did, the rest of the outlaws came calmly out from under both sides of the bridge. The engineer and fireman didn't know it, but one of the "men" they saw was Laura Bullion, wearing pants, as she always did. She and one of the others started firing randomly down the sides of the train, pinging bullets off the sides of the cars and rails to make sure everybody stayed inside. The railroad's auditor leaned out a door to scold the gunmen and was shot in the shoulder. One woman looked out a window and was shot in the arm. The brakeman jumped off the train and ran, and was shot in the shoulder. In fact, it was the shooters' dead-eye aim that made sure the passengers had wounds that were painful, but not life-threatening. Two robbers entered the express car and blew the safe open with dynamite, put the contents in bags, and then they all disappeared, sending the train on its way. Yep, O'Neill and Smith agreed, the prisoner they saw was the one who boarded the locomotive.

Once he was identified as the leader of the robbery, authorities still had to decide what to do with him. Back in Montana, a state conviction for train robbery carried the death penalty. But even with two eyewitnesses, getting a conviction was not a sure bet, especially since nobody knew who he was. There was also a great fear that there was no jail out west that could keep the bandit safe from an escape masterminded by the rest of the Wild Bunch. In St. Louis, with its brick jail adjoining the Four Courts, and the swarms of policemen thereabouts, both prisoners were much more likely to stay around long enough for a trial, and there was a strong federal case against both of them; it was illegal to even possess federal banknotes, and Kilpatrick and Laura not only possessed them but also had forged them. Wires were exchanged with the Montana prosecutor, and in the end, everyone agreed to let federal prosecutors bring indictments in St. Louis. The prisoners were kept in St. Louis, where their trial would not be held in Four Courts, but in the federal courthouse.

The day of their arraignment, nobody was going to take a chance on a Wild Bunch jailbreak, so Kilpatrick and Laura were transferred in chains and under heavy guard by six patrolmen, two federal marshals, and the six arresting detectives, each of them making sure none of the others got any more credit than they deserved. Even when Kilpatrick and Laura had to ride one city block in the same patrol wagon from the jail to the federal courthouse, they were never allowed to speak, and they barely caught a glimpse of each other. Crowds lined the streets to get a look at the pair, and the papers reported their every move. While they waited for the judge in his chambers, every clerk, policeman, attorney, and janitor in the courthouse was allowed to walk through to gawk at them.

The grand jury returned a seventeen-count indictment against Kilpatrick under the name of Longbaugh. It was a running bluff on both sides. Everybody knew the law couldn't follow through with the trial until they knew who he was. Some thought he was Longbaugh, some Logan, but nobody thought he was who he really was. Kilpatrick said little. The *Post-Dispatch* called him "the most remarkable prisoner ever in the Four Courts," and said, "He remained a mystery as much as in the past."

Laura Bullion had no money to hire a lawyer, so Thomas P. Bashaw was appointed to represent her. She couldn't have asked for better. He had enlisted in the Confederate army at age seventeen, served in John Hunt Morgan's cavalry, and later became a state legislator, circuit court judge, and district attorney. At the age of fifty-eight he was a well-respected St. Louis attorney. By the time Bashaw met Laura she'd been in custody almost a month and had endured day after day of interrogation. Exhausted at last, and on Bashaw's advice, she admitted her identity, pled guilty to forging the banknotes, and was sentenced to five years.

After entering a plea of innocent, Kilpatrick continued to be sweated every day. Finally he was worn down, and when they took him back to his cell he told the sheriff that if he could have a day to rest, with no court appearance and no sweating, he'd start talking. The sheriff agreed, only if Kilpatrick would admit to his real name. Then he showed him a photograph that arrived that morning. Sheriff James E. Howze, in remote Concho County outside San Angelo, Texas, had telephoned Sheriff Jake Allen in Greene County, Texas, who grew up with Ben Kilpatrick, his parents, and his brothers. The two sheriffs talked about Kilpatrick's picture in the *Globe-Democrat* and agreed it was probably Ben, so Howze telephoned to tell Chief Desmond, while Allen expressed an original family photo of a younger Ben to Desmond. When Desmond showed Kilpatrick the picture from Texas, he admitted he was Kilpatrick, and Desmond gave him a day to rest.

It Ends Here

Only then did the Tall Texan hire an attorney, and he chose Charles P. Johnson, who had defended Frank James, Jesse's brother, in his trial for a murder committed during a train robbery. Johnson was quick to point out to Kilpatrick that he really didn't want to be found innocent. If the federal prosecutor failed to convict him on the seventeen counts of banknote theft, possession, and forgery, he'd be sent back to Montana to face hanging for the train robbery. Kilpatrick wasn't a brilliant man, but even he could see the advantages of a jail term over a hangman's noose. He confessed and was sentenced to fifteen years, and the Montana charges were dropped.

After the sentencing, Elliott, from the Great Northern Railroad, came back with the reward money. He was a sniveling little man who wore a bowler, a suit that was too tight, and spats over shoes with built-up heels. Even so, he was the shortest one wherever he went, and he made up for it with the railroad's money. At the federal courthouse, with reporters gathered around, he presented two-thirds of the reward money to the bank clerk Jaquemin and to Pinkerton agents who had played no significant role in the cases of Laura and Kilpatrick. Then on the steps of the Four Courts, with a grand public display of mock generosity before a large crowd, he gave a third of the remaining third to the police relief fund, leaving each of the six detectives with $222 for arresting Kilpatrick.

Ben Kilpatrick was sentenced to the Ohio Penitentiary, where he served three years. Then because of overcrowding he was sent to the Atlanta pen. That was the era when federal prisons were being established around the country, and everything was changing, especially in the accommodations for female prisoners. Laura was supposed to go to prison in Leavenworth, Kansas, which had only a few dozen beds for women, and they were all full. That's why Laura ended up in the Missouri pen.

And that's how Red Galvin ended up on a train to Jefferson City in the fall of 1903. He checked into a hotel and hired a rig for the four-mile drive out to the prison. After a long wait in a gray room with a simple gray table and two gray chairs, the door opened. A towering black guard came in following the five foot, two inch, Laura. She was slender and graceful, with raven hair and large, dark eyes that seemed to flash from brown to green. Red bowed a little. "Good day, Miss Bullion. I'm James Galvin from the *St. Louis Post-Dispatch*. People call me Red."

Laura smiled sweetly and chewed her gum. She chewed gum constantly, and there was a schoolgirl quality about her until Red got close enough to see the age in her eyes. Red had sat across the table from politicians, attorneys, policemen, Pinkertons, corporate kings, thugs, grifters, con men, gamblers, murderers, and sneak thieves. That day, for the first time, he was charged with exploring the mind and heart of a female criminal.

While they chatted about the weather and the enormous guard who brought her in, Red reached into his leather shoulder bag for a pencil and writing tablet and started writing a combination of words and his own personal shorthand, creating a document that would have been gibberish to anyone else. Once she started talking, she was a chatterbox. Red's immediate impression was that she was eager for attention, a loving person who wanted to be valued. He complemented her on her simple blue gingham dress that buttoned up the front, was tucked at the waist, and had an embroidered collar. He supposed he expected to see her in gray uniform smock of some sort.

"Thank ya," she said, and a smile brought the color to her face. "That's so nice of you to say. I always wore pants 'til I come here, and now I like dresses."

"Well, you look right at home in it," he said sincerely.

"I made this, ya know," Laura said proudly.

He didn't know.

"Yes, and one of the other ladies made the embrawdry," she added, fingering the colorful decoration. "We help each other. Some is good at one thing and some another. I like to make drawn work. You know what that is, sir?"

While in prison Laura honed her skills with drawn work, trading and selling her creations with the other women in the prison.

"No idea."

"It's mostly on hankies and little towels. . . . I takes some threads out around the edges and weaves 'em, and opens it up like lace. It's so pretty. The ladies like for me to make them things for 'em."

"Did you learn that from your mother?" Red wanted to know.

"No, sir. My momma, she died when I was still young. You see, I mostly lived with my grandma. She reared me and kept me in school, and she taught me most about sewing and such.

As Laura began telling Red about her childhood in Texas, he realized that his wasn't very different, orphaned early, growing up with little money. And yet their paths led them to the opposite sides of this table. Though her grammar was rough, she seemed clearheaded, with a resigned understanding of how she got where she was. Her mother, Fereby Byler, married her father, Henry Bullion, a Native American, probably Comanche, who was a petty criminal, always drunk, and rarely home. Fereby was eighteen when Laura was born, then she had two other children and separated from her abusive husband, who died in 1888. But the year before he died, he introduced ten-year-old Laura to outlaw Will "News" Carver and local cowboy and part-time thief Ben Kilpatrick. And that set the course for the rest of her life.

Laura's flighty mother remarried and moved away, which hardly affected Laura because she was already living with her grandparents.

"They were of eminent respectability," Laura told Red. "They taught me what little I know of dignity and clean living." Will Carver was courting Fereby's sister, Viana, and married her in 1901. She was only seventeen, and the whole time, Will was also flirting with Laura, who was fifteen. Tragically, Laura's mother and Aunt Viana both died in 1901. Laura then found a more-or-less permanent home, scrubbing, cleaning, and later greeting the customers in the upscale San Antonio brothel of Fannie Porter. She told Red, "Her house was where all the cowboys and such a-went for sportin'. As I got older I stayed with her a good bit of the time. You know how it is in small country places. There ain't much for a girl to do, and when a girl ain't got no parents to look after her and tell her how to do right, she just naturally gets to runnin' wild."

At the brothel Laura met prostitute Della Moore. They became good friends, though Della soon left as the girlfriend of the Wild Bunch's Harvey Logan, aka Kid Curry. Carver and Kilpatrick both courted Laura, but like Logan, could never stay around for long. They always had another job to pull or another posse to evade. Amazingly, with little encouragement or family she could rely on, she went to school off and on until she was almost nineteen, made good marks, and completed at least the sixth grade. Possibly the thing that saved her was the fact that she had a loving extended family, aunts, uncles, and cousins, who were always happy to see her.

For years Laura was in love with Carver and begged to travel with him until he finally took her along to join the Wild Bunch. She alternated affairs with Carver and Kilpatrick, and was going by Laura Casey, using one of Carver's alias last names, when Carver took up with another prostitute and broke Laura's heart. She became Kilpatrick's girl, but always grieved the loss of Carver, her first love, who was killed by lawmen.

At twenty-eight, as she sat in prison visiting with Red, she could look back and say that Ben was a true gentleman, and the only man who had ever treated her decently. They became a couple in 1900 and spent time traveling, first to the Kilpatrick family ranch in Texas. When he was in town spending money, and especially when he was with the Wild Bunch, he played the reckless desperado. But there on the ranch Laura got a glimpse of Ben the cowboy, an uneducated but skilled working man who was completely at home with his brothers, around horses, cattle, and ranching. They visited some of Laura's kin on a ranch in Arizona, and then went to Fort Worth, where they lived for a while like the rich folks do.

As the money played out, Ben contacted Butch Cassidy. It was time to rejoin the Wild Bunch. When the Wild Bunch made their raids on banks and trains, Laura had the company of Della Moore and Etta Place, the girlfriend of Harry Longbaugh. They kept busy working for the gang, fencing stolen goods, cashing stolen checks, hiding caches of supplies, and going into town to buy food, medicine, and ammunition. Laura became a deadeye shot and handy with all sorts of guns, but she swore to Red that she had never participated in the gang's crimes until the Great Northern robbery.

"A man like you might think it's odd that I could be with a man all that time and not question more about him," she said, smacking her gum. Indeed, Red thought, it was odd. But it began to make a little more sense as she talked about it. Ben spent money on Laura, gave her money to spend, and didn't ask her any questions, so she didn't ask him any questions. They were just together, and kind, and that was a new delight for both of them.

When Laura's father introduced her to Ben years before, Ben was going under the name of Cunningham, and later he used other aliases. "They all used different names," she told Red. "At first I thought he was Mr. Longbaugh. That's funny, 'cause Ben is fair and Mr. Longbaugh is dark-headed. It was later I was a-findin' out who everybody was."

"Everybody . . . Longbaugh, Curry, Cassidy, and the rest?" Red asked.

"Yes, all them. Ben, he wasn't foolin' me a-purpose with his name. That's just the way they all did.

"You know, I ain't a-been with many decent men. There's really only two that I loved, but him most of all. The first was Mr. Carver, and he was shot dead whilst he was a-robbin' a train on the border. You want to know a secret?"

Red nodded.

"You can't write this. You promise?" she insisted, narrowing her eyes.

"Oh, yes, of course," Red said, laying down his pencil. He could hardly believe that this robber, prostitute, and forger, this criminal, was reaching out to him like a child, yearning to tell something intimate about herself, wanting him to know who she really was, deep in her heart. He felt odd in his bow tie, looking for angles, analyzing. The idea isn't to fool her, he reminded himself, but to draw her out and help her reveal what it was like to be Laura.

"When they arrested me, I had a bundle of letters wrote to me by Mr. Carver. I tied a blue ribbon around 'em. It was awful when I set there and watched them St. Louis law officers readin' through 'em." She paused.

"That must had been hard," Red offered.

She nodded. "But they was real nice, and didn't laugh nor make fun of me for havin' 'em."

"They were looking for clues about who you and Ben are," he supposed.

"I reckon. Do you think that was bad to be a-keepin' them when I was with Ben?" she asked, earnestly looking for reassurance.

"No, no," Red was quick to reply. "They . . . your love for him was still alive . . . and that only taught you how to love Ben more."

She stared at the table. "That's purdy."

Red waited.

"So I was alone for a while after Mr. Carver, and then here comes Mr. Kilpatrick."

"Tell me about him," Red encouraged.

"He was so quiet. Did you know he couldn't hardly read?"

No, Red didn't know that.

"He could a little. But he would spend maybe ten minutes to read a little menu in a café, so sometimes I'd order fer him. He could read 'beans,' so he ordered that a lot. That's why Mr. Longbaugh gave him that dictionary, but he couldn't use it much."

She looked toward the barred window, and for a moment the only sound was the scratching of Red's pencil. "He didn't have no temper. Never hit me, ner yelled at me. Was just good to me, that's all. He was polite to any woman. A real gentleman. Cowboys're like that, you know. The other men, the miners and rough ones that ain't got no regular trade nor job, they ain't like that. But real cowboys they mostly are."

Turning back to Red as if the most important thing in the world was for him to understand, she said, "So that's why I just went along. It was just fine to be with him and have him look at me so sweet, like I was somebody."

Red wrote and studied her face, reading the story beyond her words.

Laura grinned, remembering. "In Fort Worth he bought a real nice fountain pen so's I could sign them banknotes. Then he up and give it to me. No reason. Just give it to me. Nobody never done that," she said, looking the happiest she'd looked all morning.

"When we had them banknotes me and Ben stayed at the best hotels and ate oysters and whatever we wanted. He always had money. Then we came to St. Louis. That was my fault because I wanted to see St. Louis."

"Have you written to him?" Red asked hopefully.

"Oh yes, I'm a-writin' to him a lot, and he writes me back . . . but I reckon somebody is a-doin' the writin' fer him," she responded eagerly. "I'm a-writin' with his mamma in Texas too, and she writes me back. Her sisters, they write and encourage me, too."

"And your family?" Red asked compassionately.

"Oh, all I have is my sister," Laura said without emotion. "She has only wrote once, because her husband tells her not to write no more. I understand that, but you know, a woman can have her own way if she wants. I always did."

"What does he say in his letters?" Red asked. "Ben, what does he say?"

"He's sweet in his letters," Laura said. "And when I get out of here—you know I'll get out afore he does—I'm a-gonna go to Atlanta and wait for him so's we can be together again just like before."

They were both quiet for a moment, then she added, "I truly love him, and he truly loves me."

Red and Laura spent the next morning together, and then Red had to catch the train to St. Louis. By that time she was comfortable with him and said, "Before I come in here, goin' back to after my momma died, I had visited my uncle in Arizona, and I'd a-been around New Mexico and different places in Texas. But that was the prairie, and I knew the prairie. It's not as bad as the cities. I didn't know the wickedness of cities like St. Louis. There's a lot of folks out there who should be in here." She mentioned again how kind the prison guards and other prisoners had been. "But there's some young girls here who shouldn't be here," she added. "They learn things in here they shouldn't learn."

Later, as Red drove the rented rig back to the livery by the depot, he was glad she came clean with him. In the end, she knew exactly what she was doing. There was no lying about firing a Winchester to terrorize people, and putting a bullet in the shoulder of the one who ran away. She was fully aware that if her bullet was just an inch off target, she could have taken a life. Willingly, she learned to steal and spend other people's money. In fact, Red thought, she faced her personal truth better than most, more honestly, and without self-pity. After all, she still hoped to finish her life in the arms of her beloved.

Headed back to St. Louis with the Missouri River over his left shoulder, the typewriter on the facing seat, Red pecked the keys in

It Ends Here

a syncopated rhythm with the wheels on the tracks, humming, rumbling, clicking, and clacking back to St. Louis. Like a song, Laura's parting words echoed, "I don't mind the time I'm giving up in prison. I only regret the disgrace of it."

Chapter Two
Where's O'Kelley?

Red dropped the Laura Bullion interview on Johns's desk with a smile. He knew it was good work. "I hope you like it, sir," he said. "Now, that was exhausting, and I'm going to have some pasta and a beer and then get some rest."

"Just a moment," Johns spit past his cigar as he reached for the manuscript. "Tiring trip, eh? I never expected you to get it in this early, but that's good. This looks perfect. Can't wait to get it in print. People never tire of reading about the Wild Bunch lovebirds."

"Yessir."

"But about getting some rest . . . I'd like for you to take another trip."

Red sighed.

"Another trip for another great story," he enticed.

Red wasn't excited. "I thought I'd stay home and write about the World's Fair. After all this is 'the World's Fair City,'" he teased.

Johns frowned. St. Louis was indeed the "World's Fair City," although the *Republic* coined that phrase in an editorial and Johns winced every time somebody said it. He knew it was good, but he refused to use it in the *Post-Dispatch*, instead insisting on the Fair's proper name, the Louisiana Purchase Exposition. With the Fair opening in April of 1904, preparations were already in their third year, and they yielded a constant stream of innovations, inventions, mechanical marvels, personalities, and engineering feats, all of which deserved an article in the paper. Exposition visitors would see a wireless telegraph, a 265-foot-tall "observation wheel," and the world's biggest pipe organ. Tlingit Indians were bringing a dozen totem poles from Alaska. Puffed wheat would be introduced. Westinghouse Electric was building a theater that would show moving pictures of their factories.

Red looked thoughtful. "Mr. Johns, I'd like to go to the Fair and do an in-depth, exclusive, advance interview with Jim Key, the educated horse."

"Let the hacks cover the Fair," Johns jabbed. "You'll want this assignment. It's a once-in-a-lifetime story, and you're the only man for the job. It *must* be written in your style. Plus, you're the best interviewer in the city, and you . . . well, you fit in with the criminal element better than most."

"Thank you . . . I think," Red smiled.

"Besides, you already know the background on this story."

"All right, now I'm intrigued," Red brightened.

"I want you to get the rest of the story of the man who killed the man . . . who killed Jesse James."

Red was surprised. "Kelly? No, O'Kelley?"

"That's right." Johns knew he had him hooked.

"He's in prison, in Colorado," Red said, dismissing the idea.

"Was. Was in prison. We need to find out what's next for him. Is he changed? Is he sorry? Is he glad he did it? Why'd he do it? You know, all that."

"And I suppose you know where to find him?" Red waited.

Johns looked away, then back. "Ummm . . . roughly."

+ —━—+ —+

January 7, 1904, three days after Johns gave him the Ed O'Kelley assignment, Red Galvin put on his hat, picked up his suitcase, typewriter, and shoulder bag, and stepped down from the train to get his first look at Pueblo, Colorado. It wasn't what he expected. The day was warm, and people walked around without coats. There were no pine trees. No brisk mountain air. The Rocky Mountains shone beautifully in the western sun, but they were in the distance across a flat, dusty plain. For all its interesting architecture, from stoic adobe stores to the fancy government buildings and European-style hotels, Pueblo was a sleepy place. The dominant feature of the town was the meandering Arkansas River, which folks said had a frightening propensity to flood on a regular basis. All things considered, Pueblo looked a lot like Kansas.

When George Johns told Red he knew "roughly" where O'Kelley went after leaving prison, he meant Pueblo. They didn't even know he was out of prison until a cub reporter at the *Post-Dispatch* brought Johns a news wire one-liner saying O'Kelley had been released from the jail in Pueblo.

But it didn't take long for Red to discover that he arrived too late. O'Kelley had been there after he got out of prison, sure. After all, he'd once been a Pueblo policeman, and came there thinking to get on the force again. He couldn't understand why they wouldn't hire a convicted felon. Then he went out to the coal mines in search of work as a security guard, and they refused him too. But the biggest impression he made in Pueblo was in the bars and dance halls, where he rekindled the love for liquor that had been denied for ten years while he was in prison. His temper and his love for fighting had also been locked away, and once unlocked, were just as hot.

That first evening in Pueblo, Red bought a beer for more than one barfly who told about the fight that got O'Kelley arrested. Drunk as usual, O'Kelley pulled a gun and wounded a man before another man intervened and knocked the gun away. In the fury that followed, O'Kelley bit a chunk from the first opponent's ear, broke the second man's arm with a pool cue, and nearly destroyed the saloon. And it all started over something somebody said. That was January 30 of last year, and O'Kelley was sentenced to a year in jail on assault, vagrancy, and public drunkenness. Now he was out of jail and out of town. O'Kelley figured out that he had no friends left from the old days in Pueblo, and he wasn't doing any good at making new ones, so he moved on. Red missed him by about a month.

Could O'Kelley have returned to Missouri? Unlikely.

Red hated to think he came all the way to Pueblo for nothing. Surely O'Kelley told someone where he was going. One bartender said he went to California or Alaska, he wasn't sure which. Somebody said Kansas. Another said Oklahoma Territory. California was certainly a possibility, but where would Red start? Too many towns, too far, and too big. If it was Alaska, well, that was too far and too cold. Kansas . . . maybe, Red thought. On the other hand, Kansas was home to a lot of Yankees, and hard Civil War feelings that might not suit O'Kelley. Yes, he might be more likely to gravitate to the wilds of the former Indian Territory.

O'Kelley had shown up on the news wire. He would show up again, and it wouldn't take long. Red left his beer on the bar and hurried to the telegraph office, where he sent a wire to Johns asking him to find a detail-oriented clerk to check back through the wire services for news of O'Kelley since the Pueblo release. Then there was nothing to do but wait.

A day passed with no news. But the next morning brought a knock on Red's hotel room door, and a chipper bellman handed him a telegram, which he struggled to read through a sleepy haze. Edward O'Kelley had been arrested as a suspicious character and released by the Oklahoma City Police.

+———+———+

Stepping off the train in Oklahoma City was like stepping into a whirlwind, literally and figuratively. Dust was everywhere, in the air and on everything. It stirred when people walked, and when they didn't. Just fifteen years ago it had all been Indian land, a difficult place to farm, where thousands of people had been forced to farm. While it was

Red Galvin arrived in Oklahoma City on a train pulled by engine 147, which was once held up by the James Gang.

Indian Territory the only white men allowed were federal Indian agents and a few licensed traders. Of course that made it a perfect destination for rapscallions, cutthroats, and fugitives. Then the land that had been given to the Indians was marked off and parceled out to them in tiny lots that were useless to anyone trying to farm. Red knew this because he'd written about it. Of course the *Globe-Democrat* insisted that he tell the story from the view of commerce and industry, but he knew the impact it had on the Indians. In Tulsey, a name derived from a Creek turtle clan town, which everybody pronounced "Tulsa," a former Creek slave named Alex Murrell and his wife, Eliza, were assigned forty acres in August 1903. There were plenty of rocks and trees, but no water, so the Murrells never lived there, and like everyone else, they had no choice but to sell it cheap to developers, who would go on to make fortunes slicing it into individual home sites.

Most of the Territory was opened in a series of great land runs. Army soldiers set up starting lines, handed out marker stakes, and patrolled for "Sooners," people who illegally slipped into the to-be-opened areas to stake a claim before it was time. The run that produced Oklahoma City started at noon on the banks of Kingfisher Creek, April 22, 1889, with fifty thousand hopefuls lined up for a chance to get one of twelve

The land run that produced Oklahoma City and other towns in the former Indian Territory. Library of Congress Prints and Photographs.

thousand home sites. In front of them was a gently rolling expanse of free grassland, most of it iron-rich red clay, striped with oaks and willows bordering countless streams. A cannon was fired, and thousands of men, women, and children—white, black, and Native American— ran, rode horses, drove wagons, and pedaled bicycles as fast as they could to stake out their dusty little slice of red Oklahoma clay. Wagons broke down. Horses stumbled. People fell and were trampled.

Of course, there weren't enough pieces of heaven to go around, and disputes abounded. Admirably, in the absence of any sort of law, almost all of the disagreements were mediated by eyewitnesses, decency, and a handful of soldiers. But those property claims revealed a major omission in the land rush. When President Benjamin Harrison authorized opening Indian Territory for settlement, he failed to provide for any sort of government, law enforcement, or even laws for lawmen to enforce. It was home to Natives and white people learning to live together, and was still a mecca for outlaws and con artists of every stripe, hoping to profit on the newly settled farms and towns. So it's no wonder that such a mix of independent spirits couldn't agree on how to get a government started.

The biggest split was between those who wanted a state government organized by Oklahomans right away, and those who wanted to wait for the U.S. Congress to set it up. When one group scheduled the first territorial convention for July 17, 1889, in Guthrie, twenty miles north of Oklahoma City, the other guys slated their own convention two days earlier, July 15 in Frisco, fifty miles west of Oklahoma City. The one in Guthrie, hosted by postmaster F. W. Green, attracted ninety-six delegates. But they were all free-thinking Oklahomans, determined to demonstrate their individuality, so they couldn't agree on anything except to get their picture taken, then adjourn for a month. The other convention never even convened.

It's a testimony to the people of the new territory that they survived about a year with little more than common sense to determine the public good. Towns formed city councils and hired police. Oil was discovered. And finally, in 1890, Congress set up the state government with the capital at Guthrie.

The town of Oklahoma, which everybody called Oklahoma City, didn't care much about state government. It was booming with business, starting with five thousand people who settled on the north bank of the North Canadian River. For years, Native Americans watched railroads competing and winning routes through Indian Territory, all aimed at connecting St. Louis, Springfield, and Kansas City with Colorado and Texas. So at the time of the land run, there were already two major lines. That's how Oklahoma City came to sprout up around a boxcar station on a rail line, complete with a municipal government with a police force of four men.

While traces of the Native Americans were quickly disappearing, Oklahoma City attracted the most modern versions of everything from printing presses and farm machinery to preachers and politicians. Not far from the depot Red could see a forest of oil wells, and there was already talk of building the state capitol right there in the midst of them. But in 1904 it looked to Red like someone had put St. Louis and Texas in a soda mixer and shaken them up. The whole town started with quickly built wooden buildings, but two- and three-story brick

Top: Oklahoma City is shown before the land run, when it was little more than a train depot with its water tank. Bottom: A Santa Fe train rolls into Oklahoma City on April 24, 1889. Just a week after the land rush, the tent town is booming with homes, buildings, and more construction underway.

buildings were taking over, creating an odd parade of then and now, wood and stone, past and future. Businessmen in tweed suits shared the brick-paved streets with cowboys wearing chaps and big hats and Indians with long, black hair. Some women were dressed and bejeweled like the St. Louis aristocracy, while some were as plain as any frontier homemaker, in homespun dresses and handmade bonnets. The horses were stocky and strong, bred for stamina and hard work—not speed, like the ones Red knew in Missouri. Red saw two automobiles before he'd walked a block. There was a pace to it all like everyone and everything was racing toward a deadline. As if the land run was still going on, and they were all in it.

Red's first stop was the police department in the new three-story city hall on the northwest corner of Grand and Broadway. He was sure he had the wrong place when he found himself about to enter a saloon, the Black and Rogers. Red stepped back, looked around, and was about to ask somebody, when he saw the other entrance, with stairs leading down to the basement jail and up to two floors of police and other city offices. Gambling, liquor, the mayor, and the police, all sharing the same roof with the bank next door. How perfectly Oklahoman, Red thought, smiling as his steps echoed up the narrow, pale green stairwell. When he entered the police station, the desk sergeant looked up from his paperwork, happy to talk to a smiling face amid the steady flow of drunks, prostitutes, petty crooks, and lawyers.

"A reporter," he remarked after Red introduced himself. "I see a lot of them, but you're the first from St. Lou."

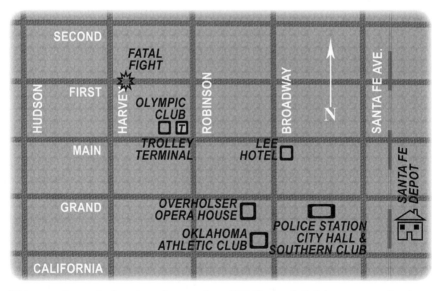

This map shows the location of every place O'Kelley and Galvin went together in Oklahoma City.

"Well, we're all the same, wherever you go," Red joked. He knew how to talk to cops, even ones he just met. "Nice typewriter," he said, pointing to the sergeant's machine. "Underwood, isn't it?" He said it was a good one, then amazed the old cop when he described his new portable, a Blickensderfer 5 from Germany. Red said the writing supplies in his shoulder bag were a lot lighter, and they laughed that they both wished they could use a pencil and paper all the time. After a while, Red persuaded the sergeant to look up an address for O'Kelley: a room at the Lewis Hotel near the warehouse district. Red was on the right track. In fact, the sergeant told him, he remembered O'Kelley's name, because he was so belligerent when he was arrested. They had nothing on which to hold him, so they had to let him go. But he threatened the arresting officer, Joe Burnett, and Burnett had told his fellow officers, "This one is trouble."

"Good to know," Red said.

Leaving the police station, Red walked two blocks and got himself a room at the Lee Hotel, on the sergeant's recommendation. The hotel clerk proudly emphasized that Red would be on the men's floor, there being a separate floor for single women, and other floors for couples and families. How progressive, Red thought, as he walked past the lobby's framed photo of New York governor Theodore Roosevelt, taken when he stayed at the Lee during the 1900 Rough Riders reunion. Red hoped Roosevelt would run for president that fall, which reminded him how glad he was to be covering crime and not politics.

It was almost dark when he walked back to the police station in hopes of locating the officer who arrested O'Kelley a few days ago. "Sure," the desk sergeant said, "come on back. Joe Burnett is back here someplace." He rose from his seat to lead Red into the offices, but stopped short. "There he is right there. Joe, this young man is looking for you."

Red extended his hand and introduced himself. "James Galvin, from the *St. Louis Post-Dispatch*."

"What brings you all this way, Mr. Galvin?" Burnett asked. "If it's that important, it must be important to us too."

"It's about a man you arrested recently, Edward O'Kelley."

"Oh yes, O'Kelley. Well . . . I'm about to start my beat. If you want to talk you're welcome to walk with me."

Red followed the cop out of the police station, turning north on Broadway. Burnett was a sturdy thirty-six-year-old, standing five feet, ten inches, with his hair cropped close, his dark blue uniform clean and pressed, and the brass buttons brightly polished. Oklahoma City cops wore the domed hat based on the English pith helmet, made of cork and covered in blue wool with the department badge on the front. Burnett's hickory baton was tucked into his belt, and his .45 caliber Colt revolver was holstered beneath the uniform coat, with another .38 caliber Colt in the small of his back.

After walking a block, a red and green streetcar came clicking, sparking, and buzzing along under the network of wires suspended

Joseph C. Burnett, pictured as Oklahoma City assistant chief, night patrol, in the years after the fatal fight with Edward O'Kelley. Courtesy of Oklahoma City Police Department.

over the street. Rail lines ran up Broadway to Thirteenth and over to Grand. They went southwest, then west to a housing development built by Anton Classen. He was a visionary who worked in the federal land office, where he watched for good deals to buy land for himself. Among the house lots in his developments he always set aside parks. He even gave the land for Epworth University and of course negotiated the streetcar line that connected it with downtown. The car stopped, and Burnett waved to the conductor as a couple of passengers climbed aboard and settled into the new leather-upholstered seats. Red tried to digest the city, noticing details of how people walked and talked. They moved in and out of buildings without speaking, but always nodding or tipping their hats, and Oklahoma City was beginning to make a certain kind of civilized frontier sense to him. It was a new town in a territory just opened to white settlement. These people were from all over America. No wonder they didn't speak. Nobody knew anybody.

Of course it wasn't very different in St. Louis, but then again it was different, Red analyzed. People there didn't know each other either, but that was because there were almost 600,000 of them. Red asked Burnett, "What do you suppose the population of Oklahoma City is?"

The Oklahoma City Police Department is shown in 1902. Joe Burnett was on the force but was not present for this photograph. Lighter-colored helmets are from their tan summer uniforms. Courtesy of Oklahoma City Police Department.

Without taking his eyes off the busy street Burnett answered dryly, "Yesterday it was 14,000. No idea what it is today."

Joseph Grant Burnett came on the force as a part-time special officer in 1897, before the land rush, and became a full-time patrolman a year later, when he was thirty. There were only eight policemen working that wild town, and two chiefs of police had been killed in its first decade. It had changed a lot since then, but Burnett's view of it, in the dark of night on streets where whiskey and desperation flowed, hardly changed at all.

"You always start your beat this time of evening?" Red asked.

"Yessir, six o'clock to six o'clock," said Burnett. "Been on nights for years. I like it."

"If you're like the police in St. Louis, you work every day," Red guessed.

"Yessir, crime doesn't take a day off, so neither do we. If we're sick we hire a replacement. There's precious few of us anyway, with seven men on days and thirteen on nights, and only two detectives," Burnett added. "My little brother Roe is a cop too.

"But you're not here to talk about me. This O'Kelley . . . ," Burnett growled. "He likes to be called Red."

"Red. That's funny. That's my nickname too," Red replied, grinning.

"Yeah," Burnett clipped seriously, "well, he's the living proof about Irish red hair and a temper. Talk about a Mick that wants to fight."

"Well, we're not all that way," the reporter reassured him.

They had left the streetcar tracks a block behind. Red noticed the buildings changing, getting farther apart, a vacant lot here and there, one with a pile of bricks, one with scraps of sewer pipe. Ahead he could see warehouses, a few homes, and the farther they went, the smaller the houses and the poorer the construction.

"That back there was all the city was for almost a year," Burnett said, as if he were reading Red's mind. "It all went up in three months, growing out from the Santa Fe depot to Harvey, and from California up to about

Third. Then all this came along, stretching out to the river. It curves around the south end of things. All kinds of business in these buildings here. Some of them are almost all storage with just an office or two."

"Funny," Red observed. "St. Louis is so old, and there are so many stone and brick buildings, seems like it's always been there."

A cat ran across the brick-paved street and Red realized how much quieter it had grown. People were home having dinner. Or out having drinks and gambling. The blazing western sky had given way to darkness. Passing from one pool of yellow light to the next, Burnett observed, "Cops sure like these street lamps. Sometimes people are using so much electricity, the power company can't keep up. Then they cut the power to the streetcars to be sure these stay on."

"How long does the power stay off?" Red asked.

"Oh, just until it builds back up. A few minutes. An hour maybe. While it's off, the folks in the bars can't get a car home." Burnett smiled. "Most of 'em don't seem to mind."

Red marveled at how Burnett was able to talk about such things as the city's electricity and still note the changing details around him, his eyes darting into every dark corner and scanning every face. "Next year, they say we're going to have streetcars run all the way to Guthrie. That's the state capital, ya know. I'll have to see it. That's almost forty miles."

For another block the only sound was their steady footsteps, until Burnett broke into Red's thoughts. "O'Kelley. What's your interest in him?"

"Well, he's from Missouri."

"That so?" Burnett deadpanned. "Well then, we're all from Missouri . . . for me it was a little farm in Greene County, near Springfield."

Suddenly, Burnett was gone. Red turned to see that the cop had wheeled back into an alley they just passed. About thirty feet back in the darkness were three men, and Red saw that two of them had the third pinned against the side of a brick wall. Their voices were muffled as Burnett strode up, unhurried, as if to talk about the weather. The three figures tensed, then moved apart a step. Red could make out the words "trouble" and "pleasant evening" and "no, sir." On a cue from Burnett, the man who'd been against the wall quickly walked toward Red, emerging onto the sidewalk and heading toward town. The muggers went the other way, and Burnett checked the side door on the wooden building to make sure it was locked.

"I saw how you handled that," Red offered. "You walked in at a controlled pace so you could take in the situation . . . see who was doing what, and if there was an immediate danger, if they had any weapons in their hands."

"Is that right?" the cop said.

"You were careful not to escalate the situation if you didn't have to. You never even pulled your baton."

Burnett surveyed his beat in silence. Red had never been that close to a cop like Burnett. "Anything could have happened. One of them could have had a gun or a knife, but you just sauntered up and visited like they were old friends."

With nothing from Burnett, he went on. "Your manner must have knocked their guard down. They had to stop what they were doing and figure out what you were doing."

"Is that what I did?"

"Yes, I'm sure of it."

"Well, Red, you don't always control a situation by controlling the situation. Sometimes you have to let the situation control itself."

"And what was the situation?" Red asked. "What was that about?"

Burnett pursed his lips. "Aw, a gambling debt. It'll get paid, I imagine. Or not. Anyway, they'd all had a little booze. I could smell it."

Red paused. "The hotel clerk told me there's talk about prohibition here."

"That's right," Burnett said, shaking his head. "With all the hard cases and get-rich-quick boys and failed farmers and the poor Indians, my God, there is a bunch of drunks around here."

"I'll bet," the reporter sympathized.

"But at least we know where they are. We've got saloons down this way and out on the fringes. But if they made that illegal, we'd be trading thirty saloons for three thousand bootleggers."

"Hmm."

"Oh, you'd have haberdashers with a gambling room servin' bootleg booze in the back. If ya know the right door to try, you could duck into the back door on one of these warehouses and buy a case o' whiskey at night, and they'd be runnin' a legitimate business out the front door during the day."

"It would be hard on the cops, I see that," Red nodded.

"And the jail and the judges," added his guide. "Better to give 'em their saloons."

They let the night settle between them, then Burnett spoke. "So let's get back to you and . . . O'Kelley. I had the durndest time figuring if 'O' was his middle initial or if he was O'Kelley. Of course first time I met him, he came out of Charlie Balzer's Saloon, tight as Dick's hatband. Intelligent conversation was hard to come by."

Red checked, "You know who he is, right?"

"That's what I'm asking you. What brings a reporter for a big city paper down here?"

"Most people don't know . . . even in Missouri, people don't know who he is."

"Is he who people say he is?"

"He's the man who killed Robert Ford, who's the man who killed Jesse James."

"Are you sure?"

"If it's the same Edward O'Kelley who came down here from Colorado, yes. I wouldn't know him by sight. But that's what he went to prison for."

Burnett shook his head.

Red went on. "May I ask how you came to arrest him?"

"Surely," Burnett said matter-of-factly. "There's a fellow who a lot of the officers know . . . kind of a busybody . . . name's Otto Ewing. And he came down here from Colorado."

They turned the corner in front of a beautiful, new three-story red-brick building with a stout cement block foundation, and Red whistled.

"Pretty, huh?" Burnett responded. "Brand new." Then his face darkened as he continued. "So one day Ewing stops me on my beat and says he was in a bar and ran into this O'Kelley fellow. Ewing worked for Bob Ford up in Colorado, until this O'Kelley killed him, like you said. Ewing says O'Kelley is a real hothead."

"That's what I hear. So you arrested him?" Red offered.

"Not right off. You see, we're trying to clean up these gambling halls and such. The worst ones are at the foot of Broadway near the Santa Fe depot. Most of the brothels are on Second. It's fine for folks to let off steam, but the ones without jobs are the ones that get into trouble. So we're all the time on the watch for vagrants. And once in a while we'll make a sweep and pick up a bunch of them. Maybe 150 in a night. Or we might hit a club, a bunch of officers all at once. We keep the pressure on 'em to have a day job, and that keeps them out of trouble at night. Not entirely, but it helps.

"The first time I saw O'Kelley was on the beat with Bunker—another night patrolman, H. E. Bunker. It was late, and O'Kelley comes out of Balzer's like I said. I ask him his name and he tells me. I ask him what he's doing in town and he says he's been working on the section gangs for the Katy and the Rock Island, putting in a lot of overtime. He says, real mean-like, we can check up on it, like we were arguing with him. But there was no need for him to be that way. And that was about it.

"But we had our eye on him and some others. Then there was a burglary at the Alton-Dawson grocery house, and we suspected some of the locals. That was about a month ago.

"I'm walking down here and Bunker comes up with O'Kelley by the collar. Hands him off to me and says the chief wants him for this robbery, so I take him to the station. We round up seven of 'em." He paused, and Red could tell the cop was aggravated. "But we couldn't prove anything on any of them."

"How'd he take being arrested?" Red asked pointedly.

"Oooo, he was hot. Still hot when we let him go. Claimed he was a cop by profession, a fellow officer of the law, and we shouldn't have arrested him."

"No more trouble from him?"

"No, we just keep our eye on a bunch of the regulars. One of our detectives, Fred Hagen, is on the day shift in this part o' town, and we both see O'Kelley with the same crowd, in and out of these saloons."

Later, back at the hotel, Red looked out his window at the saloons glowing like so many fallen stars. O'Kelley was out there in one of those places. He was an odd vigilante. Never raised a mob. Never avenged anybody but Jesse James. What kind of a man could make such a historic statement as the killing of Bob Ford, and yet spend the rest of his life in drunken obscurity? Red laid back, studied the tin ceiling, and fell asleep hoping that in the morning he'd be able to locate the man he'd come so far to find.

Chapter Three
Growing Up O'Kelley

January 10, 1904, dawned cold, and Red realized he'd need to ask for one more blanket if he was going to survive another night at the Lee. Soon enough he was at the *Oklahoman* office, warm and feeling right at home. Newspapermen love newspapers. Searching past editions he found stories about the grocery robbery and O'Kelley's name among the men who were arrested. Then he kept browsing; the night owl O'Kelley wasn't likely to be up and around for some time.

The pages of the *Oklahoman* were spotted with unwashed men like O'Kelley who skulked and loitered, waiting for an easy strike. Political storms, tornadoes, and battling desperadoes dominated every page. There were also plenty of stories of families, schools, and town builders. The year 1903 saw the completion of the Overholser Opera House at Second and Grand, with its seventy-two-foot ceiling, seven hundred electric lights, and leather seats for 2,500. And right behind the opera house was the Oklahoma Athletic Club, a gym for developing boxers. The offices upstairs were home to the Big Four gambling bosses, men who had their fingers in most bets that went down in the city. The Big Four owned gambling clubs, including the Olympic, a couple of blocks away on Main; the Southern, in the same building with the police station on Grand; and the Monte Carlo, around the corner on Robinson. To keep it all afloat they operated behind the scenes in politics, local government, and even the police department, or so it was said.

A lot of the Big Four's work was illegal, done with a handshake or the stroke of a pen, and if it was less dangerous than the kind of instant crime that exploded around men like O'Kelley, they also used thugs to keep their hold on the city. The previous summer, Larry Reedy, a prize-fighter turned political fixer who went for hire to the highest bidder, tangled with Charles Swinghammer, who quit the local horseshoeing union because the union restricted how many hours he could work. "No wonder," Red thought. "They limited his identity. His last name was an Americanization of the German word for blacksmith."

Larry Reedy and his brother watched for Swinghammer, catching him in the alley between the athletic club and the hardware store. There was already bad blood between them from union meetings, and then Reedy wrote an article in the union newspaper, the *Labor Signal*, denouncing non-union workers and naming Swinghammer as a scab. When the two men confronted Swinghammer in the alley, he wasn't intimidated. He was a massive man, every bit the equal of Larry the boxer, and he beat both Reedy brothers to the ground. That gave Larry a chance to claim self-defense, and he pulled a .38 Colt from a shoulder holster. He knew exactly what he was doing when he fired at point-blank range into Swinghammer's right arm, breaking it. As Swinghammer fell to his knees and raised his left arm to shield his face, Reedy ended his horseshoeing career, firing again and breaking his victim's left arm with a bullet that passed through and also broke his jaw.

Reedy was charged with attempted murder, but a fix was on and he never went to trial. Because Reedy had no apparent source of income, he had once been jailed for vagrancy by Joe Burnett's brother, Roe. But the charge was dismissed by Judge J. T. Highley, who scolded Roe to leave Reedy alone, saying if not for Reedy, "None of us would have a job." It was no coincidence that Judge Highley was also the publisher of the *Labor Signal*.

It seemed like he just sat down, but when Red looked at his watch it was almost noon. Perfect, he thought. Pulling on his coat, Red walked over to the Lewis Hotel. Though it dated to the opening of the city, it was one of many buildings that had never been painted or even white-washed, and it already looked older than its fourteen years. The lobby was empty, except for a surly clerk who didn't bother to get out of his chair but directed Red to room 137. A minute later, Red was watching the door creak open, and there was the man he had chased across the country and back.

A few boxing fans had seen heavyweight champ Bob Fitzsimmons fight in New Orleans and Chicago, and because the English boxer was frequently pictured in the papers and talked about in the gambling clubs, plenty of loud talkers were sure they knew all about him personally. From what Red heard in the bars of Pueblo, it was universally agreed that O'Kelley was every bit his physical equal. Red didn't doubt them now, for O'Kelly stood every bit of six feet tall and was broad at the shoulders, though his neck was long and thin.

With the door open just enough to reveal that he was still wearing nothing more than his dingy white long-handle underwear, O'Kelley eyed the man who'd interrupted him so early. Red was sure there was a pistol in the hand behind the door, so he smiled and quickly introduced himself as being from the *Post-Dispatch,* adding, "I understand you like to be called Red. That's what people call me too." The icebreaker worked, as O'Kelley took notice of Red's neatly combed head of thick auburn hair and gave his first grunt of the day, followed by, "Wait a minute," and he closed the door.

"Okay," Red said to himself. "We're off to a great start."

O'Kelley was amenable to letting the reporter buy his first meal of the day. So Red waited downstairs for his interviewee to appear, wearing a simple shirt, buttoned at the neck with no collar, black and gray striped pants with suspenders, and dusty boots, all under a heavy, tan, knee-length canvas coat with huge pockets. He had close-set green eyes, auburn hair, and a matching handlebar mustache that was too big for his face. But at least, Red thought, it improved the looks of his weak chin and big ears. He was one of those people who look naturally sloppy. He could have put on the nicest suit in town, and he still would have looked like he just rolled out of bed after a fitful night, wearing someone else's clothes. They found a café right next door, where Red started to sit near the big window, but O'Kelley directed him to a corner table at the rear, and made a point of sitting with his back to the wall. Red hung his black wool greatcoat, but Ed sat down without removing his.

The place was a beehive of bundled-up people coming in from the cold and ordering hot food. Steak and eggs were the order of the day, and O'Kelley also called for two shots of rye, one to wash down the breakfast and one added to his coffee. The conversation was sparse, Red not wanting to appear too eager, and the other man in no hurry to talk. He ate quickly, constantly scanning the room, then rolled a cigarette. "Them factory-rolled cigarettes is trash," he grumbled.

Then he was the one who got down to business. "What is it you want?" he asked, expecting to answer a couple of questions and be on his way.

"I'd like to get to know you," Red said flatly.

O'Kelley stared blankly at him.

Red went on. "I think people will be interested in reading about you and your life. Not much has been written about you, and I'd like to write a nice long piece . . . you know, who is Ed O'Kelley?"

Ed looked at him like he'd lost his mind. "*I'm* Ed O'Kelley."

Red shook his head. "Umm . . . I just thought you might like to tell your story so people can read about it in the papers. Has anybody ever asked you to tell your story?"

"Nope."

"Well, would you like to tell it?"

"Sure," O'Kelley said. "Not much of a story."

Red smiled. "Let's find out."

Ed O'Kelley's father, Thomas Katlett O'Kelley, was the firstborn son of a struggling farm family in the mountains of western North Carolina. When he was still a boy they moved to Buncombe County, then across the line into Georgia, and then to east Tennessee, near Benton, following their wealthier neighbors, the Capeharts. Hugh and Eliza Capehart continued to prosper in Tennessee, where they had a big farm and slaves to work it. Their daughter Margaret Ann once remarked that when she was a little girl she was so attended by house slaves she never had to put on her own shoes. But those days would soon be gone, as Hugh was a poor manager of their ample income. He and Eliza spent money like there was an endless supply. The tide against slavery rose in eastern Tennessee until slaves were leaving almost at will. Without enough workers, crops were left in the field, or harvested but never taken to market. At last, unable to hold on to the huge farm, they moved to a smaller place near Patton, and the O'Kelleys moved near them.

By that time Thomas O'Kelley had grown to be a principled young man who was intent on becoming a doctor and was deeply in love with Margaret Ann. In 1856 he graduated with a two-year degree from tiny Barret College, a Christian school in the Cumberland Mountains, then continued to study medicine. When Margaret Ann turned up pregnant, Thomas was terrified, knowing he had no prospects for supporting a wife and child. Still, he finished his school term, and after a little more soul-searching chose love and honor over escape, and proposed to Margaret Ann. She said, "I do," and little red-headed Edward Capehart O'Kelley was born in 1858.

Life was hard for the new family, as Thomas picked up work wherever he could while still trying to help his parents. He and Margaret Ann were barely accustomed to being parents when she became pregnant with a second child. By that time her parents were struggling to hold on to their handful of slaves. Hugh and Eliza had three other daughters and no sons to help with the farm work. One morning

It Ends Here

Hugh went to the barn to harness the horses. As he reached for a collar, he accidentally knocked over a bucket, which startled one horse so much that it bolted and lunged into the other. That horse whirled and kicked, catching Hugh squarely in the thigh. He had to crawl to the house, where he found himself unable to stand the next day, and he was laid up for almost two months. By that time they had sold off most of their land and were about to lose the house, so it was time for another change. Both the Capeharts and the O'Kelleys had relatives in northwestern Arkansas who had written about how much they loved the life they'd found there. Land was cheap, and people were scarce. So the Capeharts sold their place, and Hugh, Eliza, and Margaret Ann's sisters, Mary, Sarah, and Amanda, all moved to Arkansas.

Then a decision was made that would shape baby Edward's life, and possibly change history. Thomas and Margaret Ann agreed that life would be a lot easier for them without the baby. After all, there were four Capehart women to take care of him. Everyone agreed it was best, so little baby Edward went with the Capeharts. For two years he didn't see his parents. Then Thomas, Margaret Ann, and their second son, Harry, moved west, and they were all living in Madison County, Arkansas, on the banks of the Kings River in the Boston Mountains. But the die had been cast, with the baby separated from his parents while they bonded with the second child. A year later a third son, Zachary, was born.

The little family couldn't afford a riding horse but had a well-matched pair of mules. That was hard country to farm, with little patches of flat land in the hollows, along the creeks, and on the hilltops. Nobody in the area had enough flat land to grow wheat, so vegetable gardens and small stands of corn were tucked in wherever they could fit five rows or more. There were blackberries, huckleberries, apples, and peaches. Every family had a milk cow, and sheep did well, but the main crop was hogs.

Those were the days leading up to the Civil War, and northwestern Arkansas was on the periphery of the national argument about slavery.

It had long been a slave state but, like Missouri, had few of the sprawling plantations that characterized the Deep South, and it was even more
thinly populated than Missouri. In some counties slaves constituted almost half of the population, whereas in others they comprised barely 3
percent. Many people opposed secession but favored slavery. Western
Arkansas had seen a significant German immigration, who were almost
all strongly Union and anti-slavery. It was an odd mix, but not a violent one until the war started. Then Arkansas joined the Confederacy
and contributed a sizable army to the cause, including eleven infantry
and four cavalry regiments. And like Missouri, pro-Union and pro-
Confederate militias roamed, along with guerrillas of both sides, particularly in the northwest corner of the state where the O'Kelleys and
Capeharts lived.

There were no pitched battles around Madison County, but there
were plenty of Union patrols trying to root out the bands of rebel guerrillas who roamed the area, raiding into southwestern Missouri, then
escaping to hide in rural Arkansas, where Southern sympathies ran
strong. The soldiers were little more than vigilantes, enforcing their own
laws, making their own decisions, assigning their own missions, and
arresting and punishing whomever they wanted. In January of 1863 at
Huntsville, Union troops captured nine men suspected of being guerrillas. They removed them from the guardhouse in the predawn hours
of an icy morning and took them to a field on the banks of Vaughn's
Branch where they were lined up and shot by members of Company
G of the Eighth Missouri Cavalry, commanded by Lieutenant Colonel
Elias Briggs Baldwin. One man survived until the next day, and another
crawled away to the home of a compassionate widow who nursed him
while he recovered. Those two men told the tale of the crime. Hatred
for the Union exploded in the area, and hundreds of men who had
been holding out and trying to avoid the war kissed their wives, left
their children to tend their farms, and joined the Confederate cause.
Among them were Margaret Ann Capehart O'Kelley's cousins Silas K.

It Ends Here

Capehart, a private in Company C, Thirteenth Arkansas Infantry, and James Capehart, a private in Company I, Fourth Infantry. They saw some of the bloodiest fighting in the Civil War, including the battles of Stones River, Atlanta, Shiloh, Chickamauga, and Bentonville.

In the wake of the massacre at Huntsville, Southern guerrillas grew more active and even more violent. They targeted not only the Union Army but also civilians who were willing to help the Federals. Everybody knew the O'Kelleys owned no slaves but were outspoken Unionists, and the local secessionists suspected them of telling Union patrols which men in the neighborhood were guerrillas. So late one night in the winter of 1863, four men, Thomas's own neighbors, crept up to the house, poured coal oil around the foundation, and set it ablaze. Thomas awakened to thick smoke filling the house, and quickly woke Margaret Ann. They got the babies from their beds, wrapped them in sheets, and ran through the flames into the yard. There was nothing they could do but shiver in the cold watching their little log home burn to the ground, then walk through the snow to the Capehart home for shelter.

It had all grown too dangerous, so Thomas moved his family deeper into the mountains. They took Harry and Zachary, leaving little Edward behind with Hugh and Eliza. Unfortunately, it was even harder to keep Margaret Ann and the boys fed at the new place. It wasn't yet time for spring planting, and there would be no crops for five months. In the mountains, there was even less tillable land, and it was harder to make a few dollars at day labor. In his righteous anger with the guerrillas, Thomas determined to join the Union Army, creating an even greater burden on Margaret Ann to keep the two boys fed without him.

On March 27, 1864, Thomas and his brothers William H., James S., and Joseph M. O'Kelley all walked to Berryville, where they enlisted with the Union Army, Company A, Second Regiment Arkansas Volunteer Cavalry. With his college education, Thomas was quickly promoted to quartermaster sergeant.

The Second was constantly on the move, scouting and skirmishing with guerrillas. They were in country populated by hostile people, and it did no good to knock on doors and ask for help or information. But people like Thomas knew who was sympathetic to the Union cause and might shoe their horses, sell supplies to them, and tell them where the guerrillas were hiding. That's how most of the war was for the Second: constantly on patrol, with seamless days in the saddle punctuated by the sheer terror of clashes with bloodthirsty guerrillas who appeared from nowhere, killed, and then vanished into the hills.

Throughout the war, Missouri's Southern sympathizers continued hoping for a savior who would wrest control of their state from the Federals, reinstate the duly elected government, and kick the Yankees out of Missouri. The man they looked to was former governor Major General Sterling Price. The loyal Price had fought wherever Confederate president Jefferson Davis sent him. He and his Missouri Confederates were placed under the command of other officers and continued to serve deep into the South. It was September of 1864 when Davis finally commissioned Price to return to Missouri and retake the state. However, he had to raise a new army specifically for the invasion. As impossible as the mission seemed, Price couldn't refuse. It turned out that legions of men had been waiting for that opportunity, and they flocked to serve under him. Price made his move with twelve thousand cavalry, mostly from Arkansas. His plan was to seize St. Louis, then St. Joseph. But first, he thought, the Union stronghold at Fort Davidson, some eighty miles south of St. Louis, offered an opportunity for a possible easy victory with his overwhelming numbers against a fort held by less than 1,000 men. But he was wrong. The fight cost Price 1,500 men, and he still couldn't take the fort. Then, that night, the Union troops quietly slipped away and blew up their own fort. Price had accomplished nothing and lost a great deal.

With Union troops blocking the way north, Price had to turn west, to the only remaining significant objective, West Port, the future Kansas

It Ends Here

City. That's when Thomas O'Kelley's Arkansas regiment became part of the force that chased Price's army from the state, defeating the Confederates at the Big Blue and Little Blue rivers before they could reach West Port. When they finally got to West Port, Price sent his depleted army against some 10,000 Yankees, losing another 1,500 men. There was nothing to do except run south through Kansas, with 2,600 Union infantry and cavalry still on his tail, relentlessly forcing him to stop and fight. At Little Osage Creek, Mine Creek, Marais des Cygnes, the Engagement at the Marmiton, and Newtonia, they fought five battles in a week, and the cold plains of Kansas became the final resting place for many an Arkansas Confederate volunteer who came to fight for Missouri.

Thomas O'Kelley's regiment was mustered out August 20, 1865, and he returned to his family on the little Arkansas farm. It was difficult for all of the Union supporters because after the war the state was filled with Southern veterans. Thomas was sick of living in poverty, and he knew he'd never make a living on a hard-rock Arkansas farm. Most important, he still dreamed of being a doctor. Back in Missouri, his father had died in 1865, leaving his mother alone, aging and needing him. In 1868 another son was born, and as soon Margaret Ann could travel, Thomas packed up his family and moved them back to his parents' farm in Bollinger County, near the town of Patton. He finished medical school, his medical practice flourished immediately, and the specter of poverty would never again darken his door.

During the war, Bollinger County had been home to horrible raids, murders, and home burnings by Rebel guerrillas, countered by equally horrible raids, murders, and home burnings by Union militia. As armies and bands of guerrillas came and went, the county seat at Dallas was occupied by both armies at different times. The O'Kelleys' neighbors knew Sam Hildebrand and Pete Smith, notorious guerrillas who lived nearby and had raided throughout southeast Missouri. In February of 1863, Union cavalry surprised a Confederate force of more than twenty men in their Mingo Swamp camp and killed them all.

At Doniphan in neighboring Ripley County, the Wilson Massacre occurred on Christmas Day of 1863. Confederate colonel Timothy Reeves, a Baptist minister, was hosting an outdoor Christmas dinner for three hundred people, including soldiers and their families. Only a few of the men were armed, guarding about one hundred Union prisoners. While every head was bowed for Reverend Colonel Reeves to bless the food, thundering hoofbeats interrupted. Heartless major James Wilson and his Union troops rode through and killed thirty-five soldiers and sixty-two civilians, some of them infants, freed the Union prisoners, and captured some one hundred Confederates.

Colonel Reeves was one of the survivors of the vicious attack, and he set his sights on Major Wilson. At the Battle of Pilot Knob in September 1864, Wilson and six of his men were captured and then quietly turned over to Reeves. Reeves let his men have the prisoners, and no order was needed. Major Wilson was taken out and hanged, and his men were shot. When the news reached General William Rosecrans, who commanded the Union's Department of Missouri, he flew into a rage and gave orders to retaliate. His Confederate prisoners were marched into a room and forced to draw lots to determine which seven of them would be hanged. Rosecrans even specified that one of them had to be a major to avenge Wilson.

It's no wonder that after the war feelings of loyalty and anger lingered among the Confederate families. Veterans of Southern service were not allowed to hold public office or vote, and yet, the newly freed slaves could do both. There were many jobs the veterans weren't allowed to hold, and they were not even allowed to preach, although that's one prohibition that was broken with regularity in the little country churches.

That backdrop set the stage for the O'Kelleys and Capeharts in ways they could never foresee at the time, in a quintessential American family Civil War experience. The two families were torn apart by the violent conflict, but when it was long over, in 1874, Margaret Ann wrote to her parents in Arkansas, telling them that she and Thomas would build a home for them on their land if they would move back to Bollinger County. The Capeharts moved, and not only were they and the O'Kelleys able to put their political and military differences behind them, but they also bound together with a closeness they didn't have before the war. As Margaret Ann's sisters married, Thomas and Margaret Ann generously built a home for each of them on the corners of their farm, which had by that time grown to one thousand acres. The houses were in walking distance of one another, and they would all gather for meals and socials at the big house of Thomas and Margaret Ann.

Even though their home had many extra rooms, their own son Edward never felt welcome, and he continued to live with the Capeharts. Fortunately for him, the brothers loved each other, and that helped lighten Edward's burden. He would often sneak into the big house, staying for days on end in one of the spare rooms, and they laughed when their father got up, ate breakfast, and went to his office every day, never knowing Edward was there.

Chapter Four
Jesse, Frank, and Jim

Jesse James was born ten years before Edward O'Kelley, but like Edward, he and his big brother Frank were farm boys too. Growing up outside Kearney, Missouri, thirty miles northeast of Kansas City, one of their favorite playmates was Jim Cummins, who lived nearby. Jim's father died when he was ten, about the same time the James boys' father died after heading for the California gold fields. As a result, the James boys and Cummins became grown men before their time. And in the middle of the Civil War, Frank, then Jesse, then Jim, left home as teenagers to ride under the command of William Quantrill.

Quantrill was a charismatic and bloodthirsty guerrilla fighter who cast his lot with slave owners and Southern sympathizers along the border with Kansas in the years leading up to the Civil War. Missourians waged an ongoing struggle to hold on to their slaves, who were legal in Missouri. In a fight that started in the early 1850s, slaves were stolen by Kansas Free-Staters, then recaptured and returned to Missouri by slave owners and bounty hunters, often amid gunfire and acts of terror. Farms were burned and people were threatened, tortured, and killed in a deadly version of the debate taking place in Congress over whether Kansas and other U.S. territories should enter the Union as slave states or free.

Quantrill and the other guerrillas were unbridled vigilantes, taking the law into their own hands to protect their homes, property, and

Jesse (left) and Frank James are pictured as teenagers. Below: Jesse and Frank grew up in this farmhouse outside Kearney, Missouri. Library of Congress Prints and Photographs.

Left: William Quantrill was the most charismatic and successful leader of the South's guerrillas in the Civil War. Right: Jesse James is shown shortly after joining Quantrill's guerrillas. He sports three Colt .44 Army revolvers and wears a home-made tunic in the traditional style of the guerrillas, with big pockets for cartridges. Courtesy of Missouri Historical Society.

neighbors from the violent aggression of Free-Staters, slave stealers, and even the U.S. Army. Kansas guerrilla raids on Missouri farm families and towns were repaid by Missouri guerrillas with ever-escalating raids on Kansas farm families and towns. Then when the Civil War started in spring of 1861, President Lincoln threw out Missouri's newly elected government and filled the offices with his appointees. The state was under martial law for the duration of the war, so as many people saw it, they'd been invaded. Violence begat violence, until vigilantism was lost in the fog of vengeance. And that's the world in which the James boys and Cummins lived.

Rather than join the regular Confederate army, Quantrill and others chose to continue fighting as they had in the years leading up to war, attacking targets of their own choosing, with their own merciless rules of engagement. The guerrillas had the best horses and guns, raiding in lightning attacks, each man armed with three or more pistols so they could keep firing while their victims reloaded. They stole Union uniforms, spied, and killed civilians as readily as uniformed Union soldiers. Of course, some Union soldiers and many of the state's cavalry militia units made equally violent raids on Southern-sympathetic families.

Jim Cummins was slender with a kind face, a man who tended to overthink things. He talked incessantly about philosophy, politics, and what was right and wrong, earning him the name "Windy Jim." But he rode alongside Jesse and Frank, often under the command of Bloody Bill Anderson, who was even more bloodthirsty than Quantrill. In 1864, Cummins was convinced that General Price's impending return to Missouri meant Price would retake the state for the Confederacy, and the best way to help was in the regular Southern army. Jim quit the guerrilla business and joined the Twelfth Regiment Cavalry under General Joe Shelby. His experience in bushwhacking, coupled with his supreme skills as a horseman and marksman, qualified him to enter service as a sergeant. He was in Price's invasion, which all came to a bad end as the Rebels were pursued, captured, and killed by a Union army that included Thomas O'Kelley and his kin. Cummins was with his unit when they surrendered.

With the Southern cause in defeat, and Quantrill and Anderson both dead, many of the guerrillas tried to surrender and take the oath of allegiance to the Union, just as Confederate soldiers were required to do. But people were gunning for them, and trying to surrender was dangerous business. Cummins thought it all through, reasoned it out, and talked Jesse and Frank into surrendering to U.S. Army troops. Unfortunately, the soldiers fired on them, almost killing Jesse with a bullet through his lung, and they had to run for their lives.

After the war Jesse, Frank, and many of their closest friends still had a price on their heads. Authorities as well as bounty hunters were

Jim Cummins. Charcoal drawing by Elmer Stewart. Courtesy of Missouri Valley Special Collections, Kansas City Public Library, Kansas City, Missouri.

out to kill or capture them. All of them wanted the reward money, but some were pure vigilantes who cared more about avenging the guerrillas' war crimes. The former guerrillas couldn't surrender, couldn't live in peace, and always had to be wary of their surroundings and who was watching them. There was little choice for them but to adopt aliases, stay on the move, and visit their parents and family farms infrequently and secretly. They were afraid to take regular jobs for the risk of being discovered and arrested or ambushed, and that's why men like Jesse James turned to a life of crime.

The brotherhood formed in the heat of battle was strong, so many of Quantrill's men continued riding together as outlaws. Jesse and Frank were joined by fellow guerrillas Cole Younger and his brothers Bob, Jim, and John, the Youngers' brother-in-law John Jarrett, and the James boys' cousin Robert Woodson "Wood" Hite. Also Clell and Ed Miller, Charlie Pitts, Bill Stiles, and of course Jim Cummins. Wood's brother Clarence joined them. Dick Liddil didn't ride with them in the war, but when he was introduced to the James boys in 1879, he had already done a stretch in prison for stealing horses. Robbing coaches, trains, and banks, the members of the gang varied on, depending on who was available, whom Jesse trusted, and who Jesse thought was the man for each job. The James boys' and their old playmate Jim Cummins would ride together for fifteen more years, from the first job, the Liberty Bank robbery in 1866, to the last job, the Blue Cut train in 1881.

+ — ✦ — +

Jesse James sat alone on his front porch. It was well after midnight, and he had a lot on his mind. It was nice there in that residential neighborhood of Nashville, Tennessee. The colorful houses, some frame, some brick, had all been built after the war, and there were so many newcomers to Tennessee in those days, nobody questioned that his name was Thomas Howard, or would have ever suspected that he was a notorious wanted man back in Missouri. In his hands was a month-old copy of the *Jefferson City Times*. He saved it to re-read the editorial berating the Pinkerton agency for their horrific raid on the farmhouse of Jesse's mother, Zerelda, and stepfather, Reuben Samuel. Pinkerton spies were sure Jesse and Frank were there, though they had actually left the day before. So when the agents surrounded the house in the dark of night, calling for the two boys to come out, there was no response from the frightened family inside. An agent threw a bomb through the window, and it rolled into the fireplace and exploded, wounding the old man and a maid, severing Zerelda's arm at the elbow, and killing Jesse and Frank's mentally disabled half brother.

The *Times* was livid over the inept efforts of the Pinkertons, saying that whenever a bank or train is robbed anywhere in the country, James and Younger are "the first names mentioned." It said out-of-town detectives were "riding roughshod over the farming population of Western Missouri," and that they "hunt outlaws on special trains and fancy carriages." It concluded by saying, "[The detectives] carry off peaceful citizens, kill twelve-year-old boys, and blow off the arms of old women, and waylay reporters with their nonsensical questions. The James and Younger boys would have been caught long ago if the job had been undertaken properly." Jesse kept that paper around because it reminded him that folks back home understood them. Of course the part about being caught long ago was also a reminder that local people defending their homes could be far more dangerous than Pinkerton agents.

It was almost five years previous, on September 7, 1876, when Jesse led the James-Younger Gang from their homes northeast of Kansas City all the way to Northfield, Minnesota. Bill Chadwell, who was from that area, had already scouted the bank with Jesse, and everything looked perfect. Instead, it turned out to be a job where everything that could go wrong went wrong. Jesse shot and killed Joseph Heywood, a bank clerk who refused to open the safe for them, even after being pistol-whipped. Out in the street, mounted gang members fired pistols and yelled threats intended to scare the townspeople. Cole Younger killed a young Swedish immigrant who didn't obey his command to get out of the street; Cole didn't realize the young man didn't understand English. The alarm spread, the robbers had to run from the bank with nothing, and by that time there was a citizen vigilante pointing a rifle or shotgun from every window and alley in town. Some were veterans of the Union army who were thrilled at the chance to prove they still knew how to shoot. A couple of them were deadly accurate. In the fusillade that followed, everybody in the gang was wounded except Jesse and Frank. Clell Miller was killed, along with Chadwell.

The plan had been to escape through the swamps outside of town, and then return home by a circuitous route so nobody would know who pulled the robbery or even where they came from. The problem was, they were counting on Chadwell to guide them, and he was dead. After stopping in the woods to assess their situation, with a posse surrounding them, Jesse and Frank rode off on one horse, leaving Cole Younger and his brothers to be captured in a wooded ravine after two more weeks on the run.

As Jesse and Frank put their heads down and galloped through the posse's line, a shot hit them both in the right leg. Though in pain, they stayed on the move and stole a second horse. Each time their horses wore out, they would steal two more. One dark night they stole two from a field, not realizing that one of the horses was blind in one eye, and the other was completely blind. But they eventually made it to Dakota Territory, where they recovered from their wounds, then found their way back home with nothing to show for the raid except misery and loss. The good people of Northfield had perpetrated the West's ultimate act of spontaneous vigilantism.

+ — + — +

Frank and Jesse began traveling to Nashville in 1875, and after Northfield in 1876, they spent more and more time there. Frank would later describe his early years in Nashville, saying: "The first place I went to there was the widow Harriet Ledbetter's, who lives over on White's Creek . . . I put in a crop of wheat and moved there and lived in the place known as the Jesse Walton place. I lived on this place one year, that was up to [the end of] 1878. Next year I rented a place from Felix Smith, on White's Creek also, but nearer to White's Creek than the place I have just mentioned. I remained there a year, and made a crop in the meantime—a general crop, as farmers raise—corn, oats and wheat. The next year I lived on what is known as the Jeff Hyde place, on Hyde's Ferry, about three and a half miles from Nashville. I remained there a year. During that year I didn't farm any. I was working for the Indiana Lumber Company" (From *The Trial of Frank James for Murder. With Confessions of Dick Liddil and Clarence Hite and History of the "James Gang,"* Kansas City: George Miller Jr., 1898).

On his leased farm, Frank raised chickens and vegetables, grew a long beard, and enjoyed the rural life with his wife, Anne. Jesse and his wife, named Zerelda like his mother but who went by "Zee," rented a farm in nearby Humphreys County, where their son, Jesse Jr., was born. In 1878 Zee gave birth to twins, but they only lived about a month. She could no longer bear to live on the farm where they were buried, especially during the long periods when Jesse traveled. When Jesse talked to big brother Frank about her heartbreak and what to do next, Frank convinced him that it was safest to hide in plain sight, in town. That was fine with Jesse, because he didn't like farming anyway. So Jesse and Zee rented a little house in East Nashville. Later they moved to a two-story brick house on Fatherland Street. It was a place where they could live as Mr. and Mrs. Thomas Howard, Jesse Jr. could play in the yard, and Zee

Left: Jesse and Zee's East Nashville house, photographed in the 1970s. It was later demolished. The house in which Frank lived was later destroyed by fire. Right: Jesse and Zee lived at this house on Fatherland Avenue in East Nashville in 1881. Dick Liddil and Jim Cummins sometimes stayed there.

could go to market in the buggy. A year later, their daughter, Mary, was born there, and it was longest period of happiness they knew.

Jesse's diversion was his racehorse, Red Fox. He wasn't a great one, but win or lose, Jesse enjoyed the excitement of race day, especially at the track across town at West Park. He liked smoking cigars and talking horse breeding and racing with the wealthy people he met in Nashville, and he felt like an expert when he stopped to visit horse farms on his trips through Kentucky.

Frank took the same advice he had given Jesse, gave up the farm, and moved into town, a couple of blocks from Jesse. He was such a serious man, always looking out for his younger brother, and there was some security for both of them in being closer. Frank went by the name B. J. Woodson, they kept to themselves, and people knew he and Mr. Howard traveled sometimes for their work as livestock traders. Frank loved to read, and he entertained people by sprinkling his conversation with Scripture and quotes from Shakespeare. He had a wry sense of humor, and his idea of fun was making friends with the local police officers. He knew several of them by name and nurtured a friendship with Nashville detective Fletcher W. Horn, beginning in 1877. Even when he was living on the farm and picking up extra money hauling logs for the lumber company, he'd come into Nashville for a cup of coffee with Horn. One day he introduced Horn to Jesse, calling him J. D. Howard, of course. Horn was a horse-racing fan—he already knew exactly which horses Mr. Howard owned. To the brothers' surprise, he joined them at their table and talked at length about everything associated with horses and racing, with no idea he was actually talking to the notorious Jesse James. Seeing Horn tricked while Jesse squirmed amused Frank no end, but the humorless Jesse later let his big brother know he didn't think it was one bit funny.

Also living in Nashville during the summer of 1881, sometimes at Jesse's house and sometimes in a hotel, were Dick Liddil and Windy Jim Cummins. Liddil was a man Jesse held close so he could keep an eye on him. After all, he didn't serve with them in Quantrill's guerrillas. Cummins, on the other hand, was still one of Jesse's closest confidants, partly because he was a proven man in a fight and loyal as the day is long, but mostly because Jesse was sure the meek Cummins would never be bold enough to betray his leader. On the other hand, Cummins also made Jesse nervous because he just talked too much. In the long days between robberies, when members of the gang were trying to blend into respectable society unnoticed, the last thing Jesse needed was one of his friends bragging about how much he knew.

Jesse had always been high strung, and during that time he became more paranoid. He was nervous, suspicious of everyone, and prone to fits of anger in which he accused his gang members of being lazy, being cowards, and most important, plotting against him. As time passed and the law closed in, he grew more sullen and edgy, plotting constantly, using old war logic to rationalize the gang's work, which bore no relation to the war. Though they started by stealing from railroads and Yankees, they increasingly stole from and murdered everyday people. He also had bouts of sickness throughout his young life. And all of that combined to make him unsuccessful at going straight. Frank wanted the quiet life and made it work. Jesse didn't and never could.

He wasn't ready to retire and didn't want to give the impression that he would quit outlawry because the law had whittled away at the gang. His public image and legacy were vitally important to him, and he was still campaigning in his own misguided way against Yankees, banks, the federal government, the Pinkertons, and an economic system that he saw as brutal to poor people and farmers. Jesse was highly political, he was always in the right, and every job was carefully selected to make a point. It might have been a place, or a person, or a specific railroad. Jesse was always working a vendetta of some sort, but to everyone else his crimes were far flung and random.

Gone were the days when he and Frank were surrounded by daring men who were ready to ride on a moment's notice. Men they could count to face any danger, think clearly, and know what to do in any situation. That's why in the summer of 1879, Jesse recruited Daniel Tucker Basham, a slow-witted Jackson County, Missouri, farmer and an old friend of several of the gang, for the Glendale train robbery. They needed one more man, so they brought in a drunken Irishman named Bill "Whiskey Head" Ryan. Frank detested him for his undisciplined manner, but Jesse convinced Frank that he'd be okay for one job. After all, they just weren't going to be able to find men of the same caliber as those they once rode with.

The job went off without a hitch. They captured the depot at Glendale, Missouri, piled timbers on the track to stop the train, politely introduced themselves to the passengers, robbed them, and sent them on their way. But Basham went back to his farm, and in no time he was caught with some of the gold coins stolen from the train. He confessed, and to his credit he was true to the gang's code of loyalty. He went to prison without saying a word about who else was in the job.

Everybody laid low for over a year. Then Jesse got some information about an Army Corps of Engineers payroll to be delivered near Florence, Alabama. It was the night of March 11, 1881, when financial officer Alexander Smith was riding his horse through the rain to bring a $5,000 payroll to the workers on the Muscle Shoals Canal Project. Smith dismounted to open a gate, and Jesse, Whiskey Head Ryan, and Dick Liddil appeared with their revolvers in hand and took the payroll, which included bags of gold and silver coins hanging from the pommel of Smith's saddle. Then they "invited" Smith to ride along with them. They talked about the weather, the government, Scripture, their families, and how the canal was going, and after riding twenty miles to the west, they suggested that Smith had probably gone far enough. They all shook hands and wished each other well, and Smith headed back to Florence, while the robbers turned north to Nashville.

Two weeks later, on March 25, Whiskey Head Ryan was drunk as usual, shooting off his mouth at a saloon and grocery in the White's

Creek community north of Nashville. The place just happened to be owned by magistrate and ex-constable of Davidson County William L. Earthman, who was watching Ryan closely as he claimed, "I'm the baddest bad man there is, an outlaw to state and country." He said, "I'm Tom Hill, I'm a robber, and I will rob and kill again whenever I take a notion." Considering that Ryan was sporting a pair of revolvers, Earthman figured the situation could turn dangerous at any minute. While Ryan regaled the crowd, Earthman slipped up behind him, grabbed both his arms, and told him he was under arrest. Ryan was just drunk enough to submit. When Earthman searched him he found a leather vest under his shirt, and in the vest was over one thousand dollars in gold coins.

The next morning Frank read in the paper about Ryan's arrest and went to Jesse's house, where Dick Liddil was staying. Maybe the law was on to them, and they'd be next. So each man armed himself with two revolvers and a Winchester rifle. Jesse had a horse, but Frank and Liddil didn't, so in broad daylight they stole two horses, and the trio rode north to Kentucky. When the horses gave out, they traded them for fresh mounts taken from a pasture, and when those gave out, they ended up walking the last few miles to the home of George B. Hite, father of cousins and gang members Wood and Clarence Hite, who welcomed them inside. George's deceased first wife was Jesse's and Frank's aunt. The exhausted men were glad to see a familiar face and wanted nothing more than rest.

By the next day they were refreshed enough to notice that the elderly George had married a beautiful young woman named Sarah. Also living in the house were Wood's sister Maude, and George's sister and her husband, Mr. and Mrs. Norris. Liddil took an immediate interest in Wood's stepmother. When she went out to gather eggs, Liddil helped. When she hung out the laundry, Liddil handed her the clothespins. Old George didn't seem to notice, but it kept Jesse on edge even more than usual.

It Ends Here

Hite's house was approached by a long lane that came from the main road, straight toward the house, before curving away toward other farms. One day three men came up the lane, causing a stir as they looked around them, talked, and pointed. Jesse was sure they were detectives who had trailed them from Nashville because of the horses they stole. The boys watched carefully out the windows, ready to shoot it out if it came to that. But for some unknown reason the detectives stopped one hundred yards away, then veered off along the lane, never coming all the way to the house. With that, the three fugitives felt safe, figuring if those detectives didn't think it necessary to come to the house, nobody else would. So they all relaxed and stayed there for some weeks, during which Liddil had plenty of time to pursue his romance with George Hite's wife. Then Jesse decided it was time to leave, so he and Liddil took the train to Missouri, and Frank disappeared into Virginia.

By fall it was safe to reunite in Missouri. On September 7, 1881, Jesse led the gang in what would be their last train robbery, stopping a St. Louis Iron Mountain and Southern Railway train in a thirty-foot-deep ravine called Blue Cut, very near where they had pulled the Glendale robbery eighteen months before. Jesse expected to net hundreds of thousands of dollars' worth of gold and silver being shipped from Leadville, Colorado. But they were outsmarted by the Pinkertons, who moved the valuables to another train at Kansas City, just fifty miles ahead of the robbery. The disappointed bandits had to settle for about $3,000 worth of money, jewelry, and watches from the passengers.

As usual, the robbers wore no masks and were intense, but polite. Jesse introduced the passengers and the express agent to each one of his boys: "This is my brother Frank . . . Wood and Clarence Hite, Dick Liddil, Charley Ford, Jim Cummins, and Ed Miller." However, the Pinkertons were quoted in the paper, saying Bill Ryan, Tucker Basham, and Wood Hite were there, but Frank and Clarence weren't. The confusion made Jesse laugh, because even after fifteen years of holdups and murders, very few people could identify any of them on sight.

Missouri governor Thomas Crittenden campaigned on a promise to clean up the criminal element and was active in pursuing and convicting many of them. Along the way he used vigilantes like Bob Ford and made deals that included pardoning them for crimes, resulting in the release of dangerous felons from prison. Courtesy of Missouri Historical Society.

When Whisky Head Ryan had been arrested in Nashville back in March, the gold coins he was carrying were from the Muscle Shoals payroll, but there was no way to prove it. So he was extradited to Jackson County, Missouri, and awaited trial there for the Glendale train robbery. Jesse knew he was a real risk to tell what he knew, but Ryan kept his mouth shut. Of course that was partly out of loyalty, but mostly because talking would have gotten him killed by Jesse or one of the others. On the other hand, Tucker Basham, who'd been sentenced to ten years, had spent a year in jail thinking about where loyalty had gotten him. He won a pardon from Governor Thomas Crittenden by testifying against Ryan at his trial on September, 27, 1881, in Independence. Basham described how Ryan recruited him for the Glendale job, then they met Jesse and Frank James, Ed Miller, and Dick Liddil, captured the depot, and waited for the train. Their take was over $10,000, but they only paid Basham $900. Maybe if they'd paid him more, he'd have kept quiet longer.

Ryan's trial was a sensation. Competing mobs swirled in the streets of Independence, and vigilante blood began to boil, mainly because a local man had been killed in the robbery. Some wanted to string up Ryan. Some wanted to set him free and string up Basham for testifying against him. The railroad asked the prosecutor not to call their employees as witnesses, because they were afraid Jesse would take revenge on them. Death threats were made to the prosecuting attorneys, and that was the tipping point. The sheriff wired Governor Crittenden, who came to Independence on one special train, followed by a dozen special deputies from the Kansas City Police on another train. They stood guard at the courthouse until October 15, when Ryan was convicted of the Glendale robbery and sentenced to twenty-five years, and the threat of lynching and escape was over. Crittenden had proven that he was taking a personal hand in cleaning up Missouri. It would be done his way, and without random vigilantism.

Chapter Five
Hero Worship

By the time Jesse was making the Glendale, Muscle Shoals, and Blue Cut robberies, Edward O'Kelley was twenty-two years old and had finally moved into his parents' home. Harry, always the golden child, was attending medical school. Zachary, Frank, and Mattie enjoyed the farm work and were happy to spend their lives there with their spouses, children, grandparents, aunts, and uncles.

There was no way for any child to overcome Edward's circumstances, deprived of his mother's love while the second son was treated like the first born. He would never be the kind of disciplined son Thomas wanted. No matter what Ed did or how hard he worked, or how much the rest of the family loved him, he would never win his father's respect. So in the evenings Ed would head into Patton, or Dallas, the Bollinger County seat, to drink. He was in a foul mood when he went and was not a happy drunk, so he gained a well-deserved reputation as a hothead and a fighter. Of course, that meant there were mornings when he dragged home with a hangover and a black eye to face his brothers, who had already been in the fields since before sunup.

Even though the postwar healing between the Capeharts and O'Kelleys was a beautiful thing, the Capeharts were still farmers and Thomas was, after all, the premier doctor for miles around. The Capehart fortunes had been in steady decline for twenty years, and the O'Kelleys' were booming. To make matters worse, politics remained a barrier between them. Thomas never let the Capeharts forget who was on the winning side, as he wore his uniform in local parades and became an officer in the Grand Army of the Republic, the Union veterans' organization that brought together great reunions in celebration of their victory. Ed had grown up in the Capeharts' Southern-sympathetic home, where they still talked about the brave Capehart men of the Confederacy. Even his middle name, Capehart, aligned him with his mother's family.

It was families like the Capeharts, with their lingering loyalty to the Confederacy that continued to bring Jesse James to southeast Missouri. Back on January 31, 1874, he had a good reason to choose the Wayne County hamlet of Zeitonia, commonly called Gads Hill, as the site for the nation's first train robbery. After the gang hit the St. Louis Iron Mountain and Southern Railway, and then scattered, Jesse and Frank rode into neighboring Bollinger County, where they knew they'd be warmly received. The Patton area continued to be a favorite stop on their many trips to and from Nashville.

When Jesse robbed the train at Gads Hill, Ed O'Kelley was in his teens, just about the age Jesse was when he joined Frank in Quantrill's guerrillas. Ed would have gladly joined Jesse's gang if he had the right friends who could make the right introductions. But Jesse wasn't recruiting in Bollinger County. There were too many Union men, and it was too hard to tell whom to trust.

Still, the nearness of Jesse in 1874 lit a fire in Ed, and it was still smoldering in 1881. Jesse was still robbing banks and trains, and still traveling back and forth from Clay County, sometimes alone, sometimes with Frank and others, keeping away from the big towns and public places, and stopping to visit old friends like George Gibbs, who lived near the O'Kelleys in Bollinger County. At the first shot of the war Gibbs had joined the Missouri State Guard, and later a regular artillery unit. He was captured and imprisoned at Chicago's horrible Camp Douglas, returning after the war to live in Bollinger. Also nearby was

George Gibbs was a Confederate veteran who settled in Bollinger County near the O'Kelley family and hosted Jesse and Frank James.

the home of Daniel T. Cole, a distant cousin of Jesse's mother, whose maiden name was Cole. Confederate veteran Jacob Lutes, founder of the city of Lutesville, lived there too. His brother David didn't serve in the war but was a popular local blacksmith and county treasurer who buried the county's treasury during the war to keep it safe from the invading armies. The James boys knew Jacob to be a fair-minded man, and with him as their intercessor, they stopped to rest with one family or another. Jesse and Frank would sometimes stay in someone's home, and sometimes run a cold camp at David Lutes's farm and be gone before dawn.

One cold autumn evening in 1881, when Jesse stopped for the night at the Gibbs home, Ed was there visiting. He was introduced to Mr. Howard, but he'd already been told that the man he would meet was Jesse James. Ed was awestruck. He felt a kinship with anyone who was fighting against oppression and was sure he could fit in with the bandit gang if given the chance. He felt so distant from his family, disconnected from any sort of career, and unsuccessful with women, but he knew he could do fine among men who took what they needed from the world. Ed was sure it wasn't too late to join Jesse. One one hand, he knew that if he went on the outlaw trail with Jesse he would be giving up his birthright and possibly a generous inheritance from his father the doctor. But on the other hand, there might not be much for him to inherit. He certainly was neither a farmer nor a doctor.

+ — ◆ — +

Jesse enjoyed life in Nashville with his wife and children, and he deeply wanted to recapture that way of living in Missouri. So in a move toward establishing a new, respectable public persona in November of 1881, Jesse moved to St. Joseph, Missouri, rented a house under the name Thomas Howard, and moved in with Zee, Mary, and Jesse Jr. It was a modest, two-story house with a single-story addition in the rear, built in the mid-1850s on a hillside with a commanding view in all directions.

A new recruit to the gang, Charley Ford, helped them move, and Jesse told him to take the extra bedroom. Jesse had known of Charley Ford and his brother Bob for a long time because their uncle Bill had married Windy Jim Cummins's sister Artella back in 1862. That's why Jesse had already cautiously let Charley in on a couple of jobs, including the Glendale robbery. But Charley wasn't the kind of hard-riding, quick-thinking partner he wanted. Certainly not the kind of man he once had in Frank and the Youngers. The old saying "Keep your friends close and your enemies closer" made great sense to Jesse, and that's why he asked Charley to move into his St. Joseph house.

It was all a windblown house of cards. The threat of insiders turning on each other was constantly hanging over their heads. Sure enough, about a week after the Blue Cut robbery, rumors reached Jesse that Ed Miller wanted to leave the outlaw life for good. In Jesse's mind that probably meant Miller was going to work out a deal with the law to turn Jesse in. Maybe as a pardon for his own crimes. Or maybe to collect a reward. Or both. Miller was in the Glendale train robbery in the fall of 1879, and then went straight until he joined Jesse again for the Blue Cut job two years later. For him to come back to the gang after that absence, then leave again, just didn't seem right. Besides, Jesse knew the law had been watching Ed Miller ever since his brother Clell was killed in the disastrous Northfield, Minnesota, raid. After a long search, Jesse finally located Ed Miller at a relative's house on December 4. When Jesse suggested to Miller that they ride off a ways and talk, Miller was extremely nervous, and rightfully so, but saddled up because he couldn't think of a good reason to refuse. Unfortunately, Miller's nervousness only confirmed for Jesse that he was up to no good. When they'd ridden a couple of miles, Jesse accused Miller of intending to betray his partners, and the talk grew heated. The fear in Miller's eyes was obvious, and even in the December cold, sweat poured down his face. So Jesse lowered the intensity and told Miller he understood and everything would be all right. As they turned to ride on, just when Miller thought he was safe, Jesse pulled his revolver and shot him in the back of the head.

The next day Jesse rode to where Charley Ford had joined his brother Bob, at the home of their widowed older sister, Martha Boulton. The Fords recognized the horse Jesse was leading as Ed Miller's. Jesse said Miller wasn't feeling well, so he had gone on down to Hot Springs. When Charley asked when Miller might be back, Jesse said, "I don't think he's going to get well," left the horse, and rode away.

Martha's house in Clay County had become a way station where gang members could sleep, hide from the law, and enjoy Martha's cooking. Just a few days after Jesse's eerie visit, Charley left, leaving Bob, Wood Hite, and Dick Liddil at the house with Martha. Liddil's romance with Hite's stepmother had been gnawing at Hite, and he brought it up at the breakfast table. Adding to the bad blood between the two was that Hite had been trying unsuccessfully to kindle a fire in Martha, and

Liddil had also started flirting with her. When Hite told Liddil he was a mangy dog for chasing both women, Liddil tried to dismiss it, but Hite wouldn't shut up. The needling went on until they both stood bolt upright there at the kitchen table, pulled their revolvers and, as Bob ducked beside a credenza, commenced to firing. They put several holes in the walls, along with one shot that hit Liddil in the leg and one that hit Hite in his gun arm, making him drop his revolver and fall backwards over his chair. As he writhed on the floor holding his bleeding arm, Bob saw that the fight was a toss-up. So he pulled his pistol, took two steps to stand directly over Hite, and put a .45 slug in his head. He and Liddil took him upstairs, waited fifteen minutes for him to die, then dumped him into a ravine in the woods and threw some dirt and leaves over him.

From that moment on, Bob and Liddil were scared to death. Bob had killed one of the few men Jesse really trusted, his cousin Wood Hite. Soon enough Jesse would find out Hite was missing. Then it was only a matter of time until he figured out, or somebody told him, that Bob killed him, and Jesse was sure to kill Bob. He might even consider Liddil equally guilty and kill him too.

At the same time, the law was closing in on Jesse. Governor Crittenden, who campaigned on a promise to rid Missouri of the James Gang and others like them, posted a $5,000 reward for Jesse and the same for Frank. It was an unparalleled amount in an era when the common reward for capture of even the worst criminals was $300. The reward's effect was not so much that it spurred lawmen to action. They were already doing all they could to catch him. No, Jesse's fear was that the big offer from the governor would prove too tempting to one of the James Gang insiders.

Jesse never fully trusted Liddil. There was an understood inequality, a suspicion that he was not cut from the same cloth as the former guerrillas. On December 30, 1881, Jesse and Charley Ford showed up at the Boulton home. Bob was gone, but Liddil was still there, and the

Sheriff James Timberlake was a little-known hero of the quest to capture the James Gang. He's the one who arrested Bob Ford and arranged the meeting with Governor Crittenden. When Ford failed to follow through on his promises to the governor, Timberlake laid out a plan to capture Jesse and gave Ford a deadline. However, instead of following the plan, Ford killed Jesse.

tension was thick enough to slice. They all visited a while, with Jesse dropping offhand questions about Bob, and about where to find Hite. Liddil said he hadn't see either one in a week or so. Jesse asked about Liddil's wounded leg, and he made up a story about how he got shot by accident. And finally, Jesse asked Liddil to go for a ride with him and Charley, but Liddil knew it would be the last ride he ever took, so he said he didn't feel like it, and maybe they could go later. The next morning Jesse and Charley left, and that was the last time Liddil would see either of them.

Meanwhile, Clay County sheriff James R. Timberlake was hearing reports that Wood Hite had been killed by Bob Ford, so in early January he went to the Boulton home, waited for Bob to show up, and took him in for questioning. Bob was about to turn twenty years old but looked more like sixteen. He was of slight build, with short brown hair and a poor attempt at a mustache that was almost blond. He was left-handed and carried a Colt .45 Peacemaker holstered on his left hip. It was a showy, nickel-plated piece with a seven-inch barrel, too much gun for such a man.

Timberlake actually knew little about Bob at the time, and it was only during questioning him that he discovered Bob's arm's-length association with Jesse. The questioning led nowhere with regard to Hite's disappearance. But the possibility of getting Jesse was far more important, and Timberlake was a modern lawman who knew how to squeeze what he needed out of a man. He charged Bob with the murder of Wood Hite, and then gave him a chance to save himself by delivering Jesse. Bob was terrified of prison, even more than the gallows, so he eagerly accepted the offer.

Timberlake set up a St. Louis meeting between Bob and Governor Crittenden in a room at the St. James Hotel on January 13. It was brief. They all agreed that Bob would deliver Jesse in return for the charges against him being dropped, plus a reward. Bob was really going out on a limb. He barely knew Jesse, but he knew Charley was moving into the inner circle of Jesse's confidence, and Bob was just enough of a fool to think he could do what he promised. Later, Bob would always claim that the deal was dead or alive, whereas the governor would continue to say that he only wanted Ford to set Jesse up so Timberlake and other officers could arrest him.

Also as part of the deal, Bob asked for an audience for his sister Martha to negotiate for the surrender of her sweetheart Dick Liddil. Martha met Crittenden in his Jefferson City office, but Crittenden would not negotiate, and insisted that Liddil had to surrender unconditionally. Liddil knew Jesse was gunning for him, and his best bet was to surrender and let the law protect him for a while. On January 24, Liddil surrendered to Sheriff Timberlake, and from that point on, the more help he provided to the law, the more likely they were to go easy on him.

Liddil was worried about one other man besides Jesse who might be interested in killing him to avenge Wood Hite's death: Wood's brother and Jesse's cousin, Clarence Hite. So with Liddil acting as a guide to old George Hite's home in Kentucky, Pinkerton agents arrested Clarence, brought him back to Missouri without bothering to extradite him, and delivered him to Daviess County, where he was charged with robbing the train at Winston, a James Gang job the previous summer. When the gang took control of that train Jesse ordered, "Everyone down," and the conductor, William Westfall, refused, so someone shot him through the heart. It didn't matter who, because everyone in the gang was equally guilty—and so Clarence was charged with Westfall's murder. To get the murder charge dropped, he pled guilty to the robbery and was sentenced to twenty-five years. Liddil also promised that if the law could persuade Frank James to surrender, he would testify against him. But Jesse was Liddil's real problem. Until Jesse James was locked up, Liddil's life wasn't worth a nickel.

That winter, Windy Jim Cummins was trying to find out who killed family friend Ed Miller, whose decomposed body had been found by a hunter. Jesse was the last one to see him alive, and Cummins was determined to get some answers for himself and for Miller's family. If his old friend Jesse killed his old friend Ed, Cummins might feel obliged to avenge the murder. But first, he had to know if Jesse did it and why.

He went to Nashville, where Jesse welcomed him and invited him to stay at the house. But Cummins was afraid of the invitation and got a hotel room. There was no rush. He couldn't just come out and accuse Jesse of killing Ed. He would just see where their conversations led. So he visited Frank, and even joined him in having coffee with one of his detective friends. But after he'd been in town a couple of days, during breakfast with Jesse, he brought up Ed's name, and could see by the look on his face that Jesse knew exactly what he was up to. After that, the tension mounted day after day. Sooner or later, somebody was going to make a move, and Jesse always moved first.

It Ends Here

One night Cummins sat in his Nashville hotel room staring at a glass of whiskey, unable to escape the mounting threat of a bullet from Jesse or another of the old gang, or maybe even some new recruit he'd never met, acting on Jesse's orders. So he packed up and rode out before dawn. When Jesse discovered that Cummins had left without a word, it confirmed his suspicions that Cummins couldn't be trusted, and from that time on, Cummins would never be allowed to return to the fold. Of course that was fine with Cummins. He had no thought of returning.

Jesse was running out of people to count on, but he wanted to pull another job, so he asked Charley Ford if he knew anybody else they could trust. As if Crittenden had written the script, Charley suggested Bob. Jesse had met the boyish-looking Bob and wasn't impressed. Of course when Jesse was his age, he was already a seasoned and relentless guerrilla. But Bob Ford was no Jesse James. He had grown up in a different era. He seemed indecisive, unsure of himself, and shifty. But Jesse needed men, so Bob would have to do. That's how Bob came to St. Joseph the end of March and moved into Charley's room in Jesse's house, and as far as the neighbors were concerned, they were Bob and Charley Johnson, Jesse's cousins. Jesse warned them, "I want to be able to see both of you at all times."

Of course they were both terrified that Jesse knew who killed Wood Hite, and would not only kill Bob, but also kill Charley for bringing Bob into the gang. So by the time the Ford brothers were living in the James house in St. Joseph, they were so nervous they looked even guiltier than they were. Jesse was sure they were up to some sort of betrayal.

In Bob's meeting with Crittenden and Timberlake back in January, they had discussed no details on how to take Jesse. Bob had no plan, except to wait for Jesse to be unarmed. "He's faster than either of us," he later told Charley. What he meant was not only was Jesse faster in drawing his Smith & Wesson Schofield, cocking it, and firing, but he was also more experienced and more willing. Bob had been in the gunfight with Hite and Liddil, and he knew that being willing to kill a man was a hurdle many men couldn't overcome. A split second of hesitation by Bob or Charley at the crucial moment could be fatal.

By the time Bob moved into the James house, the deal with Crittenden had been in place for two months, and still Bob hadn't come to Sheriff Timberlake with a time and place to capture Jesse. It had also been that long since Liddil surrendered, and the governor was getting impatient. So Timberlake got a message to Bob, calling him to meet under a bridge across town. There Timberlake laid out a plan for Bob to lure Jesse to a posse, which would be Timberlake and a force of special deputies from the Kansas City police, led by Liberty, Missouri, Police Commissioner Henry H. Craig. There were all standing by, and there was a deadline. If Ford didn't deliver Jesse in ten days, the deal was off, and the law would be coming for Bob. The Fords just had to stay alive and figure out a way to make it happen.

Up until that time all of them been successful in hiding their deal-making and plotting from the press. Even Liddil's surrender was a secret. Then the morning of April 3, 1882, Bob and Jesse walked to town to buy a couple of newspapers. While Jesse paid, Bob looked at the headline, and his heart leaped to his throat. He hardly said a word as they walk back to the house, where they joined Charley on the porch. Jesse opened his newspaper, furrowed his brow, he leaned in, then back, and said, "Hello, here. Dick Liddil surrenders."

He knew Liddil was going to talk to save his hide. He looked at Bob. "Where is Dick Liddil?" he asked sarcastically. After all, he had asked Bob the same question before.

Bob swore he didn't have any idea, and hadn't seen Liddil since last fall. Jesse pressed, knowing that both Bob and Liddil had been in at Boulton's house in Jackson County in January. But it was a pretty morning, he was feeling good, and he dropped the matter.

Bob was simply out of time. If he didn't act, he'd never live long enough to carry out Timberlake's plan. After breakfast, Zee cleaned

Jesse James's wife, Zee, is pictured in 1882, shortly after Jesse was killed.

up the kitchen, the children played in the yard, and the men went to the barn to brush the horses, then settled in the parlor. Jesse had been planning to rob the bank at Platte City, where a murder trial was starting. The whole town would be focused on the courthouse, giving them a perfect chance to hit the bank, and the three of them were to leave that day for Platte City. Jesse remarked that it was a hot day, and removed his jacket and vest. Then he paused, thought, and removed his shoulder holsters carrying his nickel Colt and a Smith & Wesson, saying, "I wouldn't want the neighbors to see anything if I go out in the yard." He noticed a picture on the wall and said, "It's crooked." Then he pushed a chair under it, picked up a duster, and stepped onto the chair to straighten and dust the picture. Bob and Charley locked eyes, knowing it was then or never. They both slipped their Colts from their holsters, but Charley was hesitant, and the last sound Jesse heard was the clicking hammer of Bob's Peacemaker.

Chapter Six

Bob Ford's Burden

After being introduced to Jesse in Bollinger County, Ed O'Kelley waited a couple of months, but still couldn't get the meeting out of his mind. So he packed a bag, said his goodbyes, and walked to the train depot in Marble Hill. He boarded the train Sunday night and the miles rolled away, night fell, and others slept, but Ed could hardly close his eyes. Finally, late Monday morning, the train rolled into St. Joseph. Ed picked up his bag, and his heart was pounding as he stepped down to the platform. He had never seen such a swarm of people, running and walking in every direction, shouting, whispering, some calling to each other, "Have you heard?" Ed left the depot walking in the direction most of the crowd seemed to be headed. At the foot of Lafayette Street was a mob that stretched all the way up the hill to a little white house. Ed craned his neck but couldn't make out what was going on, so he turned to the man beside him. "What's all the excitement?" he asked. Without turning, the man smiled and said, "They killed Jesse James."

Ed had unwittingly walked into the world of the Fords, and everywhere Ed turned, they were the topic of conversation. With one bullet they ended the James Gang's violent and highly profitable crime spree, something America's best detectives, sheriffs, deputies, and policemen couldn't do. And yet it wasn't done as an act of public service or to balance the scales of justice. The killing was vigilantism perverted, an act of greed. It was also an act of self-preservation; Bob shot before he was shot. And regardless of whether Jesse deserved what he got, Bob Ford shot an unarmed man in the back. That just isn't done.

When the gun was fired, Bob and Charley Ford began their lives as the premier vigilantes in America and found it was one surprise after another. The first thing they did after running down the hill yelling insanely that they'd killed Jesse was send a telegram to Governor Crittenden, Sheriff Timberlake, and a few other folks. Then they turned themselves in to Captain Craig, and sat back waiting for their congratulations and a huge reward. Instead, they were surprised to be locked up in jail, and doubly surprised when a grand jury indicted them for first-degree murder. It was a whirlwind as they pled guilty, were sentenced to hang, and were pardoned by Crittenden, all on the same day.

But there was more: that old murder charge for killing Wood Hite during the gunfight in Martha Boulton's kitchen in Ray County. A month later Bob stood trial and was acquitted. That too was part of the deal.

As for the reward money, the governor would later write, "I have paid over twenty thousand dollars to various individuals for the capture and overthrow of this band of desperadoes, and not one penny of it came from the State Treasury." He was right, the money came from the railroads. As for the $20,000, it may have been only $10,000, of which he gave some to Timberlake and Craig, and about $1,000 total to the brothers Ford. Only Crittenden knew the total reward money raised or whose pocket it lined.

The Fords were curiosities, but not heroes. An impresario quickly wrote and financed a stage play in which Bob and Charley performed a completely fictional drama of how they killed Jesse to save a poor, defenseless woman from him. They were universally met with boos, threats, and thrown tomatoes and eggs, so their show business career didn't last long. Then they supplemented their income in dime shows, appearing alongside freaks and animals with birth defects, with Bob telling his story while moralizing to a lowbrow crowd.

Bob Ford posed for this photo shortly after the murder of Jesse James. He's holding a Colt 1873 Single Action Army, which is almost certainly not the weapon used to kill Jesse. Jesse's coroner's report says the gun that killed him was a Colt pistol, but lists a serial number that matches a Smith & Wesson Model 3. At one point Ford presented a Smith & Wesson Model 3 to Captain Craig's son, saying it was the murder weapon. However, Ford, Frank James, and others were reported to have sold various pistols, claiming that each was the one that killed Jesse.

And all the while, Charley was sure that if his tuberculosis didn't kill him first, Frank James was going to hunt them down and kill them. In fact, Frank was busy with his own trial and finally getting a taste of the quiet life he'd always wanted, selling shoes at a store in Dallas. But Charley didn't know that, so he moved from town to town, changing his name each time and drinking heavily, along with the morphine he took for the pain of tuberculosis, until at last he put a pistol to his chest and shot himself through the heart.

On his own again, Bob was beginning to see that after killing Jesse, he would have to make a showing of himself everywhere he went. There would always be a James admirer, a challenger, or an aggravating loudmouth. He would have to act the hero and defend himself physically or verbally, wherever he went. Worse, he was all false bravado. Looking at the world through the eyes of fear, he couldn't let anything pass, couldn't walk away with any dignity, and like O'Kelley, had to continually prove something. As a result, he became a sullen bully, always at war with himself because he knew in his heart that he was a coward.

Bob reconnected with Dick Liddil, whose life he was sure he saved by killing Wood. By then, Liddil had testified against Frank James and generally spilled the beans about his fellow outlaws to gain pardons for all of his crimes. He and Bob began to understand how many people hated them enough to kill them, and they opted for a fresh start out west. But they couldn't run far enough to outrun their fear. Liddil was constantly looking over his shoulder to see if Frank James or one of his friends was going to gun him down. And Bob knew any day might be the day someone would shoot him for shooting Jesse.

They tried settling in West Las Vegas, New Mexico, bought the Bank Saloon, and were soon to find that the place was poorly named. Liddil had never held a job and had no business sense for the saloon. To make matters worse, in 1885, Bob also took a job as a city policeman, giving him a living wage, as well as access to benefits of working on both sides of the law. That could have been a smart plan, except that Bob was terrible at it. He was hotheaded, quicker to fight than keep the peace, and couldn't seem to make friends with either the lawmen or the outlaws. Confederate veterans, drunks, and others who thought back-shooting was inexcusable taunted him, and he didn't take it well. All things considered, he was very unpopular, so nobody wanted to go to the Bank. Then Bob, in his usual way of shooting his mouth off, challenged a man to a target-shooting contest, with the stakes being that the loser would leave town. It was a fool's bet because he had never been known as a particularly good shot at anything smaller than a man's head at more than a few feet away. When the contest started, the other man shot first and was so good, Bob walked away humiliated without ever taking a shot. He and Liddil sold the Bank at a loss, and tried again with a saloon and dance hall in the tiny town of Cerillos.

Even there, the paranoia deepened. Bob could remember when there were show business promoters and people who wanted to buy his drinks in the saloons. There were people who paid him to speak at their church or community hall. But that had all run out. Nobody cared much anymore. And that only made his bad temper worse. Again unable to make a living, they parted company. Bob headed for Colorado and never saw Liddil again.

+———+———+

Dick Liddil proved to be every bit the threat that Jesse had suspected. But not Windy Jim Cummins. When he disappeared from Nashville in 1881, he disappeared from everywhere, and he might never have been found if not for the aspiring teenage reporter Red Galvin.

Some said Cummins went west and found great adventure as an army scout and Indian fighter, among other things. Some said he returned to his old alias of James Johnson and had enough cash to establish himself on a tiny farm in Arkansas. But he was constantly reminded of how hard and monotonous farming was, and how exciting the outlaw life had been. By 1885 all the old members of the gang were in prison or dead except for a handful who had moved on to more peaceful pursuits.

But Cummins was thinking in a different direction. The heat had died down, and he figured it was the perfect time to come out of retirement, so he made an adventurous move. Using the alias of Mr. Wittrock, he traveled to Kansas and recruited a man named Haight, along with a childhood friend, Dan Moriarity, a two-bit crook fresh out of jail in Leavenworth. Moriarity was a railroad worker who knew the freight operations and which Adams Express agents might be useful. The three of them arrived at St. Louis Union Station well before the westbound train was to leave with the express man Moriarity chose. Mr. Wittrock used his old Windy Jim line of patter to get the agent involved in a conversation and ended up riding in the express car with him. So when the train had to stop because of the wagon his partners had parked on the tracks at Pacific, he asked his new friend, "You don't want me to lay the cold, black muzzle of my Colt .45 against your head, do you?" Of course the agent was happy to have an opportunity to open the safe without even seeing the Colt, and Mr. Wittrock took an astounding $105,000. He then peeled off a handful of bills and stuffed them into the agent's pocket, and they shook hands and wished each other well.

In a cave above the Missouri River, Mr. Wittrock paid the two accomplices $1,500 each, an incredible amount of money to them, and hid most of the loot, taking a chunk of it to buy a coal delivery business and settle down in Chicago. Building on the self-promotion skills he learned from Jesse, Cummins mailed letters from various cities to the *Post-Dispatch*, saying he was Jim Cummins, he was the Mr. Wittrock who robbed the train, and life was grand. When editor George Johns printed the letters in the *Post-Dispatch*, the Pinkertons, working on the case for Adams Express, were quick to scoff, saying whoever wrote them wasn't the real robber. It became a running argument in the pages of the *Post-Dispatch*. Every time a letter came in, Johns ran it in the paper, feeling obliged to follow it with an interview with the head of the local Pinkerton office, who would make fun of the paper for believing the letter was really from the robber.

Finally, Johns had enough of it and called on the tenacious eighteen-year-old Galvin. "Red, we've got to prove this thing one way or another. We may be fools for running these letters, but we've got to know."

"Don't worry," Red said, "I won't quit until I find Cummins."

It was a long, wearying hunt, but Red was a man worthy of the challenge. He had friends among the Pinkertons who let him look at the evidence, and he was intrigued by a piece of a mail tag that was found in a pile of torn-up papers. The pile was found in a rowboat. And the Pinkertons found the rowboat because the letter writer told them where to find it, hidden in the weeds along the Missouri river, with some coffee, sugar, and cans of dried beef. In the letter Cummins said he used the boat to travel near the point of the holdup, and still the Pinkertons insisted that it didn't mean the letter writer was Cummins or that Cummins was the robber. Besides, they were busy following every conceivable lead except the letters.

They couldn't make heads nor tails of the luggage tag, so had long since dismissed it. Red, on the other hand, saw the tag as a puzzle piece. It bore only the letters "rity," and below that "orth," scrawled in pencil. From that little scrap, he checked every angle he could on Cummins, including childhood friends. He found out Cummins knew Frank and Jesse James as childhood playmates, and they all knew Moriarity. That was the "ity." He then tracked Moriarity to jail in Leavenworth, the "orth," found him living in Kansas, and convinced him that they needed to find Cummins and prove his identity for all the doubters. "It's what Cummins would want us to do," Red told him.

The odd pair, the petty crook and the sleuth reporter, took the train to Chicago, where they made barstool inquiries until finally Moriarity spotted Cummins, and Red bought them all a fine meal at the Palmer House. Cummins indeed appreciated the attention and the newspaper's dedication to getting the story right, so Red and his editor Johns got a great story out of it.

William Pinkerton, head of the agency and son of its founder, hit the roof, which lit a fire under his agents, who covered roughly the same trail Red covered and ended up arresting Cummins. They recovered about $90,000 of the loot, and Cummins stood trial. However, there was no evidence tying him to the crime, and no witnesses. And like most of the James Gang trials, nobody, not even Moriarity or the express agent, was willing to testify against Cummins, so he went free. A. Frank Pinkerton, the only son of the agency's founder who chose to be an author rather than enter the family business, would later write a thrilling fictionalized account of the case. But William Pinkerton didn't care to sensationalize it at all, and at his urging, Adams Express refused to pay Red the $2,000 reward that had been posted for information about the robbers. At last, after Johns repeatedly bashed them in the *Post-Dispatch* for not paying what they'd promised, they gave Red $200, a token to them, but a lot of money to a street-educated bootblack.

Windy Jim decided he'd had enough adventure and wished he could settle down in his old hometown of Kearney. On a bright morning in 1902, at the age of fifty-five, he turned himself in to the Clay County sheriff, ready to take any punishment he had coming so he could put it behind him. But in fact, he wasn't wanted for any crime in Clay County. So the mayor welcomed Cummins back home, making him a local hero. The local sheriff and prosecutor promised that no charges would be brought against the old Rebel, and they got their photograph taken together for the newspaper.

Chapter Seven

Pueblo

A year passed, then a couple more since Ed O'Kelley rolled into St. Joseph. He swept out saloons and moved railroad freight, but riding with Jesse remained the only dream he ever had, his only source of inspiration in an otherwise discouraging life. He couldn't go back home with his tail between his legs. Ed had to find his own way, and that meant moving west. He was enchanted by stories of the cow towns, gamblers, fast money, and especially the riches pouring from the gold mines of California and the Dakotas. But he settled on Colorado, which had witnessed a brutally rapid rise toward statehood in 1876. The Ute Indians protested every incursion on their land, and they massacred a cavalry regiment in 1879, the same year a college was built at Fort Collins. Gold was discovered on the heels of a silver boom that started in 1878 in Leadville and only got bigger. With the smell of money in the air, every resource of the Bureau of Indian Affairs, the Army, the state legislature, and local bands of ore-hungry speculators was brought to bear, and the retreating Ute were on reservations by 1881. As promising as the gold and silver strikes were, Ed was no miner. He was determined to make money from the sweat of other men's brows.

Denver was a huge, modern city. It was hard for Ed to learn his way around, and he just couldn't seem to get a handhold. So he took a train to the next stop down the line, Pueblo, and it seemed to fit just right.

Ute Chief Ouray, in his store-bought boots, and his wife, Chipeta, ca. 1880. Ouray was one of the Ute leaders fighting for their traditional lands in Colorado before surrendering and moving to reservations. Removal of the Native Americans paved the way for Colorado's silver and gold booms.

It was a town of about three thousand people, with a business district nestled along the banks of the Arkansas River, and beautiful buildings and homes for the wealthy, designed by world-class architects who incorporated design and engineering elements from around the world. There was a sprawling working class that fed on the weekly paychecks from the nearby coal and iron ore mines.

Pueblo was laid out in 1870, then waited for a railroad to get there, which meant the early speculators made a lot of money. By 1882 the town was home to a Bessemer furnace, and tiny Pueblo was equipped to mine, crush, and smelt iron ore and turn it into high-quality steel. The steel mill, with its never-ending plume of smoke and steam, dominated the horizon, giving everyone living there a sense of financial security. They were all sure they would grow quite wealthy from mining and steel and everything associated with them.

When Ed looked at that steel mill, he saw people who needed places to drink and gamble. He saw miners who needed to let off steam

The steel plant at Pueblo, with its Bessemer furnace, is pictured in this postcard. It belched fire and smoke twenty-four hours a day, every day. It fueled the local economy, which fueled O'Kelley's imagination.

after a day at the plant. He saw underpaid workers who couldn't quite support their families and resorted to petty crimes. Ed was sure he could find work as a policeman. Not only would he be appreciated for keeping the peace in the town, but he would also find opportunities to make money on the side. A little here, a little there. A little taste of the gambling action. A little something in the pocket to overlook an arrest.

Unfortunately, the police force was full, and Ed had to settle for a job as a streetcar operator. It wasn't bad, wearing a nice uniform jacket and cap, driving a horse that pulled the car along steel rails that were made right there in Pueblo. He got a chance to learn the town and people, and the whole time found himself straddling the track that divided right from wrong. He had opportunities to assist the elderly, help people with packages on and off the car, give directions, and recommend cafés. Of course he also was a wealth of information for people looking for a dice game, cheap whiskey, flophouses, and brothels. He was alert to the chatter of lowlifes and bottom-feeders, knowing at some point he'd hear of the easy burglary, the unattended cash box, or the gambling hall that was hiring shills.

And yet, there was a part of Ed that made him think he could make his father proud if only he'd do the right thing. There was a force that drove him toward doing something that Thomas would value. And in Ed's twisted mind, that course of thinking, coupled with his quick temper and love of fighting, made him a bully. He liked to surprise an opponent or attack a smaller man. He had to continually prove himself but was careful to do it only when he had the advantage. One evening, a lout climbed aboard the streetcar, and Ed smelled the whiskey on him. He was a big fellow, possibly a miner, and when Ed greeted him with "Good evening," the man only glared. They'd gone no more than a block when Ed looked back to see him standing in front of a seated young woman.

Ed couldn't make out the words, but he could tell they were getting louder, and immediately his face turned red and he could feel the heat go up the back of his neck. He stopped the horse in the same motion that he stood, covering the distance to the middle of the car in three steps. "Is this man bothering you, ma'am?" he asked firmly.

The ruffian pushed Ed firmly in the chest and told him to mind his own business. Though the man probably outweighed him by thirty pounds, Ed had at least an inch on him, and the shove was hardly anything at all. But the shove wasn't the issue. It was the principle of the thing. Ed grabbed the man's shirt front and belt and slammed his head back against the wall of the car, then tossed him to the floor in front of the door. As the dazed offender tried to stand, Ed pulled him to his feet and threw him out the door and hard onto his back on the paved sidewalk. Even that wasn't enough. Ed stepped down and straddled the dazed man, continuing to punch him in the face, on the ears, his nose, his jaw, until blood was everywhere and Ed's arms were tired.

He pulled a bottle from his coat pocket, took a long sip, tucked it away, and stood, surveying the crowd that had gathered. "You folks are safe from thugs on my car, yessir," he announced, then climbed back into the driver's seat and finished his run. The beating earned him a warning from his supervisor at Pueblo Transportation, but in fact, it wasn't the first fight for Ed in Pueblo. It was just the first one on a crowded street corner.

He was drinking steadily and liking it just fine. Every day, workers came and went in round-the-clock shifts from the mill and the mines, which meant almost everything else in Pueblo was open day and night. So no matter when Ed started or ended his hours on the streetcar, he could find a saloon ready to quench his thirst. Within a short time he'd earned a reputation as a man with a hair-trigger temper fueled by alcohol. The police saw him with men who were suspected in burglaries and livestock thefts. They saw him at the tables in gambling houses where they knew the games were fixed. And yet, he was never arrested, and the police never had anything on him.

Then late one night in September 1883, there was a burglary at a general store. The owner, who lived upstairs with his wife, awakened to the sound of footsteps running up the stairs, and suddenly two masked men burst into the bedroom with pistols leveled. They wrapped the couple in their bed sheet and tied it with binder's twine from the store, and for the next hour the helpless merchants listened to voices, banging, and scraping downstairs.

By the time the victims got loose and alerted the police it was almost dawn. The store had been practically emptied of things men would want. Every pick, shovel, hammer, chisel, and sledge was gone. Hats, boots, gloves, lanterns, four saddles, bridles, tobacco, matches, kerosene, a box of factory-made horse shoes, work shirts, rolls of fence wire and electric wire, bags of lime, and a glistening porcelain indoor toilet. And then there was the candy. All the glass jars of candy had been emptied. It was the first time the police had seen such a big haul, but they were pretty sure it was the work of the same gang that had been pulling smaller jobs, during which witnesses had seen four or five robbers. This time the police had wagon tracks leading north out of town, but there they mingled with all the others.

The next afternoon Ed O'Kelley walked in to the Pueblo police station and told a detective he could lead him to the loot and the looters. Sure enough, they found four men exactly where O'Kelley said they'd be, in a warehouse on the other side of the river, reclining on a wagon-load of stolen goods, eating candy. With the goods recovered and the men in jail, they all said O'Kelley was in on the robbery, so the police locked him up too. In fact, O'Kelley had worked his way into the gang, and that's how he knew about the job. But at his arraignment O'Kelley explained in his simple, gruff way that he did it to prove he could be a good policeman. It worked—he wasn't charged, and the chief of police decided that was the kind of man they needed on the force. By the end of the year, O'Kelley had his first law enforcement job.

+ —— + —— +

Bob Ford left Dick Liddil and New Mexico in hopes of richer prospects, taking the Denver & Rio Grande train to Denver. But a man he met in the car told him about the mining and steel mill at Pueblo, which people were calling "the Pittsburgh of the West." Ford thought about the business going on in that little town, how many miners and steel workers were drinking up their hourly wages, and how many people were getting rich off of the steel, and it sounded like a place he should investigate. So at Denver he changed trains for Pueblo, with no idea that fate was about to bring him face to face with the man who would change not only his life, but also the story of vigilantism in the West.

Ford dropped his suitcase with the stationmaster and walked from the Pueblo depot to the part of town he knew best, the saloons, gambling parlors, and dance halls. There he could get the most information the quickest, and he could survey his prospects for making a lot of money with minimal effort. He liked what he heard. He liked all the suckers at the gambling tables. He liked the overpopulation of saloons. It was getting late when he left a poker game and sidled up to the bar beside an out-of-work policeman. It was Ed O'Kelley. "Why would a policeman be out of work?" Ford asked. "Looks to me like there's a lot of lawbreakers here."

O'Kelley eyed him sideways. It was not the kind of question he favored from a man he just met. "Maybe I don't want to be workin' right now," O'Kelly snapped.

"Oh, don't mean to offend, friend," Ford offered. "Your business."

This photo shows Edward Capehart O'Kelley the day he became prisoner 2970 at Colorado State Prison. At thirty-four, he still had a mustache, but had long ago given up the rakish handlebars that characterized him in his twenties. He was well behaved, and got to keep his blue uniform. Courtesy of Colorado State Archives.

That seemed to satisfy O'Kelley. After all, he didn't have anybody else to talk to. After they drank for a minute or so more, he said, "They didn't like my drinkin' habits."

"Oh," Ford nodded. "Yes, police chiefs can be judgmental about a man's recreation, can't they? I was an officer of the law myself in New Mexico."

"That so?" O'Kelley muttered, uncaring. "Tell the truth, I don't mind a scrape now and then. But they got their own ideas about how to take a man down and I take 'em down my way."

Ford's brow furrowed. "That's just wrong. If a cop can't fight, who can?"

"When you've got a rattlesnake by the tail, you'd best start smackin' the head," O'Kelley agreed.

"Bob Ford," he introduced himself, reaching to shake hands.

"O'Kelley," the other one grumbled, taking a drink without noticing the hand.

Of all the people in the world, in all the saloons, in all the towns, here were Ford and O'Kelley, two men more alike than different, meeting hundreds of miles from the home state they hated to leave behind. O'Kelley was more of a drinker and brawler, Ford more of a talker and gambler. O'Kelley didn't care much how he looked and couldn't seem to hold on to money. Ford enjoyed dressing like he had more money than he really had and always had a knack for finding money. But they both lived on the quick dollar, had hair-trigger tempers, and had never learned how to make and keep friends.

They drank into the night, while O'Kelley acted as eager tour guide and Ford looked for opportunities. At last they wore out. It was a just a couple of blocks to the Lamplighter Hotel, where they each paid a dollar to share a room with two other men who barely opened their eyes, then went back to snoring loudly.

Soon enough, sunlight crawled across the quilt until it fell on Ford's eyes, forcing them open just before noon. He was alone, so he took his time washing his face, slicking down his hair, and dressing. But when he put on his tie, he couldn't find his diamond stickpin. He searched everywhere. Around the pitcher and bowl. Down on the floor and under the bed. It was gone, and he was sure O'Kelley took it. It wasn't the other two men. It was O'Kelley. He was mad as a hornet, and there was nothing to do about it. The thief was gone, he had a terrible headache, and his mouth tasted like yesterday's hog slop. That O'Kelley. Didn't he know who he was dealing with?

Yes, O'Kelley knew exactly who he was dealing with. They didn't have to talk about Jesse or mention Ford's notoriety. People in the bar recognized him, and one toasted to his health, while many more sneered and turned away from him. O'Kelley hated him for what he did. Still, he was willing to play host to him for the evening, just to see where it would lead. And that morning, it was nothing at all to take his diamond stickpin. He pawned it and went to drink up the proceeds at a saloon across town. He figured a man like Ford deserved what he got.

He also figured wrongly that Ford would move on down the line, and he'd never see him again. Ford landed a low-paying job running a faro game in a saloon on the river, one of the places on his tour with O'Kelley. A few days later, from his table at the far end of the bar, seeing O'Kelley enter the place, he quickly closed down his game. He covered the distance to O'Kelley, spun his right arm behind him before O'Kelley knew what was happening, and slammed his head down on the bar.

"Remember me, O'Kelley?"

O'Kelley couldn't even see who had a hold of him, but he knew as soon as Ford said, "We had a real good time, didn't we, O'Kelley? Until you stole my diamond tie pin, remember?"

With that he released the hold so he could strike a blow. They were the same height and O'Kelley outweighed him, but Ford was quicker. Plus, he was deep into the rage for which he'd become known. O'Kelley didn't have any thought that he was beat, and he whirled with a roundhouse blow that missed. Ford instantly drew the Colt from his left hip and laid it hard up against O'Kelley's head. The Irishman hit the wooden floor with a two hundred-pound thud, and Ford was on him like a mad dog, punching him twice in the face, opening up a gash above O'Kelley's left eye.

"Sold it, didn't you?" Ford yelled, spit spewing from his mouth, his eyes wide and searing. "Let's see what you have to pay me." Ford was straddling O'Kelley, kneeling on his arms. He got O'Kelley's revolver from its holster and tossed it on the bar. "That'll do to start," he jabbed. He reached into the dazed man's pockets and found nothing but a pocketknife. The saloon's owner and bouncer hovered over them, and O'Kelley didn't dare do more than submit.

Ford stood up, satisfied with the toll he'd taken, and O'Kelley slowly got to his knees, then stood, swaying a moment before getting his balance. Ford dismissed him with a wave of his hand. "Now get out of this place. And you better leave town, Irish, because if I ever see you again I'll kill you on sight," Ford snarled, and pushed his victim toward the door.

After a month, Ford had been unable to get an investor to go into business with him, so he gave up on Pueblo and took a train south to the next town, Walsenburg. Like Pueblo, it was built on coal mining, but it had an advantage in its location: the last place miners could pick up supplies as they headed into the mountains and the first place they could get a drink when they came out. It was also a good stopping place on the road between Santa Fe and Denver. It was just his style, so he sent a wire to Dot, whose real name was Nellie Waterson, a dancer and prostitute he left back in New Mexico, and she soon joined him. Ford landed a job running the gambling in the Charles Mazzone Saloon.

Managing gambling operations was a frontier occupation that paid extremely well. Saloon owners often didn't have the knowledge or the time or the edge it required, so it was common to hire someone to take charge of that. Ford decided which games were played, who ran them, who managed security, and who collected, counted, and distributed the money. While Ford watched his hirelings run the games, he also watched the losers and winners to find an investor for himself. In time he found a mark, a man who had won a great deal of money at the tables. Ford showed him that in spite of the occasional winner like him, the house always won. If he'd invest in a gambling hall of his own, he could make all that money. The man was so impressed with Ford's knowledge that he became Ford's partner, and together they opened another saloon and dance hall near the train station, with prostitutes in the rooms upstairs. Of course Dot was one of the girls.

Ford was in his element and making money hand over fist. He seemed to be controlling his temper better. His confidence grew, and he began to think maybe he could live there in peace. But then the October 25, 1889, issue of the *Walsenburg World* reported that Earnest Curry, a Texas cowboy newcomer who was drunk on his fourth night in town, walked into Ford's saloon and right up to Ford. "Look out, Ford, I'm going to kill you," he said, as he pulled his New Army Colt. "Blam!" he fired just as Ford ducked.

Ford carried a Colt .45 pistol in a holster on his left hip. He skinned it and came up from behind the bar shooting, and as the *World* said, "took three shots at Curry, one striking him in neck, one in breast [sic] and one in the arm." Ford had emptied his gun, so he grabbed a second one from under the bar and was about to end the life of the man writhing and bleeding on the floor, when other men protested and talked Ford into letting Curry live. After all, he was just drunk. "Ford at once gave himself up and in the hearing was acquitted on the grounds of self-defense," the *World* wrote. "Curry even asked that Ford should not be prosecuted, as it was all his [Curry's] fault."

But in Canadian, Texas, the paper carried the story with the headline, "Slayer of Jesse James is Too Quick for the Gentleman." That's the way it was. Everyplace Ford went, people knew what he'd done to Jesse, everything he said or did was framed by that moment in St. Joseph, and life continued to be extremely dangerous for him. With Christmas coming, he sold his interest in the saloon and took a trip to visit his Missouri family, stopping to gamble in a Kansas City casino. As he told *The New York Times:*

> One man made himself particularly obnoxious to me. He referred in an insulting manner to the Jesse James affair, but I took no notice of him, preferring to escape a row if I could. He continued to abuse me all the evening and I continued to take no notice of him. After I had been sitting at the table all night, I felt cramped and uncomfortable and leaned back in my chair. As I did so I threw my head back, and at that instant my abuser drew a knife from his pocket, held my head back by my hair, and was about to draw the knife across my throat when my friend warded off the blow. The knife cut through my collar and grazed my neck, inflicting a slight wound. I was unarmed, or I would have shot him on the spot. As it was he took to his heels and escaped.

Chapter Eight
Hello, Creede

As an Oklahoma City streetcar clanged down Broadway, Red took another sip of coffee, checked his watch, and looked out the dusty café windows. Ed was supposed to meet him almost an hour ago for dinner and their second interview. He knew it was a lot to expect a man who'd had every decision made for him by prison guards for almost ten years to suddenly be punctual. Not that Red didn't enjoy the time waiting, watching the mix of men wearing bowlers and cowboy hats, spats, and boots. And people were loud. St. Louis is never this loud, he thought. But then, maybe in St. Louis the topics of conversation are softer, he thought, and made himself laugh.

There was nothing to do but go in search of his interviewee. It sure was hard work making some people famous, he thought, amusing himself again. First stop was the Lewis Hotel, and Ed was not in his room. Next, he started down Fourth Street, ducking his head into every saloon. Most of them were shotgun affairs, with a single door and a narrow front on the street, stretching back to the middle of the block with a long bar running down one side and tables with chairs down the other. Some of them had a pool table in the back, but he figured Ed wasn't much of a pool player. It was too easy to lose money playing with a stranger.

It was on Second Street that he stepped into a dark place called the Bucket o' Blood that was known as an Irish hangout. From the doorway

It Ends Here

Red could make out a figure in a chair with his head down on the table, resting on his arm. A black man was sweeping the floor and a couple near the door were eating bread and cheese with mugs of ice-cold beer. Otherwise the place appeared empty. Red walked in, nodded to the bartender, and upon closer inspection saw that the red hair on the table belonged to his new friend Ed.

"Ed," he said softly, walking closer. Then louder, "Ed." A pause. "Hey, Ed," he said loudly, grabbing the shoulder of the tan coat and shaking firmly. O'Kelley slowly turned his head, but the eyes didn't open.

"Red," he said. "Not Ed, Red." Then the head rolled over, as if nothing had happened.

Red called to the bartender, "How long has he been here?"

"Well sir, I can't say for sure. We're open all night, and he was here when I come in this morning. He was just like that. Hasn't moved a muscle. I thought he might be dead, but maybe not."

"No, apparently not," the reporter jibed. "Can you make some coffee?" And the next two hours were spent getting Ed O'Kelley sober enough to put together a coherent sentence.

"I want to hear more about Colorado," Red prompted him. "Tell me all about Jimtown, when you went there and what it was like."

O'Kelley stared for a few seconds, smacking his lips as if tasting the question. "Sure. Jimtown. Ya wanna know about Jimtown."

Red pulled his pencil and pad from the shoulder bag, ready to begin, but the next words out of O'Kelley's mouth were, "I need a rye."

Then he looked at Red and announced. "I want to be 'Red.'" Apparently he'd awakened with that idea and it was still on his mind.

"Allll right," the reporter hesitated. "We can't both be Red."

"Why not?" O'Kelley wanted to know.

"Well . . . I don't know. That's a good question." Their eyes locked for a moment, then Red added, "Sure, we can do that. We'll both be 'Red.'"

There, for that moment, Red saw what others had seen in those green O'Kelley eyes. It was the beginning of the anger that lay beyond. It was the sizzling fuse before the explosion. The click of a hammer before the pistol shot. Red O'Kelley was not a man who liked to be crossed, and the line was a thin one.

At last the story spilled out between alternating cups of black coffee and glasses of whiskey. "Jimtown started booming in about '90," he muttered. "We were hearin' about it where I was up in Pueblo. They even ran a rail line down there to Jimtown . . . and you shoulda seen the trains going through Pueblo headed there. Lot o' men. All of 'em talkin' about how the silver was layin' on top of the ground in Jimtown, just waitin' to be picked up."

"So you went?" Red asked.

"Not right off. But then. . . . "

Red waited for the rest, but Ed was quiet. "Then, what?"

O'Kelley hesitated. "Well, then they fired me. I was a police officer, ya know."

"Yes."

"Well, they fired me for practically no reason. Said I was drinkin' on duty."

"Umm."

"And fightin'."

Pueblo was a rough and tumble town where a lot of the men were even more intoxicated than O'Kelley was. For a few years he was able to balance periods of working as a policeman, being dismissed for fighting, working, being dismissed for drinking, and working again. Finally, in 1891, he could no longer maintain his balancing act. It happened on a morning when O'Kelley had been drinking in his usual place, the Red Lily, one of the saloons that offered free drinks to off-duty policemen. Ed Riley, a black miner, had also been out drinking, and he strode into the Red Lily thinking to have a couple more. The bartender said matter-of-factly that the saloon didn't serve people of Riley's color, and he should have known it; that kind of treatment was normal for Pueblo. Riley insisted on a drink, and grabbed a bottle from behind the bar, but the bartender was quick to grab it away. O'Kelley had seen enough. He set down his whiskey and moved to arrest Riley, thinking to take him for a little cooling off in jail. Riley was a huge man—a huge, drunken man. He went along peacefully, but as they left the bar and turned to head toward the jail, Riley stumbled back, stepping hard on O'Kelley's foot. It hurt, and O'Kelley's temper exploded. He instinctively pulled his Smith & Wesson .44 caliber double-action pistol, and Riley grabbed the weapon, so O'Kelley fired twice, killing him with a bullet to the chest and a bullet to the head. No charges were filed, but that was the end of O'Kelley as a Pueblo policemen. It was time for a change of scenery.

On down the rail line, back in the foothills, in a place called Jimtown, something exciting was happening. Silver. An overnight boom had happened, and Ed heard that people were flocking there. It would be a two-hundred-mile trip back into the Rocky Mountains on the Rio Grande River. But from what the people and the newspapers were say-

A view from the top of the canyon above Jimtown shows the steep rock walls against which everything in Creede was built.

Main Street in Creede, crowded with wagons and cluttered with construction debris, all in the shadow of towering stone walls.

ing, it would be worth it. He didn't have any place else to go, and Jimtown would be wide open, wild, and rough, with law enforcement in short supply. And just like when he came to Pueblo, Ed wasn't planning on doing any mining, but it would be a place where he could make money, possibly a lot of money, on one side of the law or the other.

Just two years before, it was pristine Rocky Mountain wilderness. Then it all changed one sunny day when Nicholas C. Creede used his geologist's hammer to peck at rocks along East Willow Creek while he ate his lunch. Looking over the glistening chips in his hand, he suddenly exclaimed, "Holy Moses," and the claim he staked would become the Holy Moses Mine. It could have caused a silver boom even faster than it did, but the place was so remote that there was no easy way to get there and there was no sort of town, accommodations, or supplies to be had. In 1891, the railroad to Creede was finally completed, and the human floodgates opened.

At the rate of about three hundred people a day, miners, storekeepers, and hangers-on flocked to Willow Creek Canyon, a geological wonder nestled against steep mountains and soaring stone towers. They threw up tents and built cabins, covering the ground from the creek to the canyon walls on both sides, and they looked for, bought, and sold silver. The village closest to the Holy Moses was called Creede, but there was also Amethyst, Stringtown, and Jimtown, the center of things. The little valley grew from a population of one to about ten thousand by 1892. The Denver and Rio Grande was running two trains a day, and saloons, dance halls, and brothels were open all night. There were two newspapers, and when the town turned on its new electric streetlights, the editor of the *Jimtown Candle* wrote, "There is no night in Jimtown."

At the same time, beginning in the late 1880s, Denver was undergoing a backlash against its criminal underworld, which had long been fueled by con men, gambling, and police corruption. When the reformation came down it was particularly hard on Jefferson Randolph "Soapy" Smith, whom the *Rocky Mountain News* said on July 29, 1889, "had" Denver. Almost every day the paper printed another version of its indictment: "The city is absolutely under the control of this prince of knaves, and there is not a confidence man, a sneak thief, or any other parasite upon the public . . . who doesn't pay to operate under Soapy's protection." Smith had a piece of all the whiskey, gambling, and prostitution in town, and he paid the cops to make sure he kept it.

Soapy got his nickname from a con he ran using bars of soap. With a loud and friendly spiel he'd gather a crowd on a street corner, all listening to him extol the benefits of his fine soap while he wrapped the bars in paper. Every so often, he would hold aloft dollar bills and tell the crowd he was putting money in some of the wrappers. They watched him wrap up the money and mix the moneyed bars with the others. Of course they all wanted to buy the soap and take a chance on getting the one with the money in it. The crowd also included Smith's shills, who would open a bar of soap at exactly the right moment and shout to the heavens, "I won, I won," waving their dollar bills in the air. That made everybody buy more soap, all while more shills were

Soapy Smith was known for his short con game with bars of soap, until he found that his real talent was in organizing. With the men he attracted he controlled the wages of sin in Fort Worth, Denver, and Creede. The Denver Public Library, Western History Collection, Z-8903.

walking for blocks around the city, sending more willing dupes to the street corner money machine.

For all his skill at the shell game and other "short game" or quick cons, Smith's true talent was organization. That, along with his belief that suckers were made to be fleeced. The West percolated with bunco men and other smooth operators who could trick, lie, and otherwise separate a fool from his money. John "Reverend" Bowers, for example, could use Scripture to entice folks to make loans for the betterment of the kingdom, which was really the kingdom of Bowers's wallet. Some shysters were pretty good magicians who worked sleight of hand. Some cheated at cards. Some owned elaborate gambling equipment that could be manipulated to control who won and who lost. And some ran confusing scams that left the victim unsure whether he'd been duped or not. All over the world, such men drifted, were arrested, run out of town, and generally found it hard to make a living. But when he was living in Fort Worth, Texas, Smith had a revelation. He organized the con men, choosing each one for his talents. He assigned them to locations so that the bustling cow town was covered, and so that his grifters complemented each another, instead of stealing business from each other. He even organized the barbers to size up their customers. Those who were well heeled got an unobtrusive *V* cut into their hair in the back. It was not enough for anyone except Smith's cohorts to notice, and they would steer the marks to the right gambling tables. Of course Smith got a percentage of everything for protecting his gang, meaning he made sure nobody infringed on their business, including the law. He put the owners of saloons, brothels, and gambling halls on his payroll, along with cops, attorneys, judges, and politicians.

When the Texas operation all came crashing down in a fever of moral restoration, Smith found a promising new home in Denver and took many of the same operators along with him. Though he was roundly criticized in the Denver press, he defended himself by saying the poor fools who chose to gamble were sure to lose so much that they'd never gamble again. "I'm a reformer," he proclaimed. He and his men promised that they would never take advantage of the permanent residents but only work their games with the drifters and freeloaders. And it didn't hurt at all that Smith was a popular philanthropist. He gave generously to every charity that came along, his name was often listed with the biggest donors, and he rubbed elbows with Denver's wealthiest. Life was good, though dangerous. Smith's own saloon, the Tivoli, was the scene of so many fights with fists, knives, and guns, the *Rocky Mountain News* called it "the slaughter pen."

Men like Smith live knowing that truly good people can't be turned, and so it was inevitable that those in Denver would rise to take back their city. Politicians who couldn't be bought began to move into office, and the end was in sight for Smith and his gang. But Smith wasn't giving up, by any means. The Law and Order League, a group of citizens bent on cleaning up the town, hired former Denver detective William Glasson, who by that time had opened his Glasson Detective Agency, to investigate Smith's empire. He was to find out which civil employees and elected officials were on the take, while snooping for specific criminal charges that could be brought against the leaders of what had come to be called the Soap Gang. To Smith it was irritating, but little more. However, when Glasson spread rumors that he had bested Smith in a fight, which was a complete lie, that was the limit. On October 3, Smith, his brother-in-law William "Cap" Light, John "Reverend" Bowers, and Felix Friend showed up at the Glasson office to confront the detective. He was out, but two of Glasson's agents were there, with two clerical workers. One of the agents told Smith to get out, and when he refused, the agent laid his pistol butt across Smith's nose. Smith flew into a rage, and his friends joined in, disarming both agents and beating them severely with their own weapons, breaking their noses, gashing their heads, and leaving them bleeding on the floor while the clerks watched them drag papers out of files and throw chairs through windows. They took the agents' pistols and badges with them and told the injured men they were welcome to try to retrieve them any time.

It all came crashing down with the mayoral election in the spring of 1889. Mayor Wolf Londoner was up for re-election, and he counted

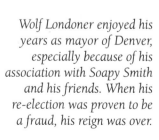

Wolf Londoner enjoyed his years as mayor of Denver, especially because of his association with Soapy Smith and his friends. When his re-election was proven to be a fraud, his reign was over.

Bat Masterson was a man who always had an adventure in progress. He was also the only one in Creede who could get away with being independent of Soapy's operation.

among his friends Smith and everyone in his circle. Among them was William Barclay "Bat" Masterson, who had already earned a reputation across the West as a town marshal, gambler, and boxing promoter. He'd been a buffalo hunter, Indian fighter, Army scout, and gunslinger. He ran in big circles from New York to San Francisco, counting among his friends vigilante lawman Wyatt Earp and author Luke Short. Masterson stood five feet, nine inches, with a stocky build and black hair and mustache. He was known for wearing a derby hat and dressing in fine style, and that, coupled with his round, young-looking face, meant that many men weren't prepared for his short patience and fast gun.

Masterson ran gambling operations for Smith in Denver and was among those who had a lot to lose if Londoner didn't win the election. The challenger campaigned on a platform of ending government corruption and cleaning up the government, and the *Rocky Mountain News* was on his side. On Election Day, Smith had men stationed at polling places around the city. He and Masterson were there too, handing out slips of paper with the names of dead men on them and paying people in cash and beer to vote often, using various names. In fact, Smith and Masterson led a group of men who walked from one precinct to another, voting over and over under the same list of names.

Londoner won, the newspaper's editor was furious and said so, and the election was challenged in court. In March 1890, Londoner was removed from office, and it was time for the Soap Gang to move on.

Smith had learned in Fort Worth how to set up quickly in Denver. In Denver he improved his organization. He also understood that he needed a town where the vices were tolerated along with everything else, simply because there was so much going on, nobody had time to decide what should and shouldn't be permitted. A place where it all was happening at such a blistering pace that anybody could make—or lose—money just by walking out his front door. And from everything he was hearing, that was a description of Jimtown. So when he knew the time was right, Smith moved and took most of his gang with him.

With the help of the prostitutes who came with him from Denver, Smith quickly contracted dozens of land and building leases at low rates, so that he controlled most of Jimtown's Main Street, subleasing it to operators he selected. In March 1892 he opened his own place, the Orleans saloon and gambling hall, which meant he had control of all forty saloons in town, except for one. That one was the Denver Exchange, which his old pal Bat Masterson ran for a Denver group. Masterson could be independent because he was Smith's friend and because, well . . . he was Bat Masterson.

Expanding on the way they ran Denver, the Soap Gang also took on role of a vigilante committee. They added burly men to their ranks, men who couldn't run a con but could make sure everybody knew who was in charge. By controlling business, politics, and the law, the Soap

It Ends Here

Gang determined not only what was legal, but also what was morally acceptable. Anybody who didn't do business their way, participating in their web of protection, found it hard to do business at all.

By the early spring of 1892, the name Creede had also come into general use for the collective neighborhoods of Jimtown, Stringtown, and Amethyst. It would be impossible to state the over-optimism, over-population, or overconsumption of alcohol in town, as Creede shipped out a million dollars of ore on the train every month. Every train that left came back full of people. *The New York Times* said, "Trains are loaded and the trails are covered with humanity flocking to the new camp." It said the streets were "so crowded travel is next to impossible," and in the hotels, "there is not room for one-third of the people." About two thousand were awake all night in the saloons and gambling halls, and the railroad left a train there overnight because the arriving passengers couldn't find a room. Actually, *The Times* didn't begin to tell the extent of the sleeping car business. For two months the Denver and Rio Grande parked cars on a siding that stretched as far as the eye could see, and charged people a dollar a night to sleep there.

In total, the tiny valley was home to two dentists, four doctors, three grocery, five general and six hardware stores, forty restaurants, most with hotels upstairs, ten livery stables, three printers, dozens of houses, five assay offices, and the telegraph office in a box car on a siding. There were five sawmills turning out green lumber that men were using to build shacks, houses, and two-story businesses, which all promised to twist, warp, and fall apart as the wood dried.

The miners weren't all crusty old characters leading burrows carrying their picks, shovels, and pans. No, Jimtown turned miners into factory workers. Every time a strike was made, a deal was made with a big mining company that brought in automated equipment, ore carts, mills, conveyor belts, elevators, and pneumatic drills. The town was filled with men who made a decent hourly wage on a ten-hour shift, then ate, drank, gambled, and slept before doing it all again. While

A miner wrangles a herd of burros for one of the early mines in Creede. All the best mines were operated like factories by big mining companies.

they toiled day after repetitive, dust-choked day, the Soap Gang took a big piece of every dollar in town and never had to get their hands dirty.

But from that time on, the explosive life of Creede, the silver boomtown, was to be measured in months. For some men, it was only days. William "Reddy" McCann was a faro dealer who had come down from Denver with the rest of the gang. About an hour before dawn, March 31, McCann shot out about a dozen of the new streetlights on Main, then dropped into the Branch Saloon because he needed one more drink before shooting out the next dozen. Deputy Cap Light came in, none too happy to be roused from his sleep at four in the morning to attend to his friend McCann. Light was the brother-in-law who helped Smith beat up the Denver detectives. He had come down from Denver with the gang, and they made him their own deputy sheriff. Because Jimtown had a cobbled-together local government and sat on state land that was not yet a county, Light's official status was decidedly unofficial. But he was a dependable man the gang called on when they needed their business handled their way.

It Ends Here

Light told McCann he was under arrest, to just come along, and everything would be fine. But McCann had a fresh drink in front of him and aimed to finish it. Light's fuse was short at that hour and he slapped McCann, knocking the cigar out of his mouth. McCann jumped away from the bar and drew his H&R .38 from its holster. Light had faced men with pistols before, and even killed two of them when he was a deputy in Temple, Texas. He was a quick draw, and he wasn't afraid of McCann. While the gambler got off two wild shots, Light drew, aimed carefully, and fired three times, cold as steel. McCann fell, hit three times, moaning, "I'm killed," and he was right.

The gang was not going to put up with behavior like McCann's, and Light did what he had to do to protect himself. Still, McCann was an old friend from Denver, and Light, who had once been a duly elected sheriff in Texas, knew he was acting on vigilante orders, enforcing unwritten laws on the orders of men who had no authority. He fell into a deep depression, drank heavily, thought over his past and what the future might hold, and finally went to Smith and quit. He was leaving the Soap Gang, leaving law enforcement, and leaving Jimtown.

From that point on, Light could never quite get his feet under him. Back home in Texas he applied to work as a railroad detective and was furious when he was turned down. He waited in the train yard for the man who refused to give him the job, beating him unmercifully. Of course Light was identified and arrested, and at his arraignment the railroad man pulled his Colt .44 and fired five times, two of the shots hitting Light in the head. Amazingly, Light recovered from the wounds and returned to drinking. Then one night, muddled by depression and booze, while idly fingering the .32 double-action Detective Model Colt in his pants pocket, he accidentally pulled the trigger, sending the bullet through his femoral artery, and in two minutes he bled to death.

Ed O'Kelley would prove to be another one for whom Jimtown was a lifetime of events crammed into a flash of lightning, a tornado from the time he rolled into town until the day he rolled out, just six months later.

+———+———+

O'Kelley's first impression of Jimtown was that it was cold outside and warm in the taverns. One night at the Denver Exchange, a bartender introduced O'Kelley to Soapy Smith. He was just the kind of man Smith liked to find: needy and cooperative. Smith gave him some odd jobs like moving beer barrels, bringing freight from the depot, and delivering messages.

Then once again, fate dealt a hand that was beyond comprehension. In the same month O'Kelley arrived, February 1892, Bob Ford stepped off the train in Jimtown. They would be thrown together again, this time with Soapy Smith and his band of vigilantes as the catalyst. Typical of Ford, he was quick to assess the power base of the town, yet he considered himself above it. He'd always been an outsider, and he wanted to keep it that way. His reputation came in with him on the train, and the Soap Gang was on guard against him from the beginning. The gang was not interested in brawls and hot tempers, which had been Ford's modus operandi, but rather in keeping a tight rein on the town's galloping business in vice. The riffraff of the Willow Creek Valley were expected to behave and spend their money, and the business operators were expected to make money. The more one made, the more they all made. Nobody wanted Ford opening a saloon like his previous ones, where commerce was interrupted by guns and blood.

In contrast to Ford, Bat Masterson knew how to be independent and still get along. He came to town with his wife-to-be Emma, whom he married in Jimtown's first wedding. They had a beautiful ceremony, and just a few months later she was divorced from her previous husband. He also brought his boxer, black heavyweight Billy Woods. Masterson loved boxing, and Woods was a good fighter who had made a lot of money for Masterson in Denver. On April 17, 1892, Woods put on the gloves again for a big match against local tough Al Johnson, and the betting was heavy. The fight was staged in an elevated ring built in the middle of the street and was under Marquis of Queensbury rules, with Masterson making sure everything about the fight, from the ring to the referee, was first class. Oddly, even though Bob Ford was a lone wolf outsider, he quickly became friends with Joe Palmer, a Soap Gang gambling operator. They were in the audience for the fight, and they were liquored up.

"This will be fantastic," the maverick Ford shouted to Palmer over the noisy crowd. "Masterson thinks he's the big dog. I'm betting Johnson will knock Billy Woods out, and I'm going to take my winnings and wave them under Masterson's nose." By the time the first bell rang they had a lot of money riding on the underdog Johnson. What nobody knew was that Ford was on edge, just as he was every April. It was the tenth anniversary of the day he murdered Jesse James. Each year at that time the scene replayed in his mind, followed by his expectations of fame, adulation, and the reward, all of which turned out to be only infamy, disdain, and a few dollars that were quickly spent. He had put himself in a trap, and there he would stay. If he hadn't made a deal with the governor, he and his brother would have both gone to prison. If he hadn't killed Jesse, Jesse would have surely killed him. If he hadn't killed Jesse, he'd have ended up like he started, a poor Missouri farm boy. He traded that life for this, waiting for Jesse's ghost to appear in the night, or Jesse's avenger to appear in the day.

When the fight ended with Ford a big loser, he exploded through the crowd and down the street with Palmer on his heels, shouting that the match had been fixed. When Ford pulled his pistol, Palmer followed his lead, and they both started shooting into the night. Soon they found better targets than the stars, reloaded, and started shooting out streetlights, then windows, signs, and water barrels. Nobody wanted to confront the two angry drunks, so every policeman on duty, one by one, decided to end his shift early, except one very patient cop, Andy Casey. It went on for almost three hours before at last they ran out of ammunition and energy. Exhausted, first Palmer, then Ford, slumped against an alley wall and slid to the ground. Patrolman Casey then walked calmly over and put handcuffs on each man. With the gunfire ended, men who'd been hiding behind tables and bars came out and helped Casey get them to jail.

For all of its wide-open, round-the-clock, make-your-own-way boisterousness, Jimtown was relatively free of violent crime. A stern talking-to from a policeman, a night in the slammer, or at worst a pistol butt across the noggin, was all it took to keep most men in line. Everybody knew they were only living there at the pleasure of the Soap Gang. So the next morning Patrolman Plunkett and another cop released Ford and Palmer from jail, put them in a wagon, took them straight to the train depot, and stayed to make sure they didn't leave. Within an hour, other Soap Gang members arrived in another wagon with all of Ford's and Palmer's belongings. They put them on the train to Denver with a warning never to return to Creede.

Ford knew very well how to weasel and play the compliant servant, and he wasn't going to give up the promise of Jimtown. He settled into a Denver hotel and immediately started sending letters to Smith, begging to return to Jimtown, knowing that Smith was the one man who could end his exile. Every day brought a new letter from Ford. Any reasonable person would have been swayed by the passionate letters in which Ford repeatedly confessed his reckless behavior and his desire to be a member of the Creede business community. So Smith relented and had one of his men send a wire telling Ford he was welcome to return, but he was expected to act like a proper businessman, which implied much more. It meant recognizing that the vigilantes were in charge, and like everyone else in Jimtown, Ford would do business according to the gang's rules. So after an exile of only ten days Ford was on the train back to Jimtown.

It was the same month the town was incorporated, officially adopting the name Creede. Ford laid low but was busy. He met people, talked about business, and set the stage for his next enterprise. He found an investor, and a month later, May 29, Ford opened his new saloon, the

Exchange. Typical of its neighbors, the Exchange was a stout, two-story building with a false front. The bar ran along the south wall, and gambling tables filled the rest of the room. One of the most famous gamblers in the West, Poker Alice, came to work as a dealer in Ford's place. She usually had a big, black cigar in her mouth and always carried a Smith .38 in a holster on her hip. Past a wall with swinging doors was the dance hall, with tables and chairs and a little stage. A wide, ornate stairway led up to Dot's brothel.

By that time, Smith really hated Ford. Ford didn't deliver on his pledge to cooperate. He remained the only saloon operator besides Masterson who wasn't part of Smith's operation, and he was doing a booming business, making money hand over fist. Not only was Ford's Exchange adorned in brilliant yellow, red, purple, and aqua blue, it was the only painted building in the whole town. He passed himself off as a gentleman, which made Smith hate him even more, because he knew him for the hot-tempered coward he was. Then there was the little group of thugs Ford hired as bodyguards and bouncers. Smith did not need Ford's boys tangling with his boys. It could interrupt the steady flow of money. To Smith, Ford was like an infection that, if not treated, would spread.

One night there was a fight in the Exchange and gunfire erupted. Of course the place was so crowded that nobody could see what happened, but that didn't keep them from telling the guy next to them what happened. By the time the rumors got to the door, people were saying Ford himself had been killed, and soon it was all over town. Of course Ford had not been shot, but a reporter put the non-shooting on the wire service and the story was printed all over the country. The *Post-Dispatch* reported the incident, saying, "Everybody was eager to believe this was true [Ford being killed], for the slayer of Jesse James is decidedly unpopular." And, "More than one grizzly miner was heard to remark, 'He'll get it yet.'"

Chapter Nine

Fate

It was some sort of miracle that in the four months since they came to town, Ford and O'Kelley still hadn't run into each other, and it's because they ran in completely different circles. O'Kelley lived in Bachelor, the neighboring town, where he was a marshal and was drunk most of the time. Ford lived in Creede, running his saloon, gambling, and a brothel. But it was bound to happen. Finally, of all the saloons in all the towns in the West, on June 2, 1892, O'Kelley strolled into the Exchange and up to the bar, so intent on ordering a whiskey that he didn't even look to see who else was in the place. Ford, on the other hand, never made that mistake. He was a man with ten years of fear under his belt. Ten years of looking in before walking in, of watching over his shoulder, and of trusting nobody.

The bartender poured the glass of rye, but as O'Kelley reached for it, a hand reached in and took it. O'Kelley's eyes opened wide and he looked up to see who would dare to . . . it was Ford. Instinctively, his hand went for his Colt, but both his elbows were suddenly pinned against the bar, and a gravelly voice whispered, "Be smart, friend."

Ford set the glass of rye aside, and said, "Mr. O'Kelley, you wouldn't like my whiskey. It's too rich for the likes of you." The bartender handed him the bottle, and holding it close under the nose of the thirsty O'Kelley, Ford poured the drink slowly back into the bottle. Then he picked up the silver dollar that paid for the drink, adding, "Nice of you to pay me this, but you owe me much more."

O'Kelley was fuming, but as the two thugs released his arms, he spun to see two more, and so was still unable to help himself. He started to walk through them, but they shouldered up as Ford said, "Eh, eh, not so fast. Let's see how much more you have. Turn those pockets out, boys."

Hands reached in and came out empty, except for four more silver dollars, which one man slapped on the bar. Then one of the men, who smelled of lavender, pulled a wad of bills from O'Kelley's coat. "Ah," Ford said, counting. "Must be payday for Mr. O'Kelley. Thirty dollars."

"You can't do this," O'Kelley blurted. "I'm a town marshal."

Ford looked closely at the badge on his vest. "Hmm. 'Town of Bachelor City.' Well, Irish, this ain't Bachelor City and you ain't spit." Then he got right up in O'Kelley's face. "This debt ain't nearly paid. The next time you'll pay with your worthless life. Understand, Irish? If I ever see you again, I'll shoot you dead."

With that he nodded, and the four goons pushed the hapless lawman to the door and out into the busy street.

+ —— ┼ —— +

Oklahoma City bustled outside, while Red and O'Kelley had cigars in the Lewis Hotel lobby, and the reporter made notes as fast as he could. "That was humiliating," Red jabbed, angry that anyone could be so cruel.

"I don't know about humiliating, but I was mad enough to kill him right then," O'Kelley confessed. It was Red's third day with O'Kelley, and thanks to time and liquor, the ex-convict was beginning to trust him. After all, Red was the first person who'd really taken an interest in him. O'Kelley still didn't quite understand how he could matter enough for a big city newspaper to send someone to talk to him, but as long as the reporter was paying for the food and drinks he'd go along with him.

"Were you scared when Ford threatened you?" Red asked.

"Sure I was scared," he admitted, "because I didn't know who them other birds were. "I wasn't scared of Ford face to face. He just got the jump on me that day."

"But that was the second time he said he'd kill you."

"Like I said, not face to face he didn't scare me. But I knew if he saw me first, I'd be dead."

"And you didn't leave town . . . ?" Red queried.

"No. No, I went back out to Bachelor."

"You lived out there?" Red asked.

O'Kelley nodded. "You see, I'd already tried to get on the police force in Jimtown, and they couldn't use me. So I just went on out in Bachelor City. They didn't have no town marshal, and the mayor elected me right then and there."

"Elected! Well, congratulations," Red said.

"You see, Bachelor, where I was marshal, it was on the southwest side of Jimtown, over this little low hill. Then if you kept a'goin' out that way, about fifteen mile, you'd cross into Hinsdale County. It was wild country out there. Wild. As busy as it was in Jimtown, it was that empty out in Hinsdale County. They had a courthouse and a store and a blacksmith, and that's about it. And they hired me on as a deputy sheriff for the county. It made sense because you couldn't tell where the town of Bachelor ended and the county began, and it was all butted up against Jimtown . . . Creede, all that."

"So you were town marshal and county deputy?" Red clarified. O'Kelley nodded over his whiskey glass. "Sounds like they needed you."

"Yessir, I reckon. People came there to Jimtown to work in the mines, or to run a business, and there wasn't hardly nobody who wanted to be lawmen," O'Kelley said with self-satisfied determination. "I was the boss in Bachelor. But of course in Creede . . . Smith's boys ran everything in Creede.

It Ends Here

"But you know what's funny?" he grinned through yellow teeth. "A town marshal is s'posed to read and write, and I don't do neither," O'Kelley spouted, so tickled he could hardly get the words out. Then the familiar cloud fell across his face again. "I's a cop in Pueblo before, and never did read nor write, and them birds never knew.

·———■———·

From the first time Ford opened the door of his combination saloon, gambling parlor, dance hall, and brothel, the beer flowed out and the money flowed in. But it would flow for less than a week. Late in the night of June 4, 1892, a fire started in a nearby tavern and was out of control before the volunteer fire department could get there, speeding from one frame building to the next, until it finally burned itself out at the bottom of the hill. While it was raging, a crowd gathered and decided to rescue the town's alcohol from the conflagration. An unbridled party took place while the fire burned and policemen tried to stem the liquor-fueled tide of townsmen pulling cases of whiskey and barrels of beer from the approaching flames. But in the end, the cops joined in, as a huge supply of alcohol was moved to safety, and the rescuers rewarded themselves by drinking as much as the rescue required.

By mid-morning every piece of ground in the business district was a pile of black, smoldering rubble. There was little to salvage, so they would need new lumber, window glass, hinges, nails, and tools, as well as food, clothing, and of course more beer and whiskey. The hot timbers would burn for days before any cleanup could begin, and nobody could rebuild anything until the mess was cleared, which would take days. Meanwhile, the cash flowing into saloons, brothels, and stores would just stop, people would go broke, and the whole dream could collapse. But Smith wasn't going to let that happen. After all, this was Creede. It had been built in days and could be rebuilt in days. His gang moved like a hive of bees to get back in business. They sent wires, and by noon there was a train full of supplies on its way from Denver.

Even more important, there was a large parcel of ground, eight blocks, at the edge of town that the state had provided, to be divided into lots and sold to fund the town's schools. Back when nobody cared about it, before the whole world wanted to live in Creede, it was leased to Civil War veteran major Martin Van Buren Wason, a speculator, for grazing livestock. But he turned around and subleased pieces of it to miners, who were digging holes all over it. Wason was already an enemy of not only Smith, but also almost everybody else in town, because he had owned the piece of land that contained the main road into Creede, and he made that a toll road. Anybody who wanted to come to Creede had to pay Wason's toll, and that went on for about a year before the state bought the right-of-way from him.

The town's fire had suddenly made Wason's school land important. So the local land board, with Smith's urging, announced that Wason's lease was being vacated, and they were going to auction off the school land. Of course Wason wanted to go on collecting from his miners, so he encouraged them to defend their claims by armed force. Cries of coercion and racketeering echoed off the mountainsides.

To complicate matters, most of the miners were squatters; they'd moved in with tents and pieced-together shacks. They protested that under squatter's law they had first rights to buy the property. Smith had a solution for that. First, his gang fired pistols in the air and into saloon ceilings at random times all day and night while shouting warnings that nobody should attempt to buy the land. Second, they posted fliers all over town warning the public not to buy the land. Meanwhile, Wason's attorney continued to fight the sale and started rumors that the sale had been postponed, and that if anybody tried to sell the parcels, "Wason would assert his rights," whatever those might have been. But he was under tremendous pressure from the Soap Gang, and the land board ordered that the sale proceed. Any squatter who was still holding out for squatters' rights got a visit from a member of the gang, who bought his squatter's rights, and there was no negotiation over the price. The auction kicked off, with Smith and friends buying at a discount from the land board, then selling or leasing to everyone who was hungry to get back in business, and the prices soared. One lot went for $850. It all happened in forty-eight hours, and anybody, like Ford, who needed a new place to rebuild had no choice but to come to Smith for a lease.

Ford was furious and refused to be a sucker for the gang's school land grab. Fists clinched, he stalked up the streets in the part of town that the fire missed until he found a vacant site and made a short-term lease. At least it would allow him to stay in business until he could rebuild the Exchange.

Ford and his men met the first train and bought a tent right off the train. They loaded it into a wagon, took it up the hill, built a wooden floor, and erected the tent over it by the next morning. The day after the fire, he was open for business.

———✦———

In a café on Oklahoma City's Fourth Street, O'Kelley asked Red how his life was sounding so far. Red sharpened his pencil with his pocketknife and kept writing. "Oh, it's quite a tale," Red said, then sipped his lemonade. The place served liquor, but Red hoped the fact that it was primarily an eatery might help to hold down O'Kelley's consumption.

"The gang didn't like him," O'Kelley sneered. "They said Ford wasn't one of them. He hired his own security men, he wouldn't pay the gang's protection money. They controlled everything . . . but not him."

O'Kelley emptied his beer, wiped his mustache on his sleeve, and then took a long pull on his cigarette. His gaze turned distant. "He was a proven back-shooter," O'Kelley said, as if reminding himself. "You can't be scared of that, but a man has to know what a man like Ford will do.

"From Bachelor we could see the smoke, so I walked over to see the fire, but didn't go into town. You know, because he might come gunnin' for me. And the next day, I still didn't go. It was wearin' on me. I wasn't gonna spend the rest of my life in Bachelor."

"He could have come to get you in Bachelor," Red empathized.

"I thought about that. I tell ya, I'd lay there in bed, lookin' out the window . . . kept a pistol under my pillow . . . and. . . . "

They sat in silence for what seemed to Red to be a long time. But he had to let O'Kelley tell his own story his way.

"Some of them Soap Gang boys were over in Bachelor that night. I liked them boys. So I was drinkin' with them. French Joe was there. I don't know who all . . . Joe Bowers, and another fella."

"French Joe?"

"Joseph Duvall. They all said I had to protect myself. And they said Smith would say the same thing. If anything happened between me and Ford, I had to protect myself, and they said they'd help."

"They'd help? Who's 'they'?"

"You know, Smith and them. Smith hated Ford. They all wanted to be rid of him. Duvall said I wouldn't have any legal trouble. Just do what I had to do with Ford. Smith and them would take care of me."

"You had some powerful friends," Red offered.

"They's powerful, anyway. Friends, I don't know." O'Kelley fell silent, and Red knew he had to do the same. The rest of the story had to be told when O'Kelley was ready to tell it. Minutes went by, then he spoke. "Can we go get a drink?"

After a brisk shot of night air, they settled at a table at the closest saloon, and O'Kelley seemed much more at home there, nursing his usual hand-rolled cigarette and a glass of rye.

"One of the boys, Bowers, he said, 'Ford'll kill ya if he ever sees ya again, right?' I told him that was right, and he said, 'Ya can't sit here and wait for 'im to get you.'

"Then one of 'em said, 'If you gets him first, that's self-defense.' They all said that would be righteous.

"Bowers said, 'Ya know he's gonna draw iron. So get yer pistol in yer hand and go find him. Come up a blind side and call out, and when he goes to draw, you cut loose.'

"Then French Joe, he says, 'Pistol, hell. You need an equalizer. You need a shotgun.' Then we all jess looked at one another fer the longest time."

Red kept writing.

"We didn't none of us lay down that night. At some point we quit drinkin' and started to sober up. But we was still pretty addled. Headaches and such. That was June 8 of '92. So later on, about midday, Bowers and the other fella left, and a few minutes later Joe and I went. That walk over the hill helped straighten me up some. I found Ford's new place right where they said. I waited out there on the street and I seen him go in."

That morning in Creede, the miners, craftsmen, and drunks all walked with purpose. Alcohol consumption was at its low ebb. Bob Ford's Dance Hall, opening for its first full day, had no customers yet. A repairman was inside with his toolbox, setting up a wood stove with a chimney that reached up through the canvas roof. The janitor was sweeping the wood floor, and Ford was talking to Brennan, the bartender. O'Kelley saw two businessmen, E. H. Taylor and A. L. Gray, walk in to brace themselves for the afternoon. They ordered beer from Brennan, then sat down at a table behind the canvas curtain that separated the bar from the gambling and dance hall in the back.

That morning one of Bob's prostitutes, Nellie Russell, lay dying in a boardinghouse. Like many of the girls, Nellie took morphine. The day after the fire she was even more dejected than usual, and it seemed like a good time to end it all, so she overdosed. Lillie Lovell, a big-boned, middle-aged woman who ran one of the local brothels, entered Bob's place carrying a basket, collecting donations to pay for Nellie's casket and burial. She handed Bob the list of contributors, held out the basket, and said, "C'mon, Bob, kick in two dollars. Smith did." Bob scanned the list and saw the hated Soapy's real name, Jeff Smith, with five dollars noted beside it. Bob immediately handed Lovell ten dollars, wrote his name on the list, and below it, "Charity covers a multitude of sins."

O'Kelley stopped talking to sip his rye and pull on the cigarette. He tapped a chunk of ash into the ashtray, then poked at it with the butt. Red understood that he needed to gather himself before telling the rest.

"French Joe, he went on home, and pretty soon here he was a'comin' back on his horse. Just like he promised. He had this short shotgun, short barrel and short stock, like they carry on coaches and such. It was about half hid under his coat. So I walked on over and he handed it to me right in front of Ford's place. I checked to be sure it was loaded, then walked in."

Red knew enough about the killing of Jesse James to know that Ford had been in the exact situation in which O'Kelley found himself. Jesse was a killer and a known back-shooter who had killed unarmed men. So was Ford. Jesse was determined, or would soon make the decision, to take Ford's life. In the same way, Ford had already threatened O'Kelley, and he might wait until they met, or he might come for O'Kelley when he least expected it. Ford expected a financial reward for killing Jesse. O'Kelley expected his reward to be joining Smith's circle of trusted associates for killing Ford.

"I knew what I had to do," O'Kelley said firmly. "I walked in. . . ."

O'Kelley started drawing on the table with his finger. "There was Ford talkin' to Brennan, the bartender, left of the door. Over here was the stove man and the janitor. There was a curtain across the middle of the tent, and that snake turned to walk back there. He didn't see me or hear me."

O'Kelley looked at the reporter, then back to the table. "I had the scattergun at my shoulder, and I just said as nice as you please like it was Sunday mornin', I said, 'Hey, Bob.'

"He stopped and turned back to me, and as soon as he saw it was me, just like I knew he would, he reached under his coat for that pistol on his left hip. But I was ready and I shot. Both barrels. Hit him in the neck. French Joe said it was buckshot, and I guess it was. You know . . . at that range . . . it near took his head off."

With that, he finished his drink, and Red took a long swallow of his.

"That day he roughed me up in that Pueblo saloon, he took my revolver. Well sir, he always carried a pistol on his left hip. I reached down and got that, and you know what? It was my pistol, the one he took off me.

"So I took my pistol and looked at him . . . I don't know how long . . . just a minute, maybe. Them other two fellas I didn't know were in the back. Them two come out and seen me standing there. They swore at me, but I wasn't paying any attention.

"I just walked out and there I was holdin' the pistol and the shotgun, and this policeman comes walkin' up fast. And he stops . . . right in front of me and just looks at me."

"Did you know him?" Red wanted to know, appreciating the fact that he was listening to this wreck of a man, a confessed murderer, who was telling it all to him now as he'd never told it before.

"Yessir, it was that big cop . . . Richard D. Plunkett was his name. I'll bet he weighed 240 pounds. I'm pretty big and he was bigger than me. He lived out past Bachelor, and everybody knew who he was because he had did some boxing and liked to brag about it."

"So did he arrest you?" Red asked.

"Well sir, not right off. I handed him the shotgun and the pistol." O'Kelley paused, seeing the scene in his mind. "I saw French Joe . . . he tied his horse and was standin' there, and of course Plunkett knew Joe, and he told Joe to watch me for a minute. He walked in, seen what I done, and came back out and asked me did I shoot Ford. I nodded and . . . well, he spoke somethin' to Joe . . . I couldn't hear for all the noise of people talkin' around us . . . and the three of us walked on over to the police office."

A crowd was already forming and word of the killing spread. Plunkett had told the businessmen Taylor and Gray to stay with the body, tie the flaps, and not let anybody else in. By that time the girls were coming around in their nightgowns, wrapped in their shawls. Somebody

The crowd outside Bob Ford's tent saloon while his body is removed to the under-taker's wagon at the center of this photo. At the far left a man with gloves appears to hold a new gravestone ready to have Ford's name engraved. The name of the dance hall has been written on the photograph in white. Creede Historical Society.

woke Dot and she ran from her boardinghouse. Gray let her come in, and she gave a short, blood-chilling shriek as if she couldn't breathe, then fell to her knees beside the body.

Of course Ford had a few supporters in the mob, mostly men who were on his payroll, all saying O'Kelley shot him in the back. Talk of a lynching started in the crowd. Words like shotgun, throat, Ford, and murder could be heard along with rope, hang, and justice. Some argued that it was good enough for a man who was a back-shooter himself. Others said it was an ambush, for sure, but not a shot in the back. Many insisted that Ford was a murderer who had never been punished, and O'Kelley just did what the law should have done a long time ago. And perhaps that sentiment was the only thing that kept O'Kelley breathing that day.

At the police station O'Kelley was booked for murder. Creede had no courthouse, and the only jail was a two-cell cage inside the police office, with an unpredictable group of part-time patrolmen to guard it. "We're not going to lock you up," Plunkett told him. "But you don't want to be out on the street where that mob can get its hands on you. And we don't want them fighting each other over who gets to hang you or who gets to buy you a beer." Plunkett and Joe Duvall put O'Kelley into a wagon and covered him with a blanket. Then the three of them drove south out of town, turning right over the hill, and past Bachelor to Plunkett's cabin.

Leaving Duvall at the cabin to watch O'Kelley, Plunkett drove back to town. By that time O'Kelley was starving. He found some crackers and a can of sardines and washed it down with water, which satisfied him. Around noon he fell into a deep sleep. He stayed there under guard, wondering what was going to happen to him, until dawn of the sixth day, when a wagon pulled into the yard. It was Plunkett and patrolman Andy Casey. "O'Kelley, c'mon," Plunkett hollered. O'Kelley opened the door cautiously, hoping the next words out of Plunkett's mouth would be, "You're free to go." But instead, the big cop told him to get into the wagon because they needed to get him to someplace safe.

It was all worse than O'Kelley expected. Word had spread that he was hiding at Plunkett's cabin, and the two camps of vigilantes, the "string him up" one and the "break him out" one, were still talking. Plus, considering Ford's past, there would soon be reporters, as well as lawyers coming and going. So Plunkett and Casey took him by train to the safety of the Pueblo jail. But just a week later they came for him again, taking him past Creede, another forty miles into Lake City in Hinsdale County. Hinsdale had been a county for almost twenty years, and in the seat, Lake City, stood its beautiful two-story frame court-house, with a jail that would keep O'Kelley in and any lynch-minded or escape-minded vigilantes out.

Hinsdale's sheriff, George F. Gardner, greeted them when the wagon rolled up. "Hello, O'Kelley. I never expected to see you on the other side of these bars. Reckon you didn't either."

"No sir," O'Kelley muttered, his head down. Though he'd been a deputy for three months, he still hadn't arrested anybody in Hinsdale, so the first time O'Kelley heard the key clatter in the cell door lock, he was inside. Like Ford, O'Kelley thought he'd be a hero. Or at the very worst thought he'd be pardoned within a day. But the mud was getting deeper, and he had no idea how long he'd be stuck or whether he'd ever get out. At least for the time being, he was satisfied to be miles away from the crowds in Creede.

Never one to miss a chance to make a dollar, especially on the death of someone he disliked, Smith sold Ford's collar button, which was dislodged by a shotgun pellet coming through his neck, and embedded in the nearest tent pole. In fact, Smith sold dozens of those collar buttons. The Emporia, Kansas, *Daily Gazette* ran the headline "As He Slew, So Was He Slain." Frank James was in Dallas working in a shoe store when the news reached him. A reporter from *The Dallas Morning News* asked him to comment, and he paused, but he had nothing to say and turned back to his work. Then after another moment, he looked up and said, "Bob Ford killed his best friend."

O'Kelley appeared before Judge John Calhoun Bell in the courtroom upstairs, above his cell. The prosecution brought up Taylor and Gray to tell how they heard the shotgun blast and walked out to see O'Kelley with the weapon, standing over the body. The stove man heard O'Kelley call Ford's name before the shot, supporting the fact that the killing was premeditated. O'Kelley's attorneys, J. M. Essington and Henry Cohen, mounted a passionate plea that O'Kelley acted in self-defense, fearing for his life after Ford beat and threatened him in the Exchange just a few days before the killing. Unfortunately, there were no witnesses to say they'd seen the beating or heard the threats, though Ford's bouncers testified that it never happened. He was turning and reaching for his weapon, the defense insisted; he had barely started to turn his head before being shot in the back, the prosecution countered. In the end, the defense made an impassioned plea for O'Kelley as a lawman,

Judge John Calhoun Bell.
Photo by Thomas McKee.
The Denver Public Library,
Western History Collection,
Z-1505.

acting under the shield of his badge to rid the community of a dangerous known felon. But even that was turned against poor O'Kelley as the
prosecution ridiculed him for having no authority in Creede, as well as
for making himself judge, jury, and executioner. He was a lawman, they
said, the last who should have committed such a murder.

Judge Bell was a rock. Besides his private practice in civil and criminal matters, he had been a county clerk, county prosecutor, and town
mayor. At forty-one years old, he was then in his fourth year as district
judge, and in his mind, the history of O'Kelley and Ford, where they'd
been, who they'd known, or who they'd killed before, had no bearing
on the case. The trial was swift and efficient, and when it was over
he sentenced O'Kelley to life in the Colorado State Prison at Canon
City. On July 14 the convicted man was taken in chains to the train
in Creede, accompanied by Sheriff Gardner. The entire time since the
shooting—at Plunkett's cabin, in the Hinsdale jail, at the trial, and up

Prisoners at the Colorado State Prison march in single file to the dining hall. The well-behaved inmates wore blue shirts and pants and they ate first, before the troublemakers in their black and white stripes.

until the time he stepped onto the train and sat down beside Gardner—he was sure Smith and the Soap Gang would intervene on his behalf. But there was nothing. No bail, no visitors, no witnesses in his defense, nobody offering to lie or bribe the judge or wire the governor asking for a pardon. Did they forget him? Did nobody care?

In time it became clear that he'd been set up. He didn't really matter to Smith or any of the true leaders of the gang. He didn't even matter to the lowly henchmen. And in the end he'd just been a sacrifice, someone who'd gotten rid of a thorn in their side. And when it was done, they were finished with him.

Two months after O'Kelley settled into the prison, French Joe Duvall joined him there, sentenced to five years, not for his role in the murder of Ford, but for theft. Like O'Kelley, he was a hanger-on, one of countless men on the periphery who greased the gang's way and did their dirtiest work but never reaped the rewards. And like O'Kelley, when he went to trial, his friends disappeared.

The prison was built of native stone and opened for business in 1871. Since that time it had been expanded twice and a prison for women was added, and still the convicts came ever faster. It was horribly crowded, and though the tiny cells were intended for individuals, most of them housed two inmates. O'Kelley's head was shaved, he was deloused, and his Bertillon measurements were taken. Like all new prisoners he was issued a blue shirt and pants and introduced to Warden Clarence P. Boyt. He was a portly and fastidious man, a couple of years younger than O'Kelley, who liked to personally explain the rules. "If you behave for the first thirty days of your stay with us, you can keep that handsome blue uniform," Boyt said coolly. "If you're a trouble-maker you'll wear the black and white stripes. We don't favor

Like all prisoners, when O'Kelley was brought into the prison his head and face were shaved to eliminate lice. Detail. The Denver Public Library, Western History Collection, F-22484.

troublemakers, but you'll see plenty of them here, and I don't expect you'll be one." Then he smiled.

That was the last time O'Kelley saw Boyt up close. A guard instructed him in the ten-man marching protocol, which was the way all prisoners went everywhere. He was assigned to the farm. Then, far from his hometown in Missouri, he settled in, always mindful of leaving his temper outside those stone walls. Worse yet was the craving for alcohol, which had been cut off so suddenly a month before.

And so prisoner number 2970 settled into a time of peace and mindless repetition, day after day, with no one to visit him. O'Kelley had never married or even had a serious girlfriend. His family had long since given him up; they never wrote. Though his attorneys and fellow prisoners offered to write a letter to his mother for him, he was too ashamed. He was left with plenty of time to think about the trail of superficial associations he'd left behind. Men he admired, like the veterans of Bollinger County. The sheriffs under whom he had served. The criminals he met, always weighing whether to arrest them or get involved in their low business. And the series of men he stared at across whiskey glasses or fought in allies, men with no names, whose faces were now blurred, nothing more than tracks in the dust erased by the tumbleweeds of time.

In the beginning he had fans. To thousands of people he was exactly who he wanted to be, the hero who avenged the cowardly killing of Jesse James by a man he trusted. Southerners and children of Confederate veterans in particular revered him and wrote letters of appreciation and support. His cellmate read them to him as he listened to hear a familiar name. But there wasn't one letter from anyone he knew. The well-intentioned correspondents encouraged him to trust in God and the courts to overturn his conviction and restore him to freedom. But he received neither divine nor legal aid, and soon the mail dwindled, then stopped.

He was a quiet prisoner. When a lifer, a man who had nothing to lose because he would never be released, accused him of stealing the food from his tray and started a fight, O'Kelley refused. He was pushed

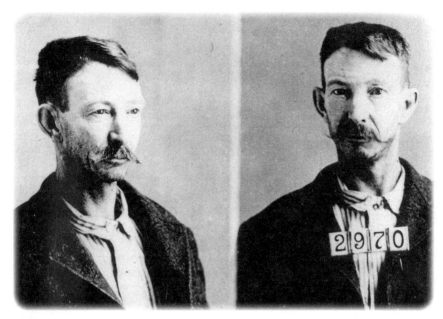

These photos were taken late in O'Kelley's term at Colorado State Prison, for unknown reasons. Another mystery is why he was photographed in a vertical-striped civilian shirt. In these photos he has aged and lost weight but restored his handlebar mustache. Creede Historical Society.

and hit before other prisoners pulled the man from him, and it was all O'Kelley could do to control his temper. But when the guards put the other man in solitary confinement, O'Kelley was glad he didn't fight. Getting out of prison was more important to him than defending his honor. His attorneys wrote appeals to the governor, which they signed for their illiterate client, misspelling his name "O'Kelly." It was sad evidence that even they didn't truly care to know him. But at last, the new Colorado governor, Jim Orman, reviewed the case and believed the court should have given more weight to the self-defense aspect. Besides, he'd been a model prisoner, so the governor commuted his sentence to eighteen years. And after serving ten years and four months, he was released into a startling world of telephones, streetcars, and double-action revolvers.

Chapter Ten

Us and Them

Outside the saloon, Oklahoma City's Second Street hosted the usual parade of men on their way to drink, gamble, and do the kind of business that's not done in the light. As usual, the decent people were home, Red thought, as he wrote and O'Kelley talked. It grew later, the storyteller ran out of steam, and they settled into a last drink. "You know," Red observed, "it's all changing. These lawmen now, they won't give up. Warrants don't go away. They've got money for travel and special deputies and shipping photographs. It's a different world."

O'Kelley nodded but wasn't sure he understood.

"And you were the best deputy you could be, Red," Red said, making sense of it all for himself. "Kept trying to get on with the police . . . you never set out to be a bad man."

"You shoulda talked for me at my trial," O'Kelley grumbled.

Red grinned. "You're not a man like George Hudson, for example. I covered his case. You ever hear about Hudson?"

O'Kelley had missed Hudson's Missouri-to-Colorado-to-Missouri life of crime. "I didn't get much news for ten years," he quipped.

George Hudson started his criminal life as a teen, when a town full of witnesses saw him kill a black man in Mississippi, and the family fled to Missouri. He enlisted in the Union army but soon deserted to become a guerrilla. He settled in Granby, Missouri, after the war, and like

George Hudson is pictured in a captured Union soldier's blouse with his Colt pocket pistol. He joined the army but soon deserted to become a guerrilla. It was perfect training for his later life of crime.

many men of his stripe, could never get a solid footing. Hudson argued with a shoemaker over a repair bill, then shot the man in the leg. Facing a jail term for assault, Hudson sent a friend to bribe the shoemaker to drop the charges, but he refused. So the next night, Hudson knocked on the shoemaker's door, and when he answered, shot him dead. No murder charges were brought, and with no witness to the repair shop shooting, the assault charges were dropped.

In 1876 the charismatic Hudson raised a gang and started a reign of terror, which included a murder he committed in nearby Neosho. Hudson was arrested, but a friend bailed him out. Then another member of his gang got drunk, shot up the town of Webb City, and was jailed for public disorder. To intimidate witnesses out of testifying against their jailed partner, the gang rode into town one night shooting pistols and rifles, and in the process killed two men. Newspapers labeled it the Webb City riot.

With the whole gang facing murder charges in Webb City, Hudson knew he had go on the run. But the friend who bailed him out on the Neosho murder pleaded with him to stay and honor his bond in that case. His arguments worked, and Hudson surrendered for the Neosho murder. The bondsman was happy, and that night, with gang member Bud Blount's help, Hudson escaped and high-tailed it to Leadville, Colorado, where he and Blount beat a storekeeper named Schultz and robbed him of $1,500. They were also suspected of a string of Colorado murders, so they split up. Hudson headed for Arkansas, where he got into a shootout with a sheriff's posse, was arrested for horse stealing, and escaped again.

While the Arkansas sheriff didn't care to chase him, an enterprising Carthage, Missouri, detective, Richard Pike, tracked Hudson to Kansas, and brought him back to face his years-old charges in the Webb City riot. Everybody in town was afraid to testify against Hudson, except one brave miner, Aaron Fishburn, who had witnessed the riot. The morning that Hudson was supposed to be arraigned, Fishburn happened to fall into an ore grinder at the mine, so those charges were dropped.

It wasn't long until the post office safe at Granby was blown open and robbed, and after the postmaster accused Hudson, he was murdered in his home, along with a friend who tried to defend him. Last, dentist L. G. Howard was killed with a pistol bullet in the head as he walked down a Joplin street one evening. Detectives determined that the good doctor had gotten himself embroiled in a lover's triangle, and a jealous husband had hired Hudson to remove one-third of the romance. However, there were no witnesses against Hudson, so he was acquitted of that crime too.

But even in 1892, after thirteen years, Colorado never forgot the beating and robbery of Mr. Schultz. By that time, lawmen had replaced endless days in the saddle with endless hours poring through files, reading reports, and exchanging wires and photographs with police departments across the country. Thanks to wire services, newspapers carried stories from around the world. As he looked through old cases, enterprising Leadville detective William Robedew found that George Hudson of Missouri had been charged in the attack on Schultz—but never arrested. An exchange of telegrams located Hudson, and the Colorado governor's request to extradite him was approved by Missouri governor David R. Francis.

By then, Hudson was living the good life. He owned a saloon in Granby and could be found most nights holding forth with a bottle of beer in his hand, loudly welcoming his fellow revelers. On August 8, William Robedew rode into Granby with Joplin policeman Carl Stout, who carried the warrant, and three special deputies. They waited until the Saturday night crowd thinned out; as Hudson was about to close for the night, they walked in and asked for a beer. Hudson turned to get the beer, and when he turned back, Stout showed Hudson the warrant and his Colt .45 revolver, telling him he was under arrest for the Schultz robbery. Hudson exclaimed, "Not by a damn sight!" At the same time, he bull-rushed Stout, grabbing the pistol barrel with his left hand and bringing the beer bottle down hard against Stout's head. As they fell to the floor, Robedew shot Hudson in the head and Stout fired twice into his chest.

"Quite a story," O'Kelley muttered.

"Yes, he was killed the same year you did the same to Ford. Anyway, Hudson never in his life tried to go straight. You're not like that."

"Damn right." O'Kelley bristled at the thought. "They have no right treating me the way they treated me here in Oklahoma."

The change in him was instant and extreme. His eyes narrowed as he told Red how he'd been arrested shortly after he arrived in Oklahoma City. He was looking for work but hadn't landed anything yet, and the police were on a campaign to arrest vagrants. "You shouldn't arrest a man because he ain't got a job!" Ed growled. "I told 'em I's a lawman and I's lookin' to get on with the law again, but they didn't listen. They rounded me up with a bunch of men."

Red wasn't afraid of Ed's anger, and he thought he could turn the tide. "Well, Red, my friend, why do you hang around with that sort of men? As soon as you got here, you were in the dives with. . . . "

"Look here, gettin' in with that low crowd is how I helped the Pueblo police, and that got me on the force there. I'm the sort who can work into those men for 'em," Ed shot back, wagging his finger in Red's direction. "They never gave me a chance in this town. I'd be a patrolman now, but 'cept they have to write them reports. They won't hire me 'cause I don't write." O'Kelley was getting louder.

"There are other lines of work," Red suggested.

"Oh I've been a'workin'," O'Kelley said with disdain. "I worked down at the rail yards and such. But they just won't let a man up. There's them and there's us."

Red looked at the crowd around the bar, then eyed O'Kelley. "I'd just like to see you get a new start, that's all. A new outlook on the world."

The whiskey glasses were empty and Red checked his watch. He got up to leave, so he could catch the last streetcar back to the Lee. He certainly didn't want to walk back across town that late unaccompanied. O'Kelley nodded, said good night, and ordered one more. He had no such trepidation about prowling the streets alone at any hour. "After all," he said, patting the .45 and the .44 bulging in his coat pockets, "I've got these two friends to keep me company."

That was Monday night. Tuesday morning came, and Red went to meet with O'Kelley about two, but he wasn't in his room. Red peeked into a couple of cafés and saloons, and then thought it was pointless. Ed could be anywhere. Red hoped someone had offered him a few hours' work, but he knew it was more likely O'Kelley had run into someone to drink with. So Red stopped in a book store and bought a novel, *The Virginian*, then sat in the lobby of the Lewis and read a couple of chapters. When it was almost five and O'Kelley still hadn't appeared, he decided to go get some dinner. Later, he sat at the typewriter in his room, working on the story for a bit, then turned in early.

It Ends Here

Lying in bed, Red pondered the role fate played in O'Kelley's story. It was as if Creede had been created just for that little window of time that Jesse's killer and avenger were both there. Creede's silver boom would not have happened without the Sherman Silver Purchase Act, passed by Congress in 1890. It required the government to buy silver, which drove the price of silver through the roof. O'Kelley, Smith, and Ford all arrived in Creede during a six-week period in 1892. O'Kelley first put on his prison-issue shirt and pants that fall, and within a year Congress repealed the Sherman Act and prices tumbled. Everybody in Creede was ruined, they moved on, and canyon winds whistled through the drying slats of decaying buildings on every street.

Thumbing through his notes, he knew he had the story. It was a story that needed to be told, of vigilantism, dreams, isolation, and betrayal. O'Kelley wasn't without values. On the contrary, the thing he feared most was not living up to his values. Or maybe, Red frowned, they're his father's values. "How fortunate I am," Red thought, "to touch history. To share a drink with this man who closed the cover on a chapter of the Old West. Here I am, staying in a room with electric lights, riding electric streetcars, and making telephone calls, writing a brand new story of a forgotten legend, possibly Missouri's last vigilante."

Was he truly a vigilante? Of course. Regardless of why he did it, he was a vigilante. Besides, Ford was a back-shooter. Did that justify his murder? Not in the eyes of the law. But in a vigilante's eyes, there may be no better reason to kill. Red realized he'd been around that tree before, and he always arrived at the same place: O'Kelley took the law into his own hands, but he still wasn't sure why.

"I'm going to ask him tomorrow," Red determined. "Tomorrow's Wednesday, my last day here. I'm going to ask him right out why he shot Ford. Was it fear? Vengeance? To atone for Jesse? To impress Smith?"

But that morning, Tuesday, Edward Capehart O'Kelley had woken up feeling better than he'd felt in a long time. The talks with his new friend Red were doing him some good, he thought. Red reminded him of his little brothers, solid like their father, but easy to talk to. O'Kelley had plenty of time before Red came at two, so he decided to get dressed and go see about more work at the rail yards. Maybe he was ready to get on full time.

It was an unusually warm day for January, and the bright sun felt good, so he left the hotel in his shirt and suspenders with a hat, and left his heavy coat, the one with the pistols in the pockets, in the room. As he approached the Frisco rail yard, a voice called from across the street. A patrolman was striding in his direction. "Kelley," he called. "Are you Kelley?"

"O'Kelley," he replied angrily. It was Bunker, the policeman who'd arrested him a month earlier and handed him over to Burnett for questioning in the string of burglaries.

"Yes, O'Kelley. Come with me," Bunker said.

"For what?!" O'Kelley demanded.

"Questioning in a robbery," the cop said, and they were off to the police station. A brothel operated by Lillian Johnson on West Second Street was held up by two men wearing masks and carrying revolvers. Lillian thought she recognized O'Kelley and his pal Bob Jackson, who had quite a criminal history. After questioning O'Kelley down at headquarters the detectives became convinced that he didn't rob the brothel because he was having dinner with the reporter Red Galvin when the robbery took place.

By the time they released O'Kelley it was after five, his whole day was wasted, and he was fuming. The sun was low in the sky, and gone were his good feelings of the bright morning. He headed straight for his hotel, and of course Red was already gone. That meant he missed the appointment and a free dinner. So he went to his room, grabbed his canvas coat with the iron-filled pockets, and walked straight to White's Saloon. He needed a drink.

For a while O'Kelley settled into the old velvet isolation he knew so well. Everybody else left him. But loneliness was a trusted companion who would stick around as long as he needed company. There were only two other men in the place. They were both too much of a crowd and not enough, and it began to be unnerving. He didn't know what time it was, and it didn't matter. The night had been his comfort for most of his life, so he stepped out into the cold January air and started walking. There were a few people on the street, and the later it got, the more interesting O'Kelley thought they were. Daytime was so predictable. But after midnight, there was no telling what might happen. That's when the hardest people were out, looking for opportunities. The easy score. The unattended suitcase. The cash left on the counter. The unlocked door. And O'Kelley had seen enough of both sides of the law to know what to look for. He always tried to do the right thing and yet couldn't please anybody. He was a lawman. He'd still be a lawman if they'd let him. Like he told Red, it was those cops. They were after him for no reason.

The alcohol? He was sure it made him sharper. It blurred the demons and dimmed the memories so the here and now could come into focus. But tonight the whiskey wasn't working. It was the last two days of conversation with the reporter, that was the problem. Sure, Red was a good man. But if he wasn't here asking questions, trying to get to the heart of O'Kelley, then the here and now would come into focus. Those questions, and those answers, kept tromping, stomping around in his head. He saw his old Missouri home. Felt his grandmother's arms around him. Heard his mother's voice. Was that his mother's voice? He turned, and there was no one there. Scenes of Creede. Faces he thought he knew. People who would help him. He couldn't quite make them out, but they'd been clear at one time. And the years taken away from him inside the gray stone prison walls. Living the same day over and over, until it was no day at all. No whiskey, no fighting, no schemes and plans. Just the same day every day. The frustration was a weight that became a burden that became an enemy. It was the enemy he couldn't see or touch, but he knew it was there, and he needed to scream at it, beat it, kill it. He walked and walked, and still the anger grew. Every muscle in his body ached to strike out, but there was no target within reach.

It was nine o'clock when O'Kelley shuffled slowly up Harvey and rounded the corner on the south side of West First Street. Coming toward him was a man in a dark coat with shining buttons, wearing the unmistakable domed hat of an Oklahoma City policeman. "Wouldn't he like to catch me doin' somethin'?" O'Kelley thought. "Well, not tonight, Mr. Lawman. Not tonight."

They drew near to each other in front of the McCord-Collins Building. The cop was a streetwise veteran who noticed everything around him, close and far away. Of course he had his eye on the man approaching, watched his hands, watched for a weapon. But the hands were in the pockets of the tan canvas coat, and the eyes were concealed in shadows, until they were separated by no more than fifteen feet, and suddenly he recognized him. At that moment, they both entered the glow of a streetlight.

"Hello, O'Kelley," Burnett said dryly.

O'Kelley's eyes widened when he recognized Joe Burnett, the man who arrested him, just when he was trying to make a new start. It was Burnett who made his arrival in Oklahoma City a nightmare. In O'Kelley's muddled, drunken mind, it was Burnett's fault that nobody trusted him. Nobody gave him a chance. Nobody.

Instantly pulling his right hand from the coat pocket with a tight grip on a Colt .45 New Army double-action revolver, O'Kelley growled, "You come with me. I'll arrest you, you sonuva. . . ." He raised the pistol high and brought it down hard against the cop's head, knocking his helmet off. The helmet offered scant protection against such a blow, and Burnett's knees buckled. O'Kelley had worked hard every day in prison, and he was strong as a mule. Burnett's left hand instinctively grabbed the gun, and he pulled the baton with his right hand and hit the assailant twice in the head. O'Kelley fired the Colt, and the shot went wild, but Burnett could feel the heat through his white patrolman's glove.

It Ends Here

At that instant, one of O'Kelley's lowlife companions, Bob Jackson, rounded the corner. O'Kelley caught a glimpse of him and called out, "C'mon, we'll murder this fellow!" As ordered, Jackson pulled a pistol and cocked it, but didn't fire because O'Kelley was between him and Burnett. Burnett dropped his baton and fought to keep O'Kelley's back to the accomplice as he cocked the gun four times, but each time let the hammer down because he didn't have a shot. Finally, Jackson turned and ran, O'Kelley turned his head to look for him, and that was Burnett's chance to reach for his own Colt New Army .38. This battle was exactly why he buttoned only the top two buttons of his uniform coat when he was on patrol.

Both men fired at the same time, both missing. O'Kelley's shot ricocheted off the pavement below them, sending hot shards of stinging lead and gravel into their hands. They wrestled and shoved nearly one hundred feet, all the way around the corner, each one trying to turn his gun for a shot without letting go of the other's gun hand. Burnett fired again, and the bullet went clean through O'Kelley's left thigh, making him growl with pain. But he fought even harder, fueled by a blend of alcohol and adrenaline.

O'Kelley yanked Burnett forward and clamped the cop's forearm under his armpit in what Burnett would later describe as "a death-like grip," making it impossible for Burnett to turn the gun on him. They wrenched each other, shoving with shoulders and butting their heads. Still, O'Kelley fired repeatedly. Shots three and four went wild. Five was against the blue wool coat, opening a smoking hole, burning orange around the edges. It tore through Burnett's hip pocket and ripped the flesh. Six, and the muzzle blast burned Burnett's left ear. And by then Burnett had answered with six shots, his gun was empty, and his left glove was nearly burned off from holding O'Kelley's blazing Colt.

It went on for fifteen minutes, both men were exhausted, and both knew they were fighting for their lives. Burnett began to yell, "Help! I'm a police officer! Help me!" People were on the street, but nobody

The fatal fight between Joseph Burnett and Ed O'Kelley. Art by Joe Johnston.

made a move to lend a hand. After all, two armed men were whirling each other around, with occasional shots going off in unpredictable directions. Burnett even heard a voice call, "How do we know you're a cop?" Another hollered, "Run! Get away from him!" But of course Burnett would have been shot in the back if he'd taken a step. He knew O'Kelley had another pistol.

O'Kelley never thought of fighting fair. He bull-rushed Burnett and bit down hard on his ear. The pain made Burnett scream out loud and jerk away. The redhead's teeth tore a gash in the ear, and he spit out some flesh. No sooner was that ear free than O'Kelley was on the other ear, biting and chewing. But the hands—Burnett had to concentrate on the hands. The teeth hurt, but the hands could kill. Just then O'Kelley realized Burnett's gun was empty, and he let go with his left hand long enough to get the .44 Smith out of his left pocket and fire another wild shot. Burnett dropped the empty .38 and got an awkward grip on his attacker's left wrist, but didn't think he could last much longer. It might be a matter of seconds until O'Kelley got a better shot, and then he'd be a dead man.

From nowhere a hulking figure approached, and Burnett recognized the muscular A. G. Paul, baggage man at the Frisco freight depot across the street. Paul had heard the gunfire, looked out the door, and seen his neighborhood patrolman Burnett. "For God's sake get hold of him," Burnett pleaded, as Paul bravely inserted himself into the fight, grabbing O'Kelley's left hand, the one that held the smoking .44.

"Is it empty?" Paul wondered. O'Kelley answered with another shot that blew a chunk out of a paving brick, taunting, "Does that sound empty to you?!" He kept firing, but Paul kept a hold on his hand, and that was Burnett's one chance. His right hand quickly reached for the .38 revolver holstered in the small of his back. He put the muzzle just behind O'Kelley's left temple and fired one shot, "Blam." O'Kelley collapsed to the bricks.

Burnett fell on his left side, gasping for breath, and looked at the man who had saved his life. "Watch him," Burnett said, gasping. "He'll kill me yet." But Paul didn't think so. He could see the pool of blood and brains spilling from the hole where the bullet exploded into the right side of O'Kelley's head.

Someone working late in an office saw the fight and telephoned the police, so other officers arrived immediately and found Burnett's gloves and coat smoldering. Then they all knew just how close the cop came to being killed when they found a bleeding bullet hole in his side and four more holes in his coat. Burnett also had a concussion, but he was not going to miss the inquest, so when they got him to the doctor he said to hurry it up.

About the time Burnett arrived at the courthouse for the inquest, Red woke to Wednesday's sun slanting between the venetian blinds. He dressed quickly and headed out the door. He was picking O'Kelley up at his hotel and taking him to a photographer's studio. After all, the man hadn't been photographed since his release from prison. He deserved to have a photograph, and the article Red was writing for the *Post-Dispatch* certainly needed to be illustrated. Of course he was meeting him early enough to sober him up and clean him up if necessary.

Red jumped off the streetcar slinging the leather bag over his shoulder, crossed the street, and entered the Lewis. It was mid-morning and the streets were busy, although for the residents of the Lewis, days started slower and ended later. As he topped the stairs Red could see O'Kelley's room down the hall, with the door open. He walked quickly, stepped into the doorway, and knocked lightly. There, turning to look at him, was not O'Kelley, but an Oklahoma City police officer, and behind him was a man in a suit opening the drawer in the washstand.

Red checked the number on the door to be sure he had the right room, and by that time the patrolman had approached. "Good day, sir, and may I help you?"

"Uh . . . " Red stammered, "O'Kelley?" His mind was working quickly, and he was suddenly sure that the subject of his article had been arrested.

"And who might you be?" the cop asked.

"James Galvin, *St. Louis Post Dispatch*," he replied. "I'm a reporter. I've been doing a story on Mr. O'Kelley. Is he in trouble?"

"Been doing a story on him? What exactly does that mean?" the cop asked, while the other one barely glanced up. He was busy looking around the room, under the mattress and inside O'Kelley's trunk.

"For the last couple of days I interviewed him. You know, asked him about his past. Did you arrest him?" he asked, sure O'Kelley had been picked up in the middle of a burglary or some such.

"You have something to prove who you are?"

"Well, I freelance. I don't work for the paper. I work for lots of papers," Red said, digging through his bag. "Here you go, these are the notes I made with O'Kelley." He pulled out his notebook and flipped it open.

It Ends Here

"Were you with him last night?" the cop asked, glancing at the notebook.

"No, we had an appointment, but I came and he wasn't here. I never saw him all day. Why? Please tell me what this is about," Red pleaded earnestly.

By that time the man in the suit seemed to be finished scrutinizing the room, and he turned to join them in the doorway. "Detective Fred Hagen," he said dryly. ""Where did you see him last?"

"The night before. Monday. I left him in a saloon . . . the Four Winds. . . . "

Hagen nodded, then said, "I'm afraid I have sad information for you, sir. Mr. O'Kelley is dead."

There was a moment of silence long enough to drive a freight train through, as Red thought about his friend, his hopes for O'Kelley to get his feet on the ground and start a new life, and all the things they talked about. And his anguish for the poor O'Kelley kept going back and forth with what O'Kelley's death would mean for the story. Did he have it all? What else was left untold? Now he'd never get to ask the big question: Why did he shoot Ford?

Oklahoma City still didn't have its own morgue, but they kept bodies of the deceased in the cool and dark back room of a furniture store, and O'Kelley's body was taken there. Red told police the parents lived in Patton, Missouri, and the desk sergeant sent a wire to them. Red waited to interview the family, but when three days passed without a response to the telegram, he went back to St. Louis. Nobody in O'Kelley's family ever answered. A couple of weeks later, January 28, the city buried O'Kelley at Fairlawn Cemetery in north Oklahoma City. He traveled so many miles and lived so many dark adventures, and yet had settled in this city that was just being born, only to die at the hands of another Missouri native.

Chapter Eleven

Little Willie Rudolph

"You're 100 percent homegrown and self made," said George Johns, raising his glass. He was buying Red's dinner to celebrate the O'Kelley story and Red's new job with the *Republic*. "Here's to the best reporter in Missouri."

"The best editors make the best reporters," Red said over the edge of his beer.

"And," his editor added, "best wishes at the *Republic*."

"You know I've never had a full-time job," Red said. "I mean, other than shining shoes and selling papers twelve hours a day. I've always freelanced."

"Yes, I know," Johns answered. "That's why you need to take this job. You'll be a breath of fresh air in the midst of all their tired old hacks. I can't wait to see how you do on a regular salary with an endless stream of assignments, your own desk, and a room full of reporters."

"Maybe I'll hate it."

"Maybe. I would love to put you on staff, but you need to work with another editor . . . and with the *Republic's* lean toward the Democrats . . . "

"But you're a Democrat," Red protested.

"A Republican in principal, a Democrat in practice, and unaffiliated at the editor's desk," Johns corrected him. "Anyway, after a couple of years I fully expect to get you back. You know I did this very thing when I was younger. Went over to the *Republic* for a couple of years and came back. Best thing I ever did."

"Well, they never would have made the offer if I didn't have you as a mentor," Red replied emphatically.

"You're too kind," Johns batted back.

"They already gave me an assignment," Red said, a determined journalistic cloud descending over his face. "There's a criminal out there who's adored by women and yet hated by everyone with a soul."

"Oh, I better make sure we have someone on that," Johns said, teasing.

"Oh, you've had Frank covering him. It's William Rudolph. They want me to get the deeper story. You know: Who is he? What makes him tick? How does he always beat the police? Why is he still . . . out there?"

"You're the man for that job," Johns declared.

"First thing," Red went on, "Rudolph has disappeared. So has his partner, Collins. It's been three months, and the cops have nothing.

Johns raised an eyebrow. "And you're going to. . . . "

"Yes, find him . . . before the Pinkertons do."

"Well, if anyone can, it's you. This isn't one of your vigilante stories, is it?

Red looked at him for a moment. "Vigilantes?"

"As you said, Rudolph is hated."

"No, I'm pretty sure Rudolph and his partner left Missouri. The locals aren't going to chase them across the country," Red asserted. "Anyway, don't you think the day of the vigilante is gone?"

"Ah, but you can't dismiss the ancient desire to right a wrong, the need to control one's own destiny in the face of unseen evil," the publisher said with a grin. "Bob Ford was a vigilante."

Red pointed with his beer. "But that was over twenty years ago, and Ford was also paid, a bounty hunter. You're talking about the vigilante as a force of civilization, a public-minded person who'll risk his own neck for other people, who'll dare to do what the law can't do. That person doesn't exist anymore."

Johns shook his head, playfully condescending, "Oh, that person will never die. He's in our blood."

The banter went on long after the meal. About eight o'clock Red stood and put on his coat and hat, he grabbed his shoulder bag, and he and Johns said their goodbyes. Two days later the *Republic* ran Red's first story as a full-time staff reporter. It was a profile piece, and it started out: "William Rudolph is a throwback, a man from another time. He's a ruthless, fearless rascal who plans his jobs in broad strokes, trusting his wits, charm, and daring to figure out the details as he goes along. And it works. Whether he's lucky, smart, or both, he has truly lived a remarkable life so far. That's why they call him The Missouri Kid."

And from that time on, Rudolph was the Missouri Kid, even to the Pinkertons.

+ —— + —— +

Little Willie Rudolph was born in 1883 in a remote Franklin County, Missouri, cabin, and grew up in a huge, rotting, isolated house near Stanton. That was mining country at one time, but the lead and zinc deposits never were as rich as expected. St. Clair and Sullivan grew bigger than Stanton, and when the work for miners dwindled, people just naturally migrated to the larger towns to find work. Mines were abandoned, along with cabins, machinery, stores, and the boardinghouse that was home to the Rudolph family. It sat high on a ridge, deep in the woods, at the end of an overgrown dirt road. A speculator built the place, expecting shops and houses to spring up around it, but they never did. For a while it was home away from home for many miners who left their wives and children to go wherever the mines were providing the most work. Over the years it became harder and harder for them to scratch smaller and smaller yields from the ground, and the big mining companies pulled out. In time the boardinghouse went vacant, nobody wanted it, and the Rudolph family, though very poor, was able to afford

William Rudolph as a Missouri farm boy. He liked to spend time alone in the woods with his dog and a fishing pole or his .22 rifle. Library of Congress Prints and Photographs.

it. It was a long, two-story structure with four entry doors along the south side. Inside were a big kitchen and pantry, a big dining room, a parlor, and fourteen bedrooms. Outside, there were two outhouses, the skeleton of a shed, and a chicken coop.

There, Willie lived with his mother, Nancy Armistead Rudolph, and his stepfather, German immigrant Francis Rudolph, who preferred to be called Frank. Willie's father, William Anderson, never married Nancy. Then, when Nancy married Frank, who was almost twenty years older and a terrible drunk, he didn't want the boy. Nancy bowed to Frank, though it broke her heart, and when William Anderson moved to Arkansas, he took little five-year-old Willie with him. Nancy's pain at being separated from her first born was unbearable, and she fell into deep depression. Within a year Nancy's brother William Armistead stepped in. He told Frank what a miserable human being he was to forbid the mother and son to be together. Frank sobered up long enough to see the light and said the boy could come home. Uncle William then traveled to Arkansas and persuaded Anderson that the boy belonged with Nancy. That's how little Willie, after being given up by his mother, came back to live with her under the shadow of a man who didn't want him. Though he was given the Rudolph name, he was never adopted.

His childhood was never happy, as Nancy worked constantly to keep the family fed and clothed, while Frank, an out-of-work miner, drank heavily, and they were all isolated in their huge house in the trees. In time Nancy gave birth to two girls, Nellie and Esther. Then her sister and brother-in-law, Esther and George Harmes, who was like Frank, an unemployed, German-born miner, came to live with them. Of course the baby girls got all the attention and little Willie got a minimum of love, schooling, and direction.

When Red Galvin started digging into Rudolph's story, two things struck him. First, a boy could have no better beginning for a life of crime. And second, his background was eerily similar to that of Ed O'Kelley. Both were given up by their mothers and had judgmental, disapproving fathers. As adults, they yearned desperately for respect. The difference was that O'Kelley tried to get it as a lawman, while Rudolph chose to get it with money: other people's money.

Willie was a boy who was almost constantly in trouble. He had a brilliant mind but was given to fighting at school, and by the time he was fifteen he was done with education. By then he was barred from several local stores because he'd been caught stealing from them. With little attention from Nancy or Frank, Willie was frequently in the company of Uncle Harmes, who was known as a shiftless thug and suspected of many robberies in the area.

Joseph and Ruth Schwartz owned a mercantile store where everyone around Stanton went to buy sugar, salt, flour, canned goods, and coffee, along with clothing and household goods. Joseph and Ruth were loyal, earnest, and hardworking. Because they were thrifty, they could afford to dress better than most folks and had the finest home in Stanton.

One cold night Harmes and some of his cronies had been drinking particularly heavily in a saloon, when they started talking about how much money the Schwartz family must have hidden in their big house. Harmes and two others went to the Schwartz home and walked right in, overpowered Joseph and bound his hands with his own belt, then tied Ruth's hands in her apron strings. They demanded to know where the money was hidden, but Joseph only answered that they had no money in the house. Take the silver, take anything you want, he and Ruth pleaded, but there was no cash. The thieves didn't believe it, and jabbed the fireplace poker into the heart of the fire. When it was red hot, the men applied it to Joseph's feet over and over again, as he screamed for mercy, trying to make him turn over the riches they were sure the old couple had hidden away.

Schwartz reported the crime to the sheriff, but he didn't know the men who did it. The sheriff questioned Harmes and teenage Willie, as well as others, but there was never an arrest. At night Willie lay in his bed and thought about how he was repulsed by his Uncle Harmes, and yet he wanted to be like him. After the Schwartz questioning, he realized that people thought they were two of a kind. People didn't care about him, so he made up his mind not to care about them. "So that's how it is," he thought. "Everybody thinks I'm a crook, so I might as well be one."

In the wake of the Schwartz attack, Harmes and Willie left town for a while and found work in the lead mines of St. Francois County. Nobody bothered the Schwartzes again, so in time the sheriff dropped the case, and George returned to the old boardinghouse. But Willie had seen enough of home, so he turned his face toward his new life. At the mines, he learned how to blow open the ore seams with nitroglycerine and dynamite. It was a job favored by a lot of young men who had steady hands, steel nerves, and a boiling-point sense of adventure. No one was better suited to it than Willie, who had a daredevil edge to him. So he took his skill with explosives to the silver mines of Colorado, where he was treated as a master tradesman and paid accordingly. The physically fit and handsome Willie passed himself off as older than he was and charmed women wherever he went. Though he worked in mines from Leadville to Pueblo, he felt drawn to the high life in Denver, where he saw the kind of men he wanted to emulate. He saw men with their hair slicked down, wearing fine suits and silk ties with stick pins and gold watch chains. They walked upright, with a swagger, and not like the tired, beaten miners back home. They went in and out of office buildings and cafes with other gentlemen at their side or beautiful women on their arm. Yes, that's how Willie would be. He'd seen enough of the sweaty, dirty, dangerous life of hard labor.

With the money he saved, he took a train back to St. Louis and bought a nice suit and hat. He got a haircut and slicked his hair back with oil imported from France. Then he noticed a difference in the way people, especially women, looked at him. And he liked it. So he went to a photographer and had his picture taken in his new suit and hat.

But when the money ran out, he burglarized a store and had a head-on wreck with twentieth-century technology. The store's owner was asleep in his apartment upstairs when he heard Willie break in, so he quietly called the St. Louis police on his new telephone, and they nabbed the young thief in the act. Willie was through being Willie, and gave the police his name as William Anderson, the name of his father. He was just twenty years old. He stood over five feet, eleven inches, and weighed 160 pounds. Anyone who met him remembered his physique, good looks, brown eyes, and pale complexion topped by thick, carefully combed dark brown hair.

Jail proved to be anything but the salvation of William Rudolph. There he met the one man who was the perfect flint for his steel, the man whose talents and inclinations were the perfect complement to those of Rudolph. George Collins, who had been arrested under the alias William Lewis, was almost five years older, and to Rudolph a man of the world. He was from the East and was an army veteran. He had been part of the force under Admiral George Dewey and General Wesley Merritt that seized the Philippines from the Spanish in 1898. Even more impressive to Rudolph, he came home with a huge eagle tattooed

The broad-shouldered William Rudolph enjoyed getting dressed up and having his picture taken. Unfortunately for him, the police appreciated the opportunity to use those pictures in tracking him down.

across his chest. While Collins was muscled and heavy, Rudolph was slender, athletic, and perfectly proportioned. Collins had no direction or plan, whereas Rudolph had an abundance of both. Collins was the

The mysterious George Collins dressed in his finest for interviews with police, prosecutors, and reporters, following his arrest with the Missouri Kid in Hartford, Connecticut. Library of Congress Prints and Photographs.

brawn, while Rudolph was the brains. Collins was a burglar who could use pry bars and skeleton keys; Rudolph was trained in the use of explosives. Ironically, Collins was arrested near Desloge in St. Francois County, the mining country Rudolph had left a year before. Drifting from town to town, he had gotten just enough work with the railroads to support him while he committed burglaries. He was a simple man who was trying to get by, with no dreams of pulling off a big job. But that all changed when he met the dreamer William Rudolph.

Rudolph got out of jail first and stayed in St. Louis waiting for his new friend to get out, and they went back to the place they both knew, the mines of southeastern Missouri. Collins, being a former railroad brakeman, knew about the Yeggs brotherhood, and for two guys needing cash and a fresh start, it seemed like exactly what they needed. The Yeggs was a hobo crime syndicate founded by a hobo named Yeager, who organized the most talented and resourceful among them to commit burglaries, some of them quite lucrative, up and down the Reading Railroad. The Yeggs operated like a hobo Masonic order, with secret signs, slang, and symbols they wrote and drew on bridges, railcars, and buildings to indicate where the next Yeggs could find more Yeggs, dangerous guards, safe hiding, or easy pickings. They generally didn't care much for stealing tools or clothes or food. They preferred to steal money. And any man who identified himself as a Yegg was likely to find fellow Yeggs ready to throw in with him.

So Rudolph and Collins made themselves known in the hobo camps along the rail lines as Yeggs. They made friends with men who were willing to hide them and tell them places to hit and places to avoid. In turn, they shared the wealth from a series of petty crimes during which they stole cash, pistols, and a small supply of nitroglycerine. The law in the area had no idea who they were or where they might strike next. But the mine supervisors and security men were a vigilante-minded group, determined to do for themselves what the sheriff and police couldn't do. There were community meetings in which men were encouraged to go armed, to be on guard, and to seize and hold any strangers who came around the mines. Mines and other businesses began to post night guards where none had been before. Rudolph decided it was getting too dangerous. After all, he and Collins were virtually the only new men in the area, and they stuck out like a sore thumb. What was the joy in having money if they couldn't go out and spend it? Besides, Rudolph had experienced enough of the hobo life. He preferred to wear nice clothes and sleep on clean sheets in nice hotels. So he and Collins meandered over to Flat River, where they were welcomed at the home of Frank Byers, an old friend of Rudolph's stepfather. It was a good place to relax and establish a bit of an alibi.

After a few weeks they took a train to Jefferson City, where they were completely unknown—a town that offered plenty of places for them to blow their money. Then in fall 1902, Rudolph took Collins to meet his family. It was a safe haven, though a strange place to go for a man who shared so little affection with the folks at home. And yet the trip meant he knew their love was on some level unconditional. First he took Collins to meet his father in Maynard, Arkansas. After laying low for a while, they still had money burning holes in their pockets, and Hot Springs offered a place to relax with the baths, liquor, gambling, and women. Nobody would look for them there.

Rudolph had always envied Collins's tattoo. He wanted something like that, but better. In Hot Springs he found a dentist who advertised gold caps for teeth, and Rudolph decided that was just the thing. He ordered a dazzling set of fourteen gold teeth for himself. Then he just had to show them off, so he took Collins to meet his mother, stepfather, and sisters.

Of course for such men, life on the old home place only proved to be relaxing for a couple of months, and then they had to add some excitement to their diet. Rudolph had an idea, which he turned into a plan, and Collins thought every word from Rudolph's mouth was brilliant. On Christmas Eve, 1902, Rudolph went to rent two horses from the livery in Stanton. There were no riding horses, but there was a wagon and team, so he rented that, using his father's name, Bill Anderson. They drove to Union, the county seat, and left the wagon near the tracks, and walked to the square, where they scouted the Union Bank. As they arrived in town, one of the horses pulled up lame, but to the resourceful Rudolph, that was the sort of problem that always led to something better. They unhitched the lame horse and left it with the wagon, and rode the other one back to the old boardinghouse. It was a terrible ride, sitting double on a horse not accustomed to being ridden, and they were bareback with twenty feet of reins to manage.

That night, with only moonlight to guide them, they rode back toward Union, stopping when they passed a farm where some good-looking horses milled in the corral. They slipped in, saddled two of them, and left the rented team horse and his twenty feet of reins. At Union they tied up at the Union Bank around two in the morning. Collins, the burglar, used his skeleton keys to quietly unlock the front door. While Rudolph went in, Collins took up a post on the corner so that he could see every street leading to the bank. Inside, Rudolph rigged two nitro-glycerin charges, one on the vault and a smaller one on the safe, and when everything was ready, blew both of them. While Rudolph raked the cash into burlap bags, Collins started shooting randomly into the air in all directions, so that anyone who was awakened by the explosions would be encouraged to keep their heads down.

They took their loot and galloped east out of town. Within an hour a posse had been raised, but they never found a trace of the men or the money. That's because after riding hard for a few miles east, the thieves hit the tracks, dropped their saddles and bridles in the brush, turned the horses loose, and hopped a westbound freight train. They rode it all the way through Union, the last place anybody would look for them, and out the other side. At the big curve heading into Stanton, they simply jumped off and walked to the Rudolph home, arriving near dawn. When they stopped to count their haul, they were astonished to find that they had gotten away with $12,000 in cash, plus some $110,000 in banknotes.

They put $2,000 in a coffee can and suspended it on a rope down a well, keeping the rest hidden in their room. Nobody in the family knew where they'd gone or what they did. The officials of Union Bank knew whoever robbed them was long gone, and the local sheriff would never find out who did it, much less capture them or recover the money. So the bank brought in the Pinkerton Detective Agency.

Chapter Twelve
An Impatient Sense of Justice

Since its founding in the wake of the Civil War, the Pinkerton Agency had changed only in size and in the vast reach of their resources. Even after mistakes like the bomb that killed Jesse James's half-brother and maimed their mother, their agents were still heavily armed, well funded, and unbridled. They were relentless not only in whom they pursued, but also in how they pursued them. So it was nothing for a Pinkerton agent to bribe, beat, or threaten anyone, including innocent friends and family members of the men they wanted. It was no wonder; Pinkerton agents were vigilantes for hire, doing the law's work with no official standing except that they were licensed private investigators. Though the public stood in awe of the Pinkertons, believing they were government agents, they were actually hired by railroads and banks. With reckless disregard for the law, they crossed county and state lines where duly authorized lawmen couldn't go. It would seem that with their lack of rules, they'd catch everybody they chased. But they didn't, and perhaps the most glaring example of their misses was the Reno Brothers Gang of Indiana. After terrorizing railroad and express companies for years and being chased by Pinkerton agents from Missouri to Canada, every member of the gang was finally brought to justice not by Pinkertons, but by either local lawmen or citizen vigilantes.

It Ends Here

After the death of founder Allan Pinkerton in 1884, the agency was led by his sons Robert and William. They continued to expand the agency's scope of operations, as well as their association with big business, including mining and steel companies, and the agency was hired to break many labor strikes. In Homestead, Pennsylvania, in 1892, agents purported to be security guards for scabs who came in to work when the steel plant's workers went on strike. But the agents came down the river on barges with rifles and pistols plainly displayed. So of course the strikers armed themselves, and a day-long shooting war broke out in which seven Pinkertons and nine workers died.

As time went by, the Pinkertons better understood the value of sometimes keeping their guns holstered and working behind the scenes, away from witnesses and reporters. They infiltrated labor unions, gathering information and even rising to leadership positions. In 1903, agent Morris Friedman got control of the Western Federation of Miners (WFM) relief fund. He gave money hand over fist to families of deceased and injured workers, until he had almost bankrupted the fund. Then he withheld payments until the needy families were on the verge of starvation. WFM treasurer Bill Haywood would later write, "I discovered that the chairman of the relief committe [sic] was a Pinkerton detective, who was carrying out the instructions of the agency. . . ." It was all aimed at ruining the union's finances and reputation.

Leading Pinkerton operations in the west were Charlie Siringo, who became known as the relentless agent chasing Butch Cassidy and the Sundance Kid, and James McParlan. McParlan was the fountainhead of subversive operations, having joined Pinkerton in the 1870s and masterminded the infiltration, spying, and double-dealing that brought down the Molly McGuires, an Irish American labor activist organization. With him at the helm, Pinkertons in the west became very good at enticing and intimidating their targets. To force people to cooperate with them or set up criminals for capture, they worked elaborate stings: They would threaten a man that he could face criminal charges for not

William Pinkerton (seated) is pictured during his days as a field agent with special agents Pat Connell (left) and Sam Finley. Pinkerton spent enough time in the field to know what to expect of his agents, then spent most of his career managing operations from Washington. Library of Congress Prints and Photographs.

giving information, when really they had no power to charge him. Or they might capture a petty criminal and promise him immunity from prosecution if he helped them capture a bigger crook, though they had no such authority.

The agent in charge of the Union Bank robbery was perfect for the job, Charles Schumacher, a blend of old and new. He was a man who feared no man, a cool, deadeye shot with all sorts of firearms, who had an impatient sense of justice. He had also mastered the agency's techniques for bullying, threatening, and coercing to get any kind of cooperation he needed. He simply did what was needed to accomplish the task at hand.

The first question in an investigation was whether the locals had noticed any strangers around town. Folks had seen a young man in his twenties, some said two men, walking along the railroad tracks toward Stanton. Then there was an unknown lame horse, and a cart that had been abandoned in town, and the name stenciled on it showed that it was rented from a livery in Stanton.

Schumacher went straight to the Stanton livery and learned that the man who rented the rig was Bill Anderson. That night Schumacher stopped in the local saloons to see what else he could learn, and found that Anderson was probably Willie Rudolph. Only a few people had seen him in the past month, but lots more had heard he was back. And of course everybody mentioned the torture of old man Schwartz, and what a rotten kid Willie had been, but nobody knew where to find him . . . unless he was back home, staying at his parents' house. Schumacher had to find out.

The brave Schumacher had enough information to go to Sheriff D. B. Bruch the next morning. He didn't know that Rudolph pulled the job, but he intended to find him and question him. So far, all of the crimes of which Rudolph was suspected had him pictured as a sneak thief, but there was a lot of shooting during the bank job. That meant Rudolph's partner could be dangerous. At any rate, Schumacher said, he had an idea how to find out if Rudolph was there with his parents.

"We don't want to spook him into running," Schumacher told the sheriff. "None of them know me, so I can walk right up and say howdy and find out if he's in there."

"But how'll you recognize Willie?" Bruch asked.

"Oh, I'll recognize him," Schumacher said. "I've got a good description."

The sheriff nodded. "May be another young fellow in there too."

"Exactly," Schumacher added. "I'm hoping to get at least a glimpse of two young thugs. Then if they're in there, we'll go back with more men and bring them in."

That afternoon, December 24, 1903, Sheriff Bruch knelt in the bushes not more than two hundred feet from the house and watched Schumacher walk on through the trees. When the place was built some sixty years before, the brush had been kept cleared, and it never grew back, so Bruch had a clear view. It was a bright January day, one of those in which the brittle sun provides no warmth at all. Schumacher wore the sheriff's hunting coat, with its big game pockets. The collar of a red plaid flannel shirt peeked out below an old and weathered hat. His wool pants were laced inside the top of his boots, he carried a twelve-gauge W. W. Greener shotgun on his shoulder, and he looked for all the world like a hunter trying to bag his supper.

The sheriff shook his head. Schumacher's bravery was amazing, walking right up to the house. He could have been shot dead at any moment, but he was counting on the crooks to be weighing how much of a threat he was, and preferring not to raise any ruckus they didn't need to raise. If they killed him and he turned out to be a detective or an innocent stranger, either way the law was sure to come to look for him.

Approaching the four doors, Schumacher headed for the one that showed the most footsteps leading up to it, second from the west end. He walked right up and hollered, "Hello in the house. Hello in the house. I need help." When there was no response, he knocked.

Schumacher stood alone, then turned his back on the door and ambled in a small circle, surveying the horizon as if looking for something familiar. Suddenly the door opened a few inches. "What is it?" came a woman's voice from the darkness beyond.

"Hello." From his hiding place Bruch could hear Schumacher say, "I was out hunting, and I'm afraid I'm lost."

The door closed, and after a moment opened a little wider. A tall, dark-haired young man stepped into the doorway, surveyed the lost hunter, then the woods beyond. Schumacher knew instantly it was him. "Howdy, sir," Schumacher started again. "I think I'm lost, and I'm awful hungry. If you have something for me to eat, I can pay." Rudolph looked around again, then grinned at the stranger for being helpless enough to get lost, and told him to come in. But then he held up his hand, saying, "If you're going to come in here, unload that gun first." Schumacher emptied the Greener and disappeared into the house.

Bruch waited. And waited. Something had to be wrong. This was taking too long. Should he rush the house? Should he run back to Stanton for more men?

Just then, the door opened and out stepped Schumacher, smiling, hefting the shotgun back to his shoulder. "Thanks very much," he said. "I just head that way and I'll hit Lollar Branch, right?" he asked, taking a bite and pointing with a big golden biscuit.

The handsome young man leaned out the door and said, "That's right," and Schumacher disappeared into the trees, heading west. The sheriff waited a few minutes, then crawled backwards from his hiding place until he was sure he was out of sight of the house.

Schumacher circled around and met Bruch on the road back to Stanton. "That was him, I'm sure," the detective said coolly. "Another fellow in there too. I guess the old lady is his mother. The old man never got out of his chair and never said a word. I saw two girls too."

"That'd be his sisters, I reckon," Bruch said. "Now what?"

"Let's get some deputies."

"How many you think we need?" asked the sheriff. "Ten? Twenty?" Schumacher laughed.

With three deputies, he set out from Stanton well before sunup on January 24, a month after the Union Bank job. Leaving their horses at the bottom of the ridge, they walked the steep road to the old boardinghouse. It was still, with no sign that anyone was stirring inside. As the sun touched the hilltop, the four lawmen slowly emerged like mist through the trees. B. F. Tichener was still healing after a farm accident, hitting himself in the leg with a glancing blow from a sledgehammer, so he was heading to the northwest corner, where he could watch the back of the house. Schumacher, carrying the same shotgun he had when he was playing a lost hunter, walked a step behind and slightly to the left of Louis Vetter, who had his Winchester rifle cocked. Emmanuel Cromer was about twenty feet behind them as they headed straight toward the door second from the west end of the house, the same door

Schumacher had entered the day before. The deputies were local men, and Schumacher wasn't sure how much he could count on them. The weight of the arrest was on him.

When they were within two paces and focused on the door ahead, like a lightning flash the door to their left opened, and before the posse could react Rudolph jumped out, followed by Collins. They yelled, "Stop, put up your hands!" and Cromer did just that. He dropped his rifle and raised his hands. But Schumacher had no such intention and fired the shotgun wildly in Rudolph's direction, missing him completely. Both robbers had a double-action revolver in each hand, and they started firing as fast as they could. Rudolph had become furious when he peeked out the window, recognized Schumacher, and realized he'd been tricked. To think that he trusted the man's story and extended the hospitality of his mother's home to this liar made his blood boil. So that's whom Rudolph aimed for, sending him to the ground with .45 caliber bullets through his hip and groin.

Cromer ran one direction and Vetter the other, dropping the Winchester on the way. Then he stopped near the chicken coop and fired his revolver, grazing Collins's head. As blood gushed down Collins's face, he aimed for Vetter and grazed him with a shot to the leg. Tichener came to the front corner of the house and saw Schumacher down, so he retreated behind Cromer, stopping in the trees to shoot. Vetter lay wounded, a sitting duck, and knew he had to keep firing, but his shots went wild. Bullets were flying everywhere as Rudolph and Collins emptied their pistols at him and Tichener. Collins fired his last bullet into Schumacher, who had fallen within a few feet of the door and was writhing in pain. Then Rudolph straddled Schumacher and, as a final act of vengeance, put two more bullets through the helpless agent's head. Vetter finally got to his feet and ran, then fell again, then rose and ran until he was hidden by the trees. Tichener and Cromer ran too, and once they were out of effective pistol range met Vetter on the road and kept going. There was nothing to do for poor Schumacher.

Confident that the posse was in full retreat, Rudolph and Collins fell into kitchen chairs at Nancy's table, breathless, their adrenaline pumping hard. The Kid's mother, his sisters, old Frank, and cousin George Harmes, who just happened to be visiting, came up from their hiding place in the basement. After a minute, first one gunman, then the other smiled, and Rudolph was the first to speak. "Let's go." In no time they had their guns reloaded, and Nancy had a sack of food ready for them. As they left, Rudolph bent to pick up Schumacher's shotgun and a handful of shells from his coat pocket, and they disappeared into the woods.

The trio of deputies made it back to where Schumacher had left Sheriff Bruch and another group of deputies, just in case the bandits made it out to the road. Bruch and the posse immediately headed northeast along another road to cut off the bandits' escape. The deputies spread out a hundred feet apart and spent a cold, frightening night huddled under blankets, sure that the fugitives would cut the road somewhere along there. It was a moonlit night, and shortly after eight o'clock several deputies spotted them moving through the woods, parallel to the road some eighty yards away. The posse opened fire, and the escapees proved that their iron nerve counted for more than numbers of men, when they fired back a mighty storm of bullets that sent the deputies running in retreat.

Nearby was the home of Sid Armstrong, a farmer Rudolph knew. Though he and Collins were desperate for horses, Rudolph refused to steal from Armstrong and insisted on knocking on the door. He begged Armstrong to loan them horses, saying he'd just killed a man. "You can tell them we stole them," Rudolph said. "But you're a good neighbor and I want to be straight with you."

Half out of neighborly loyalty and half out of fear that he'd be the next victim, Armstrong nodded and pointed toward the barn. When Rudolph opened the big barn doors, he and Collins were looking at four enormous plow horses. It was another rough ride, but that didn't stop

Rudolph. They quickly made rope bridles, headed east, and then turned north, following Flat Creek, then Fenton Creek, toward the Bourbeuse River. At the river Rudolph and Collins had had enough of the plow horses and turned them loose. Later, the two men were spotted by a farmer, rowing away in a stolen rowboat, but by the time the sighting was reported to deputies and they came around to interview the farmer, the men and boat were long gone. That night they slept well in a barn loft and watched the snow fall.

The rowboat was discovered hidden in the riverbank willows, half-way to St. Louis. They stole horses, which they sold in Potosi so they could buy two different horses, which took them to Flat River and the Frank Byers farm. But then the spontaneous Rudolph had a better idea. He knew the Pinkertons would follow their trail, and it was likely they even got Byers's name out of his stepfather. At the road to Byers's place, Rudolph turned to his partner and said, "We're going to make a dead end for the Pinks right here." They turned south, and after a good night's rest in a Ste. Genevieve hotel, completely disappeared on an epic odyssey, ranging across half the country.

Chapter Thirteen

A Juggernaut

Little did Rudolph and Collins know that Charles Schumacher, the agent they killed, was the brother of Frank Schumacher, Pinkerton's director of operations in Washington, DC. Overnight, the Pinkerton agency became a juggernaut. William Pinkerton himself got involved, proclaiming, "The world is not big enough to hide Bill Rudolph," invoking the agency's pledge that no stone would be left unturned in search of anyone who would dare take the life of an agent. That pledge meant something when they were chasing Jesse and Frank James in the 1870s, and it meant a great deal more when they were armed with the men, technology, and budget of 1903. Pinkerton men everywhere were on alert and ready to walk through the flames of hell to bring Schumacher's killers to justice. One of the things that made Pinkerton men so brave was a feeling that criminals were more afraid of them than they were of the criminals. If a Pinkerton man went down, a dozen more would come in his place. It was legend, and it was true.

The new agent in charge was George S. Dougherty, assistant superintendent of operations in St. Louis. He already knew that Schumacher had identified his man as Rudolph, and with the help of St. Louis detectives and jailers, he thought the other man they were after was Rudolph's jailhouse buddy, George Collins. The next morning he and his men were there at the drafty, rotting old boardinghouse on the ridge

Pinkerton agent George S. Dougherty is pictured about ten years after he subdued the Missouri Kid in a Connecticut brothel. Library of Congress Prints and Photographs.

outside Stanton and virtually tore it apart looking for the money and the evidence. All they found was the $2,000 in the well.

With no clues to tell them where Rudolph and Collins might have gone, the Pinkertons grilled everyone in the house to see what the family knew. Nancy, the girls, and George Harmes insisted that they knew nothing about the robbery or where the pair had gone. Frank was in his usual stupor. When the cops sobered him up with coffee and walks outside in the snow, he became belligerent, but he still knew nothing. The Pinkertons threatened to arrest them all for conspiracy, and even that produced no information. So in true Pinkerton fashion, they carried through on their threats and arrested everyone in the house.

Detectives stood in the living room talking softly and looking blankly around them as if a sign were going to appear saying, "They went that way." Several of them pulled out cigarettes, and Dougherty struck a match and gave them all a light. With a clang he opened the wood stove, threw the match in, and closed it with another clang. Then he whirled back and flung the stove door open again. There on top of the ashes was a crumpled sheet of paper. He pulled it out, and saw written several times in pencil, "Fred LEWIS," along with "Fred LADUIX, Hartford, Conn." "Hello," Dougherty said, "this might be something."

The detectives would soon find out that Hartford was Collins's hometown and he had an uncle named Fred Lewis. Pinkertons also uncovered the military records of Fred LaDuix, who turned out to be the lieutenant under whom Collins served in the army, and who was killed in Manila. After getting the report, Dougherty hung up the telephone in Sheriff Bruch's office, looked again at the piece of paper, and pictured Collins writing potential new aliases and making notes, then throwing the piece of paper into the stove, expecting it to be burned up with the next fire. If the weather had been colder, if the excitement hadn't been so great, if the family hadn't been taken in for questioning, if any of those things had been different, and someone in the home had built a new fire, that clue would have been lost forever, and the fugitives might never have been caught. "Boys," Dougherty said to the other agents, "it's good to be good. But even better to be lucky." And yet, the note was just one of many leads he had to follow.

By that night the newspapers were having a heyday with the family being arrested. The arrest of women was always sensational, and the idea of a wider-ranging conspiracy made the story even more exciting. If Rudolph's entire family was in on it, maybe they were behind more jobs. Maybe there was more treasure buried at the old boardinghouse. Maybe more people were involved, loot was hidden at other homes, and they had other jobs planned. It was beginning to sound like Stanton was the hub of a worldwide crime ring.

But Dougherty dropped the charges against the family. Everybody knew they probably loaded guns for the robbers, tended Collins's head wound, and possibly even knew about the bank robbery before Schumacher's posse got to their home. But they were no bank robbers, and they knew nothing about the getaway. The one thing Dougherty got from the family was the connection with Frank Byers in Flat River. Deputies and agents had followed the trail of the stolen boat, the abandoned boat, the stolen horses, and the traded horses. Potosi, where the fugitives traded horses, was only a few miles from Byers's home.

A twenty-man posse, all armed with Winchester carbines, surrounded Frank Byers's house, and when they called out, a shaking Byers eased out the door with his hands raised. The Pinkertons finally got the poor man calmed down enough to talk, and at the kitchen table Byers told Dougherty that yes, he had seen the boys, but that was a few months back. Later, he was outside saying goodbye as the agents climbed into their wagons to leave, and he suddenly said, "Wait," ran back into the house, and returned with a letter. "This came last summer," he said. It was from Rudolph's little sister, Esther, and said only that he had written to her when he traveling, asking her to send Byers the address of their Uncle Rome, Jesse Jerome Armistead in Maynard, Arkansas. When Little Willie was living with his father in Arkansas, Rome's the one who convinced the family that the boy would be better off with Nancy and Frank, then brought little Willie to Missouri.

"This makes sense," Dougherty said, "He knew he was going to be on the lam sooner or later, with no place to get mail. He had Esther send this address to Byers in case he needs to pick it up."

"Maybe he already got the address from Esther when he was home. Maybe he's headed to his Uncle Rome's now," said one of the agents.

"Could be," said Dougherty. "His father is down there too. I'll wire for agents in Springfield to follow that lead."

Meanwhile, H. W. Minster, head of the Pinkertons in St. Louis, had asked St. Louis chief of detectives Edgar Kiely to find out if the convicts had a picture taken before or after they were in jail the previous year. Chief Kiely sent men to interview every photographer in town. They pored through files of images, lists of names, appointment books, and accounting ledgers, looking for those two faces and any of the eight aliases between them. It was tedious, but finally they got a lead, not in St. Louis, but from one of the dozens of telegrams Kiely sent to police in the surrounding towns. In Jefferson City, while the two outlaws were enjoying a spending spree and bought new suits of clothes, they posed together, looking quite dapper, for a photograph at the studio of Alan Dubois. Agent Minster ordered dozens of prints made and sent by express to newspapers, police departments, and Pinkerton offices all over the country. George Johns ran it four columns wide on the front page of the *Post-Dispatch*. And at the *Republic*, it ran over Red Galvin's story that transformed William Rudolph into the Missouri Kid.

Suddenly the whole country was on the lookout for the two dashing boys in the picture. The picture also had another unexpected effect. Women all over America were swooning over the handsome, twenty-year-old Rudolph. In the months to come, newspapers would play it to the hilt. They would run photos and drawings of the fugitives, with hand-drawn filigree borders. They ran illustrations of the .44 caliber Smith & Wesson Model 3 the Missouri Kid was known to carry, along with other pistols, shoulder holsters, belted holsters, and collections of skeleton keys. They carried long articles extolling the romantic adventures of the Missouri Kid. Collins wanted a nickname too, so he started calling himself "Black Frank" in hopes the newspapers would pick that up. But it didn't fit him, and it certainly lacked the inspiring ring of "the Missouri Kid," so it didn't stick. Meanwhile, the press was giving Rudolph his due credit as one of the most creative criminal planners in history. No matter how many times he was cornered, no matter what went wrong, he always seemed to find a way out of a tight spot. They were bad men, murderers, but their story simply captured people's imagination, mainly because of the young, strapping, calculating Kid. There was just something about him that left the image of a boy trying to look tough for his friends, but who could break out in a big smile at any time.

The Pinkertons' pursuit of the handsome killers was epic in scope, manpower, and expense. Hundreds of full-time agents across the country were assigned to the case. Three months went by—nothing turned up with the father and uncle in Arkansas. And the more detectives learned about Collins, the more sense the note in the stove made. Hartford was Collins's hometown, and he did a stretch at reform school in Meriden, twenty miles to the south. Later he was convicted of larceny and sentenced to fifteen years in Trenton, New Jersey, broke out after just six months, went to Missouri, and nobody in Hartford had seen him since. Still, the Pinkertons had to check it out.

Once again, while other reporters waited to get news of the Missouri Kid from the wire services, Red Galvin rode to Hartford on the same train with the Pinkertons. Working with local detectives the agents found that Collins had two stepbrothers there, Theodore and Edward LaPlant, and the Pinkertons started watching them around the clock, hoping they'd lead to Collins. Red took a different trail, one that had paid off for him so handsomely in the past. He worked the saloons and gambling dives, making friends and asking subtle questions. When he turned up nothing in the first two weeks, he tried a different approach. What if Rudolph had decided it was time to hide by being respectable? Red began to spend evenings at the city's finer eateries, where Rudolph might spend lavishly on a lady friend. Frank McNeil, Red's mentor, had taught him early on how to stake out a café, saloon, or hotel lobby, and stay sober in the process. He couldn't write notes or do anything else to look like a reporter, but he could fool around with a cigar or a pack of cigarettes, check his watch, and look like he was thinking important thoughts. He could hide behind a newspaper or book. And he could sip one beer and make it last an hour.

In fact, Red was on the right track. The Kid told Collins they were going to enjoy their money, dress well, associate with good people, and open a little business of some sort. "Look," the Kid told his partner. "The mistake criminals make is hanging around with criminals. To make a lot of money we have to hang around with people who have a lot of money."

Collins was not the perfect partner for that plan. He was a low-born, violent ruffian who couldn't escape his ties to his vulgar family.

The history of his New Jersey prison escape threatened to rear its ugly head. And then there were the LaPlant brothers. They were drunks and day laborers who might attract the police, and yet the Kid knew they might come in handy, especially if he and Collins needed to make a getaway. Training Collins to be a gentleman was a big job for the Kid, but the appearance of respectability was a great way for them to avoid detection and get a new start.

Using the names of Bill Anderson and Fred Lewis, Rudolph and Collins rented rooms in a nice boardinghouse, Mrs. McIntyre's, on Allyn Street in Hartford. Then they continued climbing the social ladder, enrolling in ballroom dancing classes. From the very first lesson, Rudolph was in love with their teacher, Marion Wade. She was young, beautiful, and self-assured, and she made a nice living with her dancing school, which she had opened with a loan from her uncle.

On February 28, at the Morton House Hotel, Red looked up from an empty soup bowl and a beer he'd been nursing for over an hour, and there was a beautiful young woman, diamonds sparkling on her ears, in a rich, emerald green brocade dress, walking in on the left arm of the handsome Rudolph. He strolled in smiling, his hair neatly oiled and parted in the middle, in a brown tweed suit, custom linen shirt, ivory stick pin, and a bowler in his left hand, leaving his gun hand conspicuously free.

Red ordered another beer and nursed that while the couple had their dinner. Then he followed them out, caught a hack for hire, and shadowed their hack all the way to a tidy little house in East Hartford. When another hour passed and they hadn't reappeared, that was the time to go to the police. Not only had Red seen the Kid, but he could tell the cops where his girlfriend lived with her parents.

Agents soon found out all about Wade and her dancing school, and a team of twelve agents rotated shifts to watch her house every minute. An agent enrolled in the dancing class and followed the fugitives to their home at Mrs. McIntyre's. The postman brought the Wades' mail to the Pinkertons before taking it to the house. One night, detectives spotted the Kid and Collins in a cab downtown, taking Wade and another woman to dinner. They never saw Wade or the men leave their homes or return, which meant the fugitives were still being careful with their comings and goings. Yet the dinner date confirmed that both of the murderers had found a girlfriend. Dougherty, the agent in charge, knew the pair would begin to think more about their women and their own comfort, and less about keeping their guard up.

And yet, Dougherty still didn't want to take them with the women around. He didn't want to involve Wade's parents. And above all, he didn't want a shootout. Dougherty wasn't about to repeat the mistake made in Missouri, walking boldly into the muzzles of pistols wielded by two desperate armed men. He was happy to wait for a rare moment when the fugitives were apart, but not too far apart. If agents arrested only one, the other was sure to get away, at least extending the search, and possibly never being found. So it had to be the perfect setup, where one could be captured, and then the other—without gunplay, he told the agents. It was the most tedious assignment in history. The local police officers were accustomed to long, boring stakeouts, but it was harder for the Pinkertons, whose tactics had traditionally been to boldly go in after their man. But this time they waited. And waited.

Finally one night, a lone figure wearing a suit, no tie, walked out of the house on Allyn and stopped on the front steps to light a cigarette and look at the stars. The agents agreed it was Collins. Just then, two other men emerged from the house. It was the LaPlant brothers, clearly drunk. Last, Rudolph appeared, and the foursome walked west. The men on the stakeout followed at a distance, and when the foursome went into a brothel on State Street, they sent for more officers.

A little over an hour later, the door opened and Collins came out holding one of his whiskey-soaked stepbrothers by the arm, looking for a taxi. The other LaPlant followed. Collins had left his suit coat inside, and apparently had no weapon. It was perfect. Agent Dougherty took the lead, jumping from the bushes to pin Collins's arms at his sides. The next agent grabbed his shirtfront and quickly checked to be sure there was no pistol in his pants pockets. The other officers pushed the terrified LaPlants away from the action and made sure they weren't armed.

Once the three men were in handcuffs, Dougherty and a big Irish cop named Farrell walked boldly into the house. The madam of the brothel turned to a nearby room on the first floor and yelled a warning, "Here's two men looking for you!" That was the room they wanted. Inside, the Kid was relaxing in a chair, enjoying a cigar, when a kick from Farrell burst the door open with a bang, and both officers rushed him.

As they tumbled to the floor, Dougherty pinned him, but the Kid bit Dougherty's neck, then butted his head into the Pinkerton's chin. The blow stunned him enough that he loosened his grip just for an instant, and that was enough for the Kid to get the advantage and roll on top of him. Farrell had his legs, but suddenly his fists were free. The Kid was strong, and his fists and elbows packed a wallop, sending Farrell onto his back. He reached for the pistol in Dougherty's right coat pocket, ripping the pocket, but the Pinkerton grabbed the gun away from him and flung it aside with a clatter on the wood floor. By that time Farrell had regained his balance, straddled the Kid, and pinned both arms behind him. He pulled him off Dougherty and put him down hard on his well-known face.

As he panted under Farrell, the Kid couldn't move, but he consoled himself in the knowledge that youth and healthy good looks were on his side. A jury might convict him, but then again maybe not. And of course there would be chances for escape and appeals. All things considered, from where he lay on his stomach, pinned down by 250 pounds of cop, his chances looked pretty good.

"They'll never take me back," the shackled Kid shouted to reporters who swarmed around the cops pushing him into the Hartford County Jail. "If they try to take me back to Missouri my gang'll pinch the train and turn me loose!" His audience loved it, and they all ran to their

The Missouri Kid after he was arrested in Hartford, Connecticut, confident and well groomed, as always. Library of Congress Prints and Photographs.

typewriters to predict the daring escape. Dougherty turned to Red and smirked. "He doesn't have a gang." Then he paused, adding, "I hope."

The next morning at the Hartford County jail, Red got his reward for leading the cops to their prey. While other reporters dug for the story and begged the cops to know who did what, Red was the only one allowed to talk to the prisoners. "I was a fool to let myself get trapped that way," the Kid confided. "I had guns, and if Dougherty hadn't got the drop on me when he walked in the room, I'd have dropped him sure." Collins was just as belligerent. He shook his head and said that was the first time he'd gone out of any house without a gun. He added that he planned to kill Dougherty as soon as he got out.

Red stayed and talked with the Kid a long time. They both loved St. Louis. As the Kid told about his travels, he mentioned being in Pueblo in January of 1903, and Red said he was there a year later.

"I learned mining in Missouri," the Kid said. "But the coal mines at Pueblo paid me a lot more," he grinned. "I'm a soup man."

"Soup man?" Red wondered.

"Nitroglycerin," Bill said proudly.

Red nodded and told him he went out there looking for O'Kelley. Then he had to explain who he was and why he wrote about him.

"I met that bird," the Kid told an astonished Red, adding that he had no idea about the connection to Bob Ford and Jesse James. He simply bought O'Kelley's dinner a few times. "He was on hard times, and he'd come around this place where I took my meals after my shift," he said.

"Small world," Red muttered. "So were you friends?"

"No. He just needed something to eat. I was not much more than a boy, but I could make a dollar."

Red nodded.

"He was ill tempered as a water moccasin, and I feel sorry for a man like that. I like to always expect things to turn out, don't you agree?" the Kid added, with a twinkle in his eye.

"Sure," Red smiled, glad to be with this young man who smiled in his chains.

"So . . . whatever happened to that bird?" the Kid asked.

Red looked into the Kid's eyes and hesitated. "Oh . . . he went down to Oklahoma."

+ —— + —— +

Never before had so much money and manpower been invested in assuring a clear conviction of a pair of men with such a brief criminal history. The Union Bank's cashier, Tom Hoffman, took the train to Connecticut and identified the men, which was dubious because the bank was robbed in the middle of the night while Hoffman was sleeping off an enormous Christmas dinner. Agents showed him over $2,300 in cash the men had on them when arrested, and another $6,380 from a trunk in their room, part of it in gold. Hoffman said he recognized it, that was the bank's money, and they should give it to him right then and there. Dougherty ignored that part of the identification. The trunk also held three revolvers, a huge supply of cartridges, masks, and a collection of skeleton keys. The next day, Bernard Schmuke, a thirty-two-year-old farmer whose place bordered the old boardinghouse property, arrived with Sheriff Bruch, and they both identified the Kid. And the whole time, Dougherty couldn't get rid of bank clerk Hoffman. In a rare moment of laughter from the police, the red-faced Hoffman again loudly raised his demand for the bank to get the outlaws' cash. He was informed repeatedly that it was evidence and would not be released for a while.

And the whole time, the Kid kept bragging that their friends would bust them out of jail. Dougherty was pretty sure they didn't have a gang, but he also knew Collins might be able to raise one. Collins knew a lot of hard men in the area, including some who'd been his childhood friends. It was not lost on the agents that this all started in Missouri, of all the states, the one with the nation's longest running and most violent history of vigilantism. Even in the new era of fast trains and white-collar crime, a gang wasn't out of the question. The Missouri Kid case involved drunks, Germans, torture, miners, stolen horses and boats, explosives, hoboes, a recluse, a secretive family, stepchildren, a dashing young Missouri boy, and Collins, an easterner. Plus, most of the deposits at the Union Bank belonged to poor dirt farmers and local merchants. It was all rich with potential for vigilantes of one stripe or another to take a hand, intent on hanging the pair or setting them free. So one evening after the arrest, when a crowd of men assembled, then grew, on the street corner, police became convinced that they were going to storm the jail. The police went out to disperse the mob, and a horrible fight broke out, resulting in two cops being sent to the hospital and eight men being arrested for assault. After that encounter, armed guards were stationed outside the jail around the clock.

The train ride back to Missouri was uneventful, and Agent Dougherty turned the Kid and Collins over to assistant Pinkerton superintendent George Charlesworth. They were lodged in the St. Louis jail because, as Charlesworth said, "There's no jail safe for these men in Franklin County." It meant they would have to be transported back and forth on the train to Union for every step in their prosecution and trial, but authorities agreed that there was less danger in protecting them on the train than there was in trying to protect them in Union.

On the day of their arraignment, the prisoners were taken to Union by a force of two Pinkerton agents, two St. Louis detectives, and eight patrolmen. The thought given to managing the pair's movements, both for security and for public relations, was unprecedented. Rather than surround the prisoners with bristling guns, the cops presented an image of quiet decorum. The Kid and Collins were flanked by a dozen men wearing business suits. To a casual observer, they didn't seem to be expecting trouble, and yet each officer had a pair of revolvers holstered in the small of his back. The trip to Union was uneventful, the arraignment was quick, and the cops took the prisoners straight to the train and back to the St. Louis jail.

The Kid and Collins were kept separate from each other, so there was no opportunity for them to work out a defense or plan an escape. Sitting alone in his cell, facing a likely death sentence for murder, the Kid knew he was smart enough to escape, and he was glad he didn't have to worry about getting Collins out. After all, in his brief criminal career he had been one of the most successful criminals in the modern era. He had stolen hundreds of thousands of dollars, spent a lot of it, traveled and enjoyed life in various cities, visited his little sister Esther, fallen in love with a dance instructor, and only spent a couple of months in jail. He was not even suspected in most of the dozens of robberies and burglaries he committed in his travels. And he had done it all without a mentor. His plans came from his own bright mind and knack for innovation. One of the things he knew about himself was that he was great in a crisis. Coming up with a plan in a tight spot was perhaps his best skill. So of course he was sure he'd be smart enough to get out of the St. Louis jail.

The St. Louis jail featured a beautiful and innovative design. Cell blocks stood on three sides of the "pen," at the center of which was a pylon reaching up to the domed roof with its skylights.

The jail was uniquely and beautifully designed, built in a circle, with the cells in blocks along the walls on the east, west, and south sides, leaving a large court known as the "pen," so the prisoners could have indoor exercise, no matter what the weather. The focal point of the pen was a steel pylon that held a spiral staircase leading to a second-floor observation post for the guards. The pylon continued to soar some six stories high, with a framework of steel webbing that radiated from its peak to the outer walls. Near the top was a ring of skylights.

Around five o'clock on the evening of July 6, 1903, just before dinner, seven guards were on duty holding their Winchester rifles as usual, watching the prisoners in the pen. For no apparent reason two prisoners named Walsh and Cody started fighting. All of the other prisoners gathered around, and the noise of their shouting was deafening. It was all happening in the west end of the pen, just around a corner of the cellblock, out of view of the pylon and the domed roof above. The guards came down from the observation platform, some rushed to break up the fight, and others watched nervously to make sure it didn't develop into a riot. At the same time, the Kid ran up two flights of stairs, then climbed a web of steel bars that all curved inward, going hand over hand until he reached the center. There the bars ended with points, leaving an open circle just big enough for a man to pass through. He squeezed past the points and climbed onto a soaring steel beam that arched upward, beginning three stories above the floor. He crawled across the beam to the other side of the huge room while the noisy crowd watched the fight below. The beam ended five feet above the row of skylights, so he had to hang by one hand, balancing on one foot on another beam, to kick a hole in the closest skylight, just big enough that he could crawl through onto the roof.

Broken glass clattered down from above, and the disbelieving guards looked up just in time to see the Kid's feet disappear through the hole in the skylight. Another prisoner, John Burke, had followed him and was just leaving the stairs to follow the Kid's daredevil climb. He never expected to get out, but he too was part of the plan, because the guards raced to stop him, giving the Kid a few more crucial seconds.

Emerging into the early evening sun, the athletic Kid bent over with his fingers touching the curving roof to keep his balance, and ran that way around the building, some 130 feet, then jumped 20 feet down to the roof of an adjoining building on the Spruce Street side of the jail, ran across it, and stopped. From the back of his pants he pulled a rope made from a shirt ripped up and tied into strips. But he didn't use it on the first jump and decided it would take too much time to use it on the second, so he dropped it and jumped another 20 feet to the roof of the jail's hospital. In that leap his foot caught on a telephone wire that ran along the edge of the roof, making him land awkwardly and tumble. Though his right knee was wrenched, he got up and ran the length of the hospital roof, then jumped 15 feet down to the ground. Ed Lawson, the porter for the morgue, just happened to look up and see the fugitive

The domed roof of the St. Louis jail with its ring of skylights connects three rectangular cellblocks. The Kid escaped through a skylight on the left side of this photo, ran around the roof and jumped to the roof of the hospital, the shorter building on the right side of the cellblock. Then he jumped to the shed, then down to the ground, running to freedom through Jailer Dawson's house in the right corner of the jail yard. In this photo, the brick two-story house with multiple chimneys is seen above the "Pianos and Organs" sign. A man in the morgue, at the corner of Twelfth and Spruce, bottom center, saw the escape and ran to the stables, lower left, to report it. Upper left is the roof of the magnificent Four Courts Building. Photograph by Andrew J. O'Reilly, 1888. Courtesy of Missouri Historical Society.

on the roof, and ran next door to the patrol-wagon quarters to alert officers there. In their excitement to run and tell the jail superintendent, Dawson, and Chief Kiely, nobody sounded the alarm, which of course slowed the response from other officers who had no idea there was an escape in progress.

The Kid was still inside the jail's fourteen-foot-high brick fence, and at that point he did what no other man would have thought to do. He walked confidently through an iron gate that opened into Jailer Dawson's backyard, ran across the yard with Dawson's huge dog snapping at him, and entered Dawson's back door into the kitchen. He hurried through the dining room, and there was Dawson's eight-year-old daughter Mary playing with her dolls. Because of Rudolph's notoriety, Mary's father had taken her to look at him through the bars of his cell, so she recognized the intruder, and bolted immediately for the open back window. There she screamed, "Father, Rudolph the murderer is in the house!" Her alert came at the same time guards were leaving Dawson's office after telling him of the escape, so they didn't hear her, but he did. That meant Dawson was the only one who knew which way the escapee went: through his house. The Kid ran out the front door of the house to Eleventh Street, turned left, and ran toward the railroad yards at Eleventh and Poplar. While the guards tried in vain to get organized, Dawson alone was chasing the Kid. He could see him up ahead, but lost him among the railcars. He stopped and looked back, but there were no guards coming to help.

As Dawson turned for home, the Kid made it out the other side of the rail yard and within a block found a clean change of clothes hanging on a line. Within another block, something caught his eye in the doorway of a warehouse. With no way to go but north, all the way to the riverside at Baden, possibly no other outlaw in history would have seen his salvation in a rusty blue bicycle. The best image of William Rudolph may be of the fearless escapee in a stolen plaid shirt and overalls, whistling as he peddled on rain-dampened streets, right through the middle of St. Louis, appearing and disappearing through gray shadows cast by the setting sun.

Back at the jail, Dawson immediately brought Collins in for a sweating. But Collins was in his cell when his partner escaped, and he convinced the jailer that he knew nothing about the plan. In fact, more than a week before, rumors of an escape had come to the warden, who ordered a search of their cells, which turned up chains and saws. Since then, the pair had been separated, never eating or exercising at the same time, and hadn't even seen each other.

Alexander Vogler, a fisherman on the Mississippi, was ending his day about six o'clock, when a man appeared and asked to borrow a skiff. But Vogler had only bigger fishing boats. "There are plenty of other folks along the river with skiffs," he offered, and the Kid thanked him and walked away. It was only after the police came by asking questions the next day and described the Kid—hair parted in the middle, lots of gold teeth, almost six feet tall—that the fisherman realized he had been face to face with a killer. Vogler then told the cops about the Kid's plaid shirt and overalls, and that his hands were covered with small cuts, which of course came from the broken skylight. But the information didn't help much.

The police checked all the boat owners along the riverfront, and nobody else reported an encounter with the escapee. No boats were missing, so the search never extended to Illinois. What the police didn't know is that Rudolph had found a boat under a house and dragged it down to the foot of President Street, where he crossed the river.

It was no wonder that the Kid continued to capture the imagination of the American public. Red Galvin's front-page story of the escape ran under a headline that proclaimed the convict's "skill and daring." It included a photo and diagram of the jail, and said, "The city police agree it was the most daring escape ever made at the city jail." Though the Kid was not yet twenty-one years old, the article noted, he was "capable of masterly planning and just as masterful execution."

Chapter Fourteen
Sunset in Olathe

For a month in Illinois he played it straight. Not one flirtation with the law. Sweeping floors and saving a few dollars, he worked his way to Galena, Illinois, where he made good money in the lead mines. But he never let them know he knew explosives. The Pinkertons might have had alerts out for mine operators to watch for that, he figured, and he was right. So then it was time for the Kid to see some country he'd never seen, and Kansas sounded good. He took a train to Olathe, where he settled into a nice hotel. It was a good place to ponder where he was and what was next, and he intended to take his time. He took six months.

The Pinkertons were watching over two hundred prisons and jails throughout the country and in Canada, Great Britain, and France. They inspected every ship bound for Europe, Central, and South America. They went back to watching Marion Wade, the dance instructor, twenty-four hours a day. Wade discovered a maid that her mother recently hired was actually a Pinkerton agent, and the maid was promptly fired. Pinkertons read all of Wade's mail and found one letter from the Kid telling her to meet him in Manitoba, but somehow the news got back to the Kid that they had seen the letter, and he sent word to Wade to cancel the meeting. The detectives checked every milk can that was delivered to the house, finding a note from one of the Kid's friends taped under the lid of one, but it didn't provide any good leads. The Kid's continued attempts to connect with Wade convinced the Pinkertons that their man was somewhere in the northeast, not far from Wade, possibly in Canada or probably New York. That's where they concentrated their search, and all the while, the Kid was in Kansas, planning his future.

In a small café near the rail yards, the Kid sipped his coffee, lowered his newspaper, and looked out the window at a blazing Kansas sunset. The story he just read was about him and the hundreds of Pinkertons looking for him. He couldn't see Wade, couldn't go to a big city, couldn't have any fun at all. He wasn't going to sit there and watch all his sunsets in Olathe. He was going to have to save himself again. He'd always been clever, but his new plan would impress even himself. It was brilliant, and a perfect smile crossed his handsome face. The only thing to do, the Kid figured, was to start over as someone else.

In one of the most creative plans in the criminal history of the American West, William Rudolph—aka William Anderson, aka the Missouri Kid—walked away from nice hotels, made his way into the hobo camps, and once again called upon the Yeggs brotherhood. Though he was younger than most of the men, his confidence enabled him to introduce himself as John Yegg, a name that let everyone know he was ready to lead a job. His credentials: He was a safecracker and an expert with "soup," meaning nitroglycerine. He just needed a man to supply the knowledge of Kansas that he lacked.

It was about the same time that law enforcement first learned about the Yeggs. Walsh and Cody, the men who staged the fight to help Rudolph escape from the St. Louis jail, revealed that the Kid was a John Yegg, and explained what that meant. Though Pinkertons had heard about the Yeggs, the information after the jail escape was their first verification that the organization was real, pervasive, and powerful, and they launched an unprecedented investigation into the Yeggs, while continuing their search for the Kid.

Soon, along with the hundreds of agents watching jails, prisons, border crossings, and ports for the Kid, there were hundreds more posing as hobos, riding the rails, hiding in boxcars and livestock cars, living in the dangerous hobo camps, and learning about the Yeggs. If one of them had been unveiled, he'd have been killed for sure. Soon their reports began to trickle in, and from several sources they heard about a John Yegg in Kansas who went by the name Charles Gorney and was skilled with soup. It was a highly prized ability among Yeggs because soup was easily concealed, it was quick, and it took the place of a world of heavy safe-cracking tools. In an article about the search, Red Galvin quoted William Pinkerton saying, "The Yeggs as they exist today are far more dangerous than the old-time burglars. While it took the old timers all night to crack a safe these tramps will do a similar job in two hours, and get away with it."

The Kid found the perfect accomplice, a directionless hobo named Tom Rogers. He wasn't a partner like Collins had been, but rather a willing dupe in the Kid's ingenious plan. They stole a wagon and team, then some nitroglycerin and blasting caps. Then the night of January 16, 1904, Rogers stood guard in a heavy snowfall while the Kid blew open the vault in the bank of tiny Cleveland, Missouri, right on the state line. After Cleveland, they drove five miles to Louisburg, Kansas, and did the same to the Katy Railroad safe there. The wagon left clear tracks in the snow, but by morning they were covered again.

The chase lasted three days, during which the Kid and Rogers spent most of their time hiding out. Rogers didn't realize it, but his boss was just making sure they were caught without being shot. In fact, they might not have been caught at all if not for the Anti-Horse Thief Association. The organization was started in northeast Missouri before the Civil War, suspended during the war, and then revived. By 1904 there were hundreds of members in local chapters in various states. Fortunately for the Kid and Rogers, the ones who chased them in Kansas were not the kind of Anti-Horse Thief members in some states, who rode like Old West vigilantes, chasing down their prey with smoking pistols. The ones after Rudolph and Rogers followed the organization's sworn purpose to follow reports of stolen horses, track the thieves, and bring in law enforcement for the capture. They wanted to cooperate with lawmen, not take over their job.

The bandits traveled just ten miles from Louisburg, then made camp in a deep, dry wash and slept under the wagon. Swarms of Anti-Horse Thief men, mostly with potbellies and carrying long guns that had been used for nothing more than putting a turkey or pheasant on the table, prowled the Kansas plains. They weren't so much tracking as riding around hoping to stumble across the thieves, and by sheer numbers they made it impossible for their quarry to move. On the third day they spotted them and brought in the lone policeman from the nearby town of Paola. Everything the Kid was doing depended on a low profile, and he wasn't about to go near a big town. Sleepy little Paola was just perfect. Or so he thought.

Their trials were over in a month. Because Rogers knew nothing about explosives, he was sent to prison for stealing the horses and team. The Kid gave his name as Albert Gorney, originally from Minnesota. He was found guilty of the robbery and sentenced to five years in the Kansas State Penitentiary. In fact, Gorney was a name the Kid picked up from the Yeggs. There was an actual Albert Gorney who did time in the Kansas State Prison and was released two years before, so the warden and clerks were not surprised to see him return to his life of crime. The prison would be a perfect place for the Kid to hide out in plain sight for a couple of years. Then he'd be released with a new identity and his troubles would be behind him. Ironically, the Pinkertons suspected that the devious Kid might do exactly what he did: stage a crime with the specific purpose of being arrested and convicted under an assumed name, so he could hide in prison until the coast was clear.

Three things were going on that would have amazed the Kid if he'd only known. First, lawmen were finding creative ways to use photographs. Second, businesses were increasingly joining associations to help with their mutual interests, including security. Third, and most important to the Kid, the Pinkertons were under contract with the American Bankers Association. The bank the Kid robbed in Cleveland was a member of the association, and one of the requirements of membership was that if a robber was convicted of robbing a member bank, his photo had to be sent to William Pinkerton in New York. So the dutiful police chief in tiny Paola, Kansas, had the Kid and Rogers photographed in jail, then sent the pictures to Pinkerton.

The Kid had done everything he could to change his appearance. As soon as he broke out of the St. Louis jail and made it to Illinois, he moved the part in his hair from the middle to the side. He grew a black mustache, and even popped out most of the gold caps on his teeth. He was sure it would be enough to fool even the best Pinkerton man.

Ordinarily, the pictures would have gone directly to the rogues' gallery, the Pinkerton agency's photo files in Washington, DC. But even after all those months, there was no man more wanted by the Pinkerton

Even though the Missouri Kid lost weight, moved the part in his hair, grew a mustache, and gave his name as Gorley, when the Paola sheriff sent this photo to William Pinkerton in Washington, Pinkerton instantly knew it was William Rudolph. Library of Congress Prints and Photographs.

agency than the Kid. Just in case he was arrested someplace, anyplace, William Pinkerton required all photographs to be shown to him before being filed. He even kept a photo of the Kid on his desk. The Kid's angular face was burned into Pinkerton's mind, so he recognized him immediately in the Paola picture of Al Gorney, and he sent Nelson A. Bush, head of Pinkerton's Kansas City office, to the prison. So while Pinkerton agents were all over the country watching prisons and big-town jails, William Rudolph was caught because a conscientious small-town policeman simply did his job.

Agent Bush arrived at Leavenworth, and the guards retrieved "Gorney," from his work in the prison mine. When he walked into the warden's office, Bush said, "Well, if it isn't Bill Rudolph," and the Kid's face turned red. Still, he refused to answer any questions. The prison doctor came and repeated the Bertillon measurements, which matched exactly with the ones taken when he was arrested in Hartford. Just to be sure, they compared them with those on file for Gorney. Sure enough, the Kid was almost an inch taller, and his reach about three-quarters of an inch longer.

The Kid knew his goose was cooked, but like every other time he was cornered, he was working on his next plan. That evening at about seven he and a group of other inmates finished their meal in the dining hall. As they rose to leave with guard Evan Roe, the Kid grabbed a table knife, put it to Roe's throat, and twisted his arm behind him. It was a desperate try at a rugged escape, as if the table knife could have hurt the guard. It was clearly not the Kid's usual style; no wonder it didn't work. A life prisoner who wanted to win favor from the guards grabbed the Kid, and other prisoners joined in an instant. The Kid smiled. It was worth a try.

The next day, February 23, Sheriff Bruch of Franklin County, Missouri, took the train to Leavenworth and went straight to the prison. The warden had a lineup of six men, including the one called Gorney. Bruch looked at all six, smiled, walked over to the Kid stretching out his hand, and said, "Hello, Bill." The Kid returned the smile and shook his hand, saying, "Hello, Sheriff."

Several other men were waiting in the warden's office to add their own voices to the identification. They included a Pinkerton agent who knew him and the St. Louis jailer Dawson, from whom he escaped. But even after they all said he was Rudolph, the stoic prisoner refused to confess his name or give more than rudimentary answers to their questions.

As soon as O. E. Myersieck, Franklin County's prosecuting attorney, heard that the Kid had been identified, he began to prepare his case in the murder of Agent Schumacher. But there was already a problem with bringing him back to Missouri. Extradition could mean a long delay, and the Kid's attorney was already poised to block it. The easiest way around extradition was a pardon from the Kansas governor, Willis J. Bailey, but he had already been visited by leaders of the Anti-Horse Thief Association, begging him not to pardon the Kid. His capture was a singular victory that would polish the association's reputation among law-abiding citizens and outlaws alike. The men on the chase would be able to brag about it to their grandchildren. And after all, they did something that all the lawmen and jails in Missouri couldn't do: they captured the notorious Missouri Kid. They were not going to sit by and watch Missouri steal their hard-won prize. Besides, he escaped Missouri once, and he might do it again.

The Pinkertons weren't going to let such details stop the hanging of Schumacher's murderer. In their unusual "whatever it takes" style, they launched a bold plan to make sure the Kid got quickly back to the St. Louis jail. Early the next morning a Kansas judge, with Pinkertons looking over his shoulder, set aside the Kid's conviction, making him officially a free man. He was released from the state prison, and as he walked out the gates, Leavenworth County sheriff Meyers was waiting to arrest him on a Missouri warrant. No extradition was needed, as Meyers surrendered him directly to Franklin County sheriff Bruch, who handcuffed himself to the Kid's left arm, while St. Louis jailer

It Ends Here

St. Louis detectives pose in the police department's first car, a 1904 Dorris, made by the St. Louis Motor Carriage Company. The Missouri Kid was riding with them in this car when they encountered the huge crowds around the Four Courts.

Dawson handcuffed himself to the right. They took him to the Kansas City depot, where they climbed aboard a secret special train from St. Louis with Pinkerton agent Dougherty and several St. Louis patrolmen. They left at ten in the morning and stopped outside St. Louis at Grand Station, where the Kid was loaded into the new patrol wagon, a 1904 Dorris, built in a little factory on Vandeventer Avenue by the St. Louis Motor Carriage Company. It was his third automobile ride, the first two being in Hartford, and it was exciting, even though he was trussed up like a turkey headed for the oven and pressed between two detectives in the back seat. "In the span of twelve hours I've been a prisoner in Kansas, a free man, and a prisoner in Missouri three hundred miles away," he remarked to Dawson. "What a day."

They drove across the city to Four Courts, arriving about six in the evening, and none of them could believe their eyes. Thanks to Red Galvin's story in that morning's *Republic* saying the Kid would be back in the jail before dark, the driver had to ease the automobile through a crowd of five thousand people all wanting a glimpse of the Missouri Kid. Patrolmen pushed them back as the Dorris edged forward, around the corner to the jail. The cops were all on high alert, hands resting on their revolvers. There could be an army of Yeggs in that mob, intent on breaking the Kid out. Or the prisoner himself might have another brilliant escape stunt up his sleeve. It was the perfect setup for something to go wrong. But the Kid emerged smiling from the automobile into a sea of reporters with notebooks, all shouting questions. Beyond them, the crowd was mostly women. Women of all ages, from some in their teens to many old enough to be the Kid's mother, and they were all dressed as if they were on their way to Mrs. Astor's plush ball. The Kid was exhausted, his hair dry and uncombed, his suit and shirt rumpled, with no necktie, no hat, and his hands and legs in irons. He most certainly was not the dashing prince he had once been. But that mattered little to the women, who reached to touch his sleeve, hoping to catch his haunting grey eyes looking their way. He was their darling, and they all were sure that given half a chance, they would stand by him, win his release, and lead him to a new, law-abiding life in a charming house with blooming roses and beautiful children playing in the yard.

Though some newspapers speculated that Collins had conspired with the law to recapture the Kid, Red Galvin knew it wasn't true. First, Collins had nothing to gain. He'd been sentenced to death, and nothing was going to reduce his sentence. And Red was there when the Kid arrived back at the St. Louis jail, was led past the cell of Collins, and they exchanged smiles. Collins said, "Hello, Bill," and the Kid replied, "Good to see you again." Collins had an idea of what the Kid was up to from reading the papers, and he knew the Cleveland bank robbery had all the earmarks of his old partner's jobs. Collins even knew the name Al Gorney, which the Kid had told Collins he was going to use the next time he got out. Still, Collins held his secrets to the end.

The Kid had escaped from the St. Louis jail at the end of June, just a week before he and Collins were to be tried. Officials saw no reason to delay prosecuting Collins, so they went ahead with his trial. Sitting in the audience as the trial opened in the Franklin County Courthouse at Union was little Mary Dawson, the St. Louis jailer's daughter who'd watched the Kid escape through their house. Like many girls her age, she was smitten with the two dashing outlaws. Witnesses were plentiful, including Stanton deputies Vetter, Cromer, and Tichener, but as the defense showed, not one of the deputies actually saw who shot Schumacher. They were all turning and running when he was shot. There was a valid argument that with six men firing, a member of the posse could have easily fired the fatal bullet. Finally, the defense made a lame attempt to posture Collins as the Kid's pawn. But Collins didn't take the stand, and he wouldn't say a word against Rudolph. On July 2, 1903, Collins was convicted of first-degree murder and sentenced to be hanged the following spring.

The attorneys for Collins pursued delays in his execution. The governor granted one stay, but there was no justification for another, and the execution was set for March 26, 1904. During the week leading up to the hanging, three women came to the jail at different times, begging to visit Collins. He didn't know any of them, and Sheriff Bruch refused to allow anyone except deputies inside the jail. Then, it just happened that Rudolph was recaptured and brought back to Union in time for his trial to start on March 25, the day before Collins's execution.

A group of twenty-five schoolgirls came for the trial from nearby St. Clair. Other women aged fifteen to eighty-five were there, totaling well over one hundred and making up most of the audience, and again, Jailer Dawson's daughter was among them. But it looked bleak for the Kid, as his trial started with the same parade of witnesses and the same arguments that had already condemned Collins. Deputy Cromer, of the Schumacher posse, testified that the Kid and Collins came out of the

The Franklin County Courthouse stands in the town square, and on the corner beyond is the small, two-story, brick Union Bank, the one Rudolph and Collins robbed.

boardinghouse with pistols leveled, screaming, "Put up your hands." Wide-eyed, Cromer said, "So that's what I did. I dropped my gun and held up my hands. Then Collins told me and Mr. Vetter to run and we did." The crowd chuckled when he added, "Mr. Vetter was a lot faster than me."

The Kid's cousin, George Harmes, testified that he heard the Kid tell Collins, "We'll shoot our way out," just before sending his mother and sisters to the basement, with Harmes and old Frank following. Through all the testimony, the Kid was relaxed. After all, there were no surprises. When St. Louis jailer Dawson described the escape from the jail, with the miraculous six-story climb "like a monkey," the Kid joined the whole courtroom in laughing out loud.

There was only one witness left for the defense, George Collins. Rain began to fall that evening, and like every night the outlaws were in Union, guards with Winchester rifles stood at each corner of the jail. In one of the most dramatic moments in the case, Collins, neatly dressed and sporting a shamrock in his lapel, a gift from the local priest, was brought from the jail in leg irons and handcuffed between two deputies, with a circle of deputies pointing rifles and revolvers at his chest. They emerged into a pelting, wind-driven rain and marched past the gallows that had been built to take Collins's life, then around the corner and into the courthouse. In the foyer, Red Galvin leaned around the phalanx of lawmen and asked, "Are you testifying in hope of saving yourself, or to help the Kid?"

Collins pulled up short and looked Red in the eye to say, "My friend, I can't be saved. My only hope is that I can lighten my pal's burden."

Inside the courtroom he walked past his old partner and they exchanged glances, but they weren't allowed to speak to each other. More guards ringed the courtroom, and one deputy sat directly behind the accused man. As Collins took the stand, the rain stopped and the temperature climbed toward eighty, and still the courtroom's tall windows were kept closed.

It Ends Here

While Collins described the shootout, his right hand was released from the handcuffs so he could point to a diagram of the house and surrounding land, but his left hand remained cuffed to the deputy. He described everything that happened the day of Schumacher's killing, adding that as he and the Kid looked out the window and saw the posse approach, they sent the Kid's mother and sisters to the basement because the deputies fired two shots into the house. That part wasn't true, but it was a nice embellishment. Occasionally Collins would look at the Kid, but he never looked at the jury. He never said who shot Schumacher, but only that the agent had been shot. He emphasized that the instant they ran out the door of the house they shouted to the posse, "Put your hands up!" and only shot after Schumacher cut loose with the shotgun. But in the scheme of things, it all made little difference.

The questions included details like identifying the Kid's revolvers and telling that he met the Kid while working in the mines, instead of where they actually met, in jail. The defense objected to several prosecution questions on the basis that the answer might incriminate the witness. However, each time it happened the prosecuting attorney objected, saying "Your Honor, a condemned man can't incriminate himself," the judge ruled that Collins didn't have to answer.

Collins proved to be a splendid witness. His appearance, dress, and manner were all impeccable. His speech was like that of a college graduate. He was humble, but friendly, nodding greetings to Dawson, the St. Louis jailer, and other lawmen. It was a courageous show by a man on the eve of his death, and when he rose to be led out, every woman in the audience burst into tears.

Collins was escorted out the same way he came in, chained, handcuffed, and surrounded by a gun-laden army, all leaving the idea in the jury's mind that Collins and the Kid were very dangerous men. At that point the Kid had nothing to lose, so he testified in his own defense. His attorney asked him if he shot Agent Schumacher, and he said, "Yes." The attorney then asked why, and Rudolph said, "Because he tried to shoot me."

They made it a simple matter of self-defense. The problem was that the judge had instructed the jury that they could return one of only two verdicts. Rudolph was either guilty of first-degree murder, or he was innocent. During a recess the defense pleaded with the judge to allow a verdict of second-degree murder. That would mean that in effect the jury could say that yes, the Kid killed Schumacher, but he did it in the heat of battle, which could get him a life sentence instead of the gallows. But the judge refused to allow a second-degree verdict. It was first degree or nothing.

To make matters worse, the judge allowed the prosecution to introduce an affidavit that the Kid's little sister Esther made more than a year before, right after the shootout, when she was twelve years old. She said, among other things, that after the shootout her brother came back into the house breathless and said, "I got the man I was after."

That night Father McErlane of College Catholic Church in St. Louis, who had counseled both prisoners while they were in the St. Louis jail, heard Collins's last confession and promised to stay with him to the end. Collins ordered a steak and ice cream for his last meal. He wanted a beer, but Sheriff Bruch refused it. He opened a letter from his sister in Connecticut asking if the execution had been delayed, and he looked sad when he asked the priest to mail a response for him. He then picked up a pencil and wrote neatly on the back of her letter, "All over tomorrow. Good bye, George."

There was a high board fence around the gallows to make sure the condemned man couldn't go to his death looking at the bank he robbed, which stood directly across the town square. Outside the fence, in the streets and milling around the town square were hundreds of people. Shops were busy, horse traders and peddlers came to town, and gambling games opened up in the alleys. The saloons did record business, the hotels were packed, and the courthouse lawn was full of people sleeping under the stars that night. Sheriff Bruch had invited 150 witnesses to the execution with printed cards that read simply, "You are invited by Sheriff Bruch to attend the execution of George Collins." Three men with cameras were poised on the front row, but Bruch ordered guards to escort them out of the viewing enclosure and announced, "There will be no photographs of this event."

Because of rain, the gallows railing wasn't quite finished. But early that morning under a cloudy sky, carpenters finished the job just in time for Collins to keep a one o'clock appointment with the rope. Waiting in his cell he joked with jailers, read the newspaper, and smoked cigarettes. He was handcuffed, still holding a rosary the priest had given him, and asked Bruch to mail the rosary to his sister after the hanging, saying, "She's the only friend I have." Then he was escorted outside to the gallows. As they walked, one of the guards remarked, "You're lucky to get the halter, George, instead of the electrical chair like that fellow in New York. Took them a long time to cook him." The guard was referring to William Kemmler, the first convicted killer executed in the chair, fifteen years earlier. The chair was legal in two other states but was still a horribly long and painful way to die.

"No sir, not for me. Kemmler's last words were, 'Get some rope!'" George laughed.

As he mounted the thirteen steps, he stopped briefly, tossed his hat aside, looked out on the crowd and smiled just a little. With Father McErlane at his side, he kissed the rosary before the black hood was placed over his head and the noose around his neck. Then he said to the sheriff, "Cut her loose, Bruch, and be sure you make a good job of it." The man who pulled the lever was Louis Vetter, one of the deputies in the gunfight. Nobody there had ever taken part in a legal hanging before, so nobody knew to use a rope that had been stretched. Instead, they thought it was smart to use a brand new rope. When the trap door dropped, Collin's weight stretched it for the first time, and his neck didn't break. He bounced like he was on a spring, then settled and strangled. Doctors kept checking, and they finally pronounced him dead thirteen minutes later.

When Bruch brought the news that it was done, the Missouri Kid sat on his bed and wept, unashamed.

Chapter Fifteen

The Wheel Turns

Red Galvin looked up from his typewriter and smiled. He had so many clippings, notes, and old newspapers, he couldn't even see the little desk. Well, he thought, George Collins was in the grave, a chapter in the newspaper archives closed. The Missouri Kid would soon follow. This time Red knew all the Kid's figuring and planning would lead nowhere but the gallows. And he was glad he got to know the Kid. The last time he visited him in jail, he just let him ramble, a doomed criminal reflecting on who he once was. "When I was a boy I was always out in the woods. I didn't do too much talking. I never did much play at games with the other boys. I just never had any interest in that. But I never considered it a waste of time to be alone fishing or swimming or hunting with my dog and my .22 rifle. At fifteen I quit school and worked on farms. At eighteen went to work in the mines around Joplin, then out to Colorado, and worked in the mines. I kept just enough money to live on and sent the rest home to my mother."

The Kid made it a point never to develop bad habits. He exercised habitually, even in jail, doing pushups, squats, and jumping jacks. After the escape, he was never allowed to mingle with the other prisoners and had to exercise alone, from eleven to midnight. He never smoked and never developed a taste for alcohol. No wonder he thought clearly and always thought something good was right around the corner. With a sad smile Red thought, "That outlaw was just about the most positive person I've ever known."

The Missouri Kid confirmed for Red that the wheel had turned. He was born in an era when vigilantism ruled Missouri, but that all faded as law enforcement grew into adulthood. The technology, from telephones to photographs and fingerprints, was powerful and always changing. Detectives were also scientists. The turn to psychology and patient, persevering investigation was more effective than all the blazing gun battles in history. Prosecutors worked more closely with police. The resources being brought to bear, from money to manpower to brains, were all working. And it all depended on communication.

At the same time, writers like Red emerged, doing what lawmen couldn't do. "We go where they can't go and hear things the best cops can't hear," he thought. "We keep everybody honest. We hold government accountable, like I did with Prosecutor Folk. Vigilantes of sorts, I suppose."

Because of the news, the pressure was always on both sides. Thanks to reporters like Red, people knew what the crooks were doing and whom to watch out for. And they knew how well or how badly the lawmen were doing at catching and punishing them. The newspaper was a mirror held up to law enforcement, a reflection from which they could not turn. And it kept the criminals moving and guessing, making their moves until they made the wrong move. For some, that didn't take long.

Then it hit him: The Missouri Kid was barely twenty when he killed agent Schumacher, and Ford was barely twenty when he killed Jesse James. "My God," thought Red, "when I was that age I was writing about men like them. The Kid was to hang at twenty-one. Ford was gone at thirty. Jesse James dead at thirty-five. O'Kelley made it to forty-seven, but only because he spent ten years in the safety of prison. At least the cop Joe Burnett made it to fifty.

"Some people have a rough start," he thought. "The Missouri Kid's mother gave him up to his father, and then his father gave him back.

James P. "Red" Galvin, self-made investigative journalist. Art by Joe Johnston.

His stepfather, Rudolph, was an unemployed drunk. O'Kelly's mother gave him away, then he came back and his wealthy father never liked him. Jesse James's father died when he was ten. Bob Ford's mother died when he was ten, after giving birth to ten children and watching half of them die young. But my beginnings weren't so different," Red thought. "My father died in his thirties, and I was a street-wandering newsboy at eight. As teenagers, Jesse and Frank James were guerrillas, chasing Yankees, and at that age I was chasing my first big stories.

It Ends Here

"James and Ford were both sons of preachers. Even O'Kelley and the cop who killed him were more alike than they knew. Both of their families lived in Arkansas before the Civil War, and their fathers joined the Union cavalry. After the war, Arkansas was so hostile to Union veterans, both families moved to Missouri. What made all the difference was the isolation of Edward O'Kelley, while the Burnetts stuck together, three brothers, two sisters, with their parents, spouses, and children, and they all came to be part of the exciting birth of Oklahoma.

"How we start at the same place and our roads turned out to be so different is a wonder. The high road is always there, but men like them make one wrong move after another," the tired reporter mused. "There but for the grace of God. . . ."

Red loved and hated those criminals whose names he had typed countless times, and he thought he saw them perhaps more clearly than anyone else. When he wrote about a robbery he knew the men—and women—behind it, even if they'd never met. He'd known so many of them, he knew how their patterns repeated. He felt their pain and desperation, their satisfaction when a job went right, and the emptiness that accompanied them as they moved on, one short step ahead of a bad end. Lonely people with no true friends in a world full of enemies. People who could never know peace, never fully enjoy a family's love.

For Red, writing a story was always like walking into a room and closing the door on everything outside. He became so enmeshed in the lives of the people he investigated, when he stopped writing he had to pause and remember his own story. He fingered the diamonds on his tie clasp. It was a hobby, collecting diamonds. An odd hobby, he knew, for a lowly freelance reporter. He once wore them in rings and on his pocket watch and fob. He carried a diamond-studded money clip. It was interesting, studying and trading in them. But in time he tired of the attention and the comments. Others made too much of it, so he rarely wore them anymore. Still, they were a good investment, and he was a very thrifty man, unlike most reporters. Counting the diamonds, he had about $50,000 in the bank.

He looked around at the *Republic's* long, walnut-paneled newsroom. It was empty except for him and the smells of newsprint, ink, and ashtrays. Neat stacks of lifeless paper sat waiting for reporters to breathe air into them. His desk lamp was on, and the light above the stairs, but the other lights were waiting. The typewriters waited. The editors' pencils waited. In a couple of hours it would all be a storm of inquiry and answers, from the weather forecast to the obituaries, the world's politics to St. Louis society parties.

It had been a long night. Red checked his watch, not surprised to see that it was a couple of minutes past four. He pushed his chair back and realized how tired he was. The little burgundy cushion on his chair had been a humorous Christmas present from Holy Joe Folk, but it didn't provide enough padding for an all-night reporter, he thought, smiling again. Starting a new day without sleep wasn't good for his health or his writing, but he could push on through. He would go home, wash his face, change clothes, get some breakfast, and see where the news led him next.

As he stood, something didn't feel right. A pain shot down his left arm. He couldn't quite get his breath, as if a great weight were on his chest. He collapsed back into the chair, reached toward the glass of water on the desk, and his head fell on the typewriter, mashing the keys into a knot, the final punctuation. The life of the tireless investigative reporter ended at his post, at the age of thirty-eight.

The postmaster sent flowers. Governor Charles P. Johnson spoke at the funeral, which was attended by senior editors, policemen, and elected officials. His honorary pallbearers included a Supreme Court justice, a lieutenant governor, and his old mentor, Frank O'Neil.

Chapter Sixteen
"Have You Lost Hope?"

The rainy March morning when George Collins went to kingdom come, closing arguments were made in the Kid's case. Then he was sent back to his cell, and court recessed during the execution of Collins. The Kid's jury was recalled immediately, and just as he had done for Collins, the judge gave the jury only two choices, guilty of first-degree murder or innocent. After deliberating for only thirty minutes, they found the Kid guilty, and he was sentenced to hang in just six weeks, on May 13. Before dark he was on a train back to the St. Louis jail, shackled between Jailer Dawson and another guard and surrounded by a dozen more. Though his family was not allowed to speak with him, they rode in the same car, as did Schumacher's widow.

Dawson and the Kid pointed and talked like schoolboys when the train entered St. Louis and passed the busy crowds and dazzling lights of the World's Fair. Dawson had taken his daughter Mary the first week it was open, and he told the Kid all about it. He pulled out a souvenir token from the Fair, a new 1904 Indian Head penny in a metal disc shaped like a chamber pot. The Kid smiled and said, "Yeah, that's where all my money went, in the pot." They laughed, but then the Kid's countenance darkened and he remarked, "Too bad I missed all of that. But most of the big ones who went to it have heard of me and some of them have come to see me."

Even a dark, rainy day couldn't discourage the eager crowds at the 1904 World's Fair. Library of Congress Prints and Photographs.

The Kid's lawyers appealed, but the conviction was upheld by a panel of the higher court. Because the whole court didn't hear that appeal, the lawyers won another delay from Governor Folk, pleading that the case should then be heard by the full Missouri Supreme Court. But the court refused to hear the case. Months passed, and finally the attorneys moved for the case to be heard by the U.S. Supreme Court on the very progressive argument that the Kid's constitutional rights had been violated; neither the Kid's nor Collins's case had gone to a grand jury, and the Constitution requires a grand jury before anyone can be tried for a capital offense.

It was a good argument, so the entire Supreme Court heard the case. One judge objected strongly to the conduct of the trial on two items introduced by the prosecution. One was the warrant for the Kid's arrest in the bank robbery, which was not pertinent to the murder, and the other was his little sister's affidavit in which the Kid told her he "got his man," which was hearsay. The dissenting judge said both "blackened" the character of the Kid without shedding any light on whether he was guilty of the murder. The court refused to overturn the conviction, but two of the justices wrote personal letters to Folk, urging him to commute the sentence to life in prison. However, Folk was firm, and the execution was reset for March 17.

When the Kid's attorneys told him the court's decision and the new execution date, he exclaimed, "Would they hang a man on St. Patrick's Day?"

Of course the Irish Catholic community wouldn't hear of it. Father McErlane had won the Kid's heart for the Lord, and, like he did for Collins, promised to be with him until the end. McErlane sent a letter to Governor Folk pleading for a change in the execution date, and Folk moved it to April of 1905. One last legal maneuver sent it to May 8. The Kid then wrote to Folk, asking, "I hope you will favor me with a chance to plead my case to you personally," but there was no reply.

There were many compassionate reasons to spare the Kid, including his youth, but there was also enormous pressure from prosecutors and the Pinkerton agency. Though the condemned man's mother and stepfather traveled to Jefferson City and met in person with Governor Folk to plead for the Kid's life, the governor would interfere no more. Nancy sat in the waiting room until the end of the day in the hope of seeing the governor again, and still he refused. She then went to the governor's mansion and pleaded to speak with Mrs. Folk, sure that she would prevail upon her husband to spare "her boy." When Nancy was turned away, she said, "I'll come again tomorrow and the day after and every day until he goes to the gallows. It will do the governor no good for my boy to hang." But the stepfather convinced Nancy that the battle was lost, and they boarded the late train to St. Louis, where they stayed at the home of their daughter Nellie Allen.

It Ends Here

Dawson came to the cell and told the Kid the governor's final word to Nancy. The convicted man shook his head and said in an uncharacteristically anguished voice, "I cannot to save me understand how he could refuse. It seems to me he would have considered the petitions of my friends and the personal appeal of my mother." Then, after composing himself, he sighed and added, "Well, if I must die, you will find me ready."

Mary Dawson came to say her farewell. She had been to visit Rudolph several times, and they'd become true friends. He who had no exposure to the arts in his life was always eager to hear of her piano lessons and the latest concert or play or opera she'd seen. He even asked his sister Nellie to buy a pair of engraved opera glasses for Mary, and when the girl came for their last visit, he gave her the glasses, wishing her happiness and many exciting nights at the theater.

Knowing the end was near, Nancy came to say goodbye. At night, with all the other prisoners locked away, she met with him in the pen of the St. Louis jail, but when she broke down sobbing, the warden moved them to his office. Still, guards hovered near as they spoke in hushed voices for thirty minutes. Then Nancy kissed his face and was gone.

Back when the Kid returned from Kansas he had fasted for a couple of days because he thought it would help him make the change to the starchy prison food. He was always disciplined that way. "I read a lot," he told Stephan O. Grady, a promising young reporter who had been assigned to finish Red Galvin's coverage of the case for the *Republic*. "I've read several novels. I enjoy poetry, and suppose I like the works of Wordsworth the best. I've read the Bible four times." For all his lawlessness, he just thought that somehow, some day, his regimen would make everything get better. If he could just do enough things right, he would get his feet back on the solid path. Grady asked him, "Have you lost hope?" "Not I," said Rudolph. "I'm not hanged until I'm hanged. My greatest pleasure is the visits from my mother, who comes two or three times a week, and usually stays two or three hours."

After the months of legal wrangling and delays in his hanging, punctuated with repeated "goodbyes" with his mother and his sisters, depression moved in and took an observable toll on the once-carefree Kid. He had always been polite and reserved, and he became even quieter. He stayed in his cell and stopped exercising. As a result, he gained over fifty pounds. His face was puffy, and he was no longer the debonair, daredevil bandit.

On the train to Union for his execution he was once again handcuffed between Jailer Dawson and another guard, and surrounded by a dozen more. A lone woman walked through the car, then two more. Soon two more, as the first ones returned and glanced over their shoulders at the prisoner. As the miles went by, it became obvious that the parade of women walking through the car all just wanted to get a look at the Kid. He leaned to Dawson and said, "We're going to have to charge the next one admission."

In the Union jail that evening, his sisters Nellie Allen and Esther Rudolph visited. McErlane stayed with him until about midnight, then he slept well after smiling and telling the guards, "Don't wake me up too early!" The priest was back at six for his confession and last rites. In honor of Red Galvin's interest in him, the Kid requested that the only reporter allowed in was Grady, the heir to Red's legacy. The young reporter saw Nancy and the stepfather come in for ten minutes. Then former sheriff Bruch held the door for the new sheriff, Louis Gehlert, when he came to read the execution order just before ten. Grady noted that the Kid asked to see Governor Folk's signature, then remarked to Gehlert that he had hoped there might be a last-minute commutation.

But he walked to the gallows deliberately and mounted the thirteen steps in front of a quiet crowd of 250. About 250 more milled around outside the highboard fence, unable to see, but somehow needing to be near. They were kept back fifty feet by rope barriers, while an army of guards with Winchester rifles surrounded the courthouse and lined the way to the gallows. Everybody whispered how brave he was for a man about to meet his maker. It seemed to Grady that the women present were especially well dressed, and most of them wept silently. But there was none of the circus atmosphere that accompanied the Collins hanging. Gone was the drama, the romance, the expectation of one more grand escape. Gone was the boy outlaw.

A particularly morbid Pinkerton agent had kept the rope used to hang Collins, and he brought it back to be used on the Kid. But when he handed it to Sheriff Gehlert they could see that souvenir hunters had made cuts and sliced pieces off the end, so it couldn't be used. Besides, to correct the mistake made by Bruch in using a new rope, Gehlert was ready with a pre-stretched rope. But contrary to hanging wisdom, the sheriff placed the knot upright behind the convict's left ear with no slack in the rope. He had never hanged a man before, and he didn't know that the knot should have been laid loosely on the shoulder, assuring a sharp *snap* at the end of the drop. A couple of minutes past eleven, May 8, 1905, Gehlert pulled the lever releasing the trap door, and it opened with a loud *ka-thunk*, followed by the squeak of hinges, ropes, and timbers. Rudolph dropped ten feet, rebounded up and down twice, and slowly turned to the left, but just like Collins, his neck didn't break. Doctors continued to take his pulse as the crowd grew restless and began to file out through the gate. At last, just like Collins, it took a horrifying thirteen minutes for William Rudolph to die by strangulation.

Chapter Seventeen
Beauty and Truth

On September 20, 1905, U.S. assistant district attorney H. L. Dyer walked into his office and his secretary pointed with her pencil in the direction of a thirty-year-old woman in a simple blue dress and black hat, her hair neatly arranged in a bun, seated in the waiting room. It was Laura Bullion, who had been released from the Walls the day before, after serving almost four years of her five-year sentence. While in prison she saved every penny she could from her wages and from sewing for the other inmates, giving her a nice little nest egg. She bought the new outfit and a train ticket to St. Louis, arriving that evening. After dozing on a bench in Union Station, at dawn she bought an apple from a street vendor and ate it as she walked to the federal building. There, she waited outside Dyer's door for the secretary to get to work, intent on pleading with Dyer for a reduction in Ben Kilpatrick's sentence so that they could begin their life together. Dyer wasn't persuaded. But Laura had spent years envisioning each step in this saga, so she simply moved ahead undaunted. After staying in St. Louis for a couple of days and talking with attorneys, she was convinced that her legal options for Kilpatrick were exhausted. So she took the train to Atlanta and rented a room in a boardinghouse a block from the prison.

Her first visit with Kilpatrick was filled with emotion that touched even the hardened guards. But the warden warned his staff that Kilpat-

The federal penitentiary in Atlanta, where Ben Kilpatrick wasted some of the best years of his life.

rick was as much of an escape risk as ever. After all, Butch Cassidy, the Sundance Kid, and others of Kilpatrick's old running mates were still on the loose. In fact, there was a good chance that Kilpatrick would use Laura to cook something up, something more creative than the warden or guards could dream. But such was not the case. The sweethearts declared their love for each other, talked about the letters they'd exchanged, and gazed into each other's eyes. Kilpatrick reluctantly said that he couldn't ask Laura to wait for him, and she was better off striking off in a new direction. But she wouldn't hear of it, swearing to wait for him faithfully. Still, the warden was so worried about an escape, he never allowed another visit.

True to her promise, Laura took a job as a waitress, then managed a boardinghouse, and waited for Kilpatrick. At last he was released June 11, 1911, after serving ten years of his fifteen-year sentence. For all his outlawry, Kilpatrick was a gentleman, and he would do no less

The Peabody Hotel in Memphis, shown in 1900, romantic rendezvous for Laura and Ben.

than provide for Laura the way he had before, in fine style. He would go straight, he promised her, and they would enjoy a long life together, never again on the dodge. But first he had to make a raise. No, she begged him, they would be fine without that. But his mind was made up. He whispered not to tell anyone their plans, and he would meet her in Memphis. Just get settled there, he said. Then go to the desk of the Peabody, the hotel where they last stayed so happily before all the trouble started in St. Louis, and leave him a message saying where to find her.

The law wasn't through with Kilpatrick. He still had a murder charge hanging over his head for the killing of Oliver Thornton, a rancher who was shot to death in March 1901 about a mile from where Kilpatrick was staying in Concho County, Texas. Kilpatrick was charged with the murder, even though Thornton was known to have accused two neighbors of stealing hogs. So Kilpatrick walked out of the Atlanta pen and into a Texas jail. His family got him a good Texas lawyer, and with a writ of habeas corpus asserting that he was arrested by the wrong lawman for the wrong crime and was being held in the wrong jail, he won his release.

Kilpatrick returned to Laura in Memphis, coming and going several times in the next few months. In prison he had met H. O. Beck, who was released about the same time and found a job in Memphis under the name Ole Hobeck. That fall and winter the pair were suspected in a series of bold train and bank robberies that paid very little. The thefts ranged over Oklahoma and Texas and included one in Arkansas, just west of Memphis, the day after Hobeck quit his job there. The descriptions of the two robbers matched Kilpatrick and Hobeck, though some of the robberies also included other men.

Kilpatrick and Hobeck were never arrested or even identified at the robberies by witnesses who knew them, and yet the law, banks, and railroad employees were all on alert for them in Tennessee, Arkansas, and especially Kilpatrick's old stomping ground, Texas. A woman thought she spotted Kilpatrick in Ozona, and someone suspected Hobeck was the man watching the bank in San Angelo. They were suspected when some horses were stolen. One night a man matching Kilpatrick's description chatted up the express agent at Sanderson, asking questions about the train from Del Rio, and then disappeared into the darkness.

Finally, in March 1912, Kilpatrick fell back on a plan that had worked before. He was going to rob the Galveston, Harrisburg, & San Antonio Railway Train No. 9, the same train he'd robbed with the Black Jack Ketchum Gang back in 1897. It gave a big payout before, so it should work again. The train pulled away from Del Rio about eight at night and stopped for water at Dryden. As it was pulling out, Kilpatrick and Hobeck left the passenger car, put masks over their faces and crawled over the tender to the engine with Winchesters leveled at the engineer and fireman. They ordered engineer D. E. Grosh to stop at an iron bridge about halfway between Dryden and Sanderson.

There they forced the crew to uncouple the passenger cars and leave them sitting on the track while they pulled a mile ahead with the engine, a combination baggage and mail car, and the Wells Fargo Express car. Hobeck held the engineer and fireman at gunpoint while Kilpatrick took the mail clerk, the clerk's helper, and the Wells Fargo messenger,

David A. Trousdale, poking them with his Winchester and growling commands at them. The safe in the combination car yielded just $37. After cutting open the mail sacks Kilpatrick realized there was nothing more to steal in that car so they moved on to the Wells Fargo car.

As tensions rose, Kilpatrick pushed away thoughts that this job was too big for two men. The Wild Bunch would have used six or seven. His instincts were dulled by years of gray prison routine. He didn't want to shoot anyone, and he only wanted this one strike so he and Laura could get a fresh start. But what if $37 was all he got? What if he had to shoot? Could he do it? What about Hobeck? If Hobeck was challenged, could he handle himself? Kilpatrick glanced at the Winchester 401SL in his hands and wondered if it was the right weapon. It was the newest and best semi-automatic, a high-power rifle that could bring down an elk. He had two revolvers. Maybe one of them would have been easier to handle in these close quarters. His mind whirled, when it should have been in sharp focus on the job at hand.

In the Wells Fargo Express car Kilpatrick opened a couple of boxes, then herded his three prisoners past several crates of iced oysters stacked in the middle of the car. Beside them was a wall of ice blocks, which Trousdale would periodically break up and crush, to replenish the ice in the crates as it melted and dripped through the floor of the car. The tools for that job included an ice pick and a mallet that looked like a miniature sledgehammer, with a large, round, oak head measuring six by nine inches mounted on a twenty-four-inch hickory handle.

Trousdale had never been held up, and he didn't intend to be. He was no timid clerk, like some express men. He was a baggage handler, a freight loader, and a veteran of years on loading docks working with all sorts of men. He'd won the assignment on that train partly because he could do the hard physical work of keeping the oysters chilled. He was also equal to the six-foot-two Tall Texan in stature, and he was not intimidated. On the other hand, he knew he would have only one chance, and he couldn't afford to give Kilpatrick an out.

It Ends Here

As they scooted past the oysters and Kilpatrick glanced around the car, Trousdale had an instant to grab the ice mallet, but not enough room for an attack, so he held it under his coat. It was a dangerous move, as Kilpatrick might spot it at any minute. They walked a couple more steps and Trousdale was thinking fast. He pointed to a heavy box on the floor and told Kilpatrick he didn't know what was in it, but the station agent had said it was valuable. Kilpatrick took the bait, leaning the rifle against his leg and reaching to pick up the box. Trousdale knew that was his only opportunity. Grabbing the ice mallet with both hands, he made one mighty, whirling, roundhouse swing, like he was chopping a log, catching Kilpatrick at the base of his skull, breaking his neck. The giant frame went limp, and Trousdale instantly followed with a blow to the top of the head, then another one, which made a noise like watermelon cracking on a brick floor. Blood and brains splattered everywhere. The gentleman who loved Laura so truly lay on the express-car floor in a heap.

Trousdale picked up the Winchester, took Kilpatrick's twin Colt .45 revolvers, and gave them to the crew men. He turned out the lights, and then all three men took cover at the other end of the car. Trousdale aimed the rifle at the door. About thirty minutes passed, but he would later say it seemed like two hours. When Kilpatrick still hadn't come back to the engine, Hobeck had to go investigate. Approaching the express car, he paused outside the door, where Trousdale could see him silhouetted in the window. Hobeck called out, "Kilpatrick, what's taking so long?" With no answer, he went in ready for trouble. Though he opened the door with his Winchester leveled, cocked, and ready to shoot, he never had a chance to pull the trigger. Trousdale dropped him with one shot that entered above the left eye, went out the other side and lodged in the wall of the train. When Trousdale found six sticks of dynamite on Hobeck and a bottle of nitroglycerin in Kilpatrick's pocket, he knew the day could have been a lot worse.

By the time the engineer got the steam back up, the crewmen got the cars coupled, and Trousdale and the clerk secured the money, mail,

Freight agent Trousdale, left, helps the other crewmen from the train hold up the dead bodies of Ben Kilpatrick, center, and H. O. Beck, on the station platform at Sanderson, Texas. Library of Congress Prints and Photographs.

and cargo, they finally rolled into Sanderson about five in the morning. News of the attempted holdup spread like spilled beer. Trousdale was hailed as a vigilante hero, as he and other men held up the bodies of the two would-be robbers for a photographer. Within an hour, telegrams and phone calls confirmed the identity of Ben Kilpatrick. Trousdale was presented with thousands of dollars in reward money from the railroad, the county, and Wells Fargo, which also gave him an engraved watch, plus a chain and engraved gold fob from the passengers on the train.

Kilpatrick was only successful when he fit himself into the mold of the Wild Bunch. He lacked the mental capacity for planning, and the leadership and charisma to attract dependable people. Without the gang, he could never make a big raise, but only stole enough money to get him to the next raise. He was always too hungry, too desperate for money, and that's why he was careless on the train, giving the vigilante express man a chance to end his life.

That was the end of one of the Old West's great outlaw romances, a love story that had an opportunity for beauty and truth, but that Kilpatrick threw away on one shortsighted, terrible idea. He could have spent his better years with the love of his life, instead of wrapped in a sheet with a common criminal whom he barely knew, buried together in one big wooden box at Cedar Grove Cemetery in dusty Sanderson, Texas.

The ever-romantic Laura took a room at the Peabody and cried until she could cry no more. Then she went back to her little boardinghouse and her job, sewing and upholstering for a furniture company. She was only thirty-one years old. She took the name Freda and, in time, met a man. Then another. She filed a military pension application as the widow of Maurice Lincoln, who was a veteran of a state militia, not the U.S. military, so the pension was denied. When her hands became too weak to sew in the 1950s, the furniture company kept her on as an interior designer. Laura lived into her eighties, though she adopted a habit of reporting her age as ten years younger. She was laid to rest in Memphis with both the names Freda Bullion Lincoln and Laura Bullion on her gravestone. But for all her aliases and fictional biographies, Laura knew exactly who she was, as evidenced by her epitaph, the "Thorny Rose."

Epilogue

With great fanfare Frank James surrendered to Governor Crittenden, handing over his pistols before hundreds of reporters and politicians. He then stood trial for the murder during the Glendale train robbery. Dick Liddil was a stooge for the government and railroads, testifying against the man who once trusted him with his life. But Frank was found not guilty, largely because he had lived long enough to be a legend, rather than a threat. That, and the fact that on the witness stand he quoted the Bible and Shakespeare and had a procession of witnesses who were eager to provide alibis. Alabama then charged him with the Muscle Shoals payroll job, and again, the only witness was Liddil. But by that time he was a confessed, convicted, and pardoned felon, so that case never went to trial. In one clever stroke Frank was arrested in Missouri for the Northfield, Minnesota, bank robbery. When no one could testify against him, a Missouri judge found him innocent, meaning Frank never had to return to Minnesota for trial.

He enjoyed a varied career, from selling shoes in a Dallas store to clerking and starting races at a horse track, and he even did a little amateur Shakespearean acting. Around 1909 he settled with his wife and son on a one-hundred-acre farm in Fletcher, Oklahoma. But at his age farming was hard, and after a few years they moved back to Excelsior, Missouri, and he gave tours of the old James-Samuel family farm. He

Left: Frank James in 1898. Right: Zerelda James Samuel, mother of Jesse and Frank, is shown in 1892. Both from Library of Congress Prints and Photographs.

died in 1915 at the age of seventy-two, leaving his wife, Annie Ralston James, and a son, Jesse.

In her old age, Zerelda James Samuel, mother of Jesse and Frank, spent the winters with Frank in Fletcher, Oklahoma, and the summers with John Samuel, a half-brother to the James boys, in Excelsior. The afternoon of February 11, 1911, she was with Frank's wife, Annie, in a sleeper car on the Frisco train, on her way to visit Frank's son, Jesse, in Kansas City. As the train reached Oklahoma City, she died, almost exactly seven years after Ed O'Kelley, Jesse's avenger, was killed in the same city.

+——+——+

James Robert Cummins, like Frank, was one of the few who truly changed his life. After settling down in Kearney, Missouri, the sixty-three-year-old Cummins married local widow Florence Sherwood. Tragically, she died later that year. Since Windy Jim was not only a former guerrilla, but also a veteran enlisted Confederate soldier, he was entitled to move into the Confederate Soldiers Home at Higginsville, Missouri. There, he wrote a book about his exploits that was published in 1906. One day in 1909 another resident attacked him, and his old instincts kicked in. In a clear case of self-defense, when the other man wouldn't stop throwing punches, Cummins clubbed the man with a chair, killing him. Cummins became the oldest surviving member of the James Gang, dying at the home in 1929.

+——+——+

Bill "Whiskey Head" Ryan, who was sentenced in October 1881 to twenty-five years for the Glendale train robbery, was pardoned and re-leased in 1889. One night not long after his release, he was drunk as usual and galloped his horse full speed under a tree branch, which hit him in the head, killing him instantly.

+——+——+

Dick Liddil disappeared after parting company with Bob Ford in the mid-1880s, showing up in Kansas City in 1891. Then, when he went to visit friends in Ray County, site of Martha Boulton's house where Wood Hite was killed ten years before, he was surprised to be arrested for the Hite murder. However, the prosecutor quickly determined that there were no witnesses and no evidence, and honestly, nobody cared any-more, so the charge was dropped. Three months later Liddil keeled over dead from a heart attack at a Kentucky racetrack at forty-eight years old.

+——+——+

Margaret Ann O'Kelley, Ed's mother, died in 1903, deprived of ever seeing her firstborn after he left more than twenty years before. Ed's father, Thomas, applied for his veteran's pension in 1915, and when asked to name all his children, living or dead, he omitted Ed—and it wasn't because Ed was deceased, as evidenced by the fact that he listed Hugh, who was also deceased. It was a final affront to the son of whom he was ashamed. In his declining years Thomas was on crutches and unable to practice medicine. He parceled out his sprawling farm to his living children and passed away in 1925.

To support his military pension application, Thomas O'Kelley wrote his children's names in his Bible, something he apparently failed to do as each one was born. Again, he left Edward out.

After the life-and-death fight with O'Kelley, Officer Joe Burnett spent six weeks recovering from his wounds, then returned to duty, and was in another running gun battle two months later. In 1910 he was in chase and gunfight with a man who had murdered a fellow officer. Burnett, a Democrat, was promoted to assistant chief, night shift, until the change to a Republican city administration led to his firing along with many other officers. Two years later the politics shifted again, and he was reinstated as assistant chief. In 1917 he suffered a stroke, which doctors believed was the long-term effect of the pistol whipping he received from O'Kelley. He died two weeks later and was buried in the same cemetery that contains the pauper's grave of O'Kelley. The *Daily Oklahoman* honored him as Oklahoma City's longest-serving policeman. He left a wife and six children. There were twenty automobiles in the funeral procession, and the force operated on a skeleton crew that day so officers could attend.

Joe Burnett's parents and siblings all outlived him. His youngest sister moved with her husband to Colorado, about 150 miles from Creede, and his other sister moved with her husband to Fletcher, Oklahoma, where they were neighbors of Frank and Annie James.

+———+———+

After the crash in silver prices, Soapy Smith re-established himself in Denver, but he began to wear out his welcome after a series of run-ins with the law. In one scrape, Bob Ford's drinking buddy Joe Palmer saved Smith from an irate drunk trying to kill him, and got both his thumbs shot off in the process. In 1897 Smith and Joe followed the get-rich-quick crowds to Skagway during Alaska's gold rush. There he tried to build another vigilante empire, but in the face of an already-entrenched vigilante empire. One of their men killed him in a gunfight at the snowy Juneau waterfront in 1889.

+———+———+

Two months after Red Galvin died, the people of Missouri showed their appreciation for his corruption-busting with Holy Joe Folk by electing Folk governor. Red never got to cover the Missouri Kid's hanging. But he knew how the story would end. In fact, he knew it was only a page in the final chapter that the hand of history had written across the face of Missouri. Men like Jesse James, Ben "the Tall Texan" Kilpatrick, Edward "Red" O'Kelley, and William "the Missouri Kid" Rudolph, and even women like Laura "Desert Rose" Bullion, were anachronisms. As soon as they came into existence, they were doomed. It was an era of committing crimes on horseback and riding to jail in an automobile. Though there had been a time when outlaws like them feared vigilantes, the day had come when they truly and rightly were more afraid of the law.

It Ends Here

Some figured out that they could outrun local people who might take the law into their own hands. Once the Kid and Collins left Stanton, they didn't have to worry about a lynch mob any more. The Wild Bunch traveled from Wyoming to New York, Texas, and Bolivia, on endless rail lines and improved gravel roads. They lost themselves in big towns with dozens of hotels and crowds of people. There were so many men in the James Gang, and even more men and women in the Wild Bunch, nobody knew for sure who participated in which jobs.

The men and women in those gangs were wildly individual, but willing to follow orders to accomplish their crimes. They had superior scouting and planning, and never pulled a robbery unless they had enough people to execute the plan. And when it was done they traveled great distances to preselected hiding places, then waited a long time before the next job. That's why the James Gang rode for seventeen years, the Wild Bunch for five years, and longer for Cassidy and Sundance. Though individuals in the gangs committed murders, most of their robberies were carried off without killing. And they went for big, impersonal hauls from railroads and banks, not from individuals. A local lynch mob would go after a cattle rustler or hog thief, but it was a lot harder to get the neighbors to travel three hundred miles to avenge the railroad's losses.

As much as some, like the Kid, thrilled at having their picture taken in fine clothes, they hated seeing those pictures in the newspapers. They knew change had come. There were more lawmen, highly trained, with time and resources to stay on a case like a dog on a bone. And they specialized; there were detectives, city police, county investigators, insurance investigators, private eyes, Pinkertons, and U.S. marshals, and they all became increasingly savvy about what it takes to assemble the evidence that would ensure a conviction. They were constantly connected by a web of telegrams, telephones, trains, automobiles, and photographs. Police in Springfield could trust the police in Denver to help hunt Missouri fugitives before they became Colorado criminals.

And once the Kid's photograph was discovered in St. Joseph, it was only an express train ride away from the Connecticut police.

Red was wrong about one thing. Edward O'Kelley was not Missouri's last vigilante. Maybe there will always be another someone willing to take up that sword. But the old-style vigilante became a man with a schedule: He works at a regular job that provides a regular paycheck to support his family. Mothers don't want their husbands trading gunfire with fugitives. They want someone else who's paid to do that. The wilderness has filled up with people, roads, fences, and towns, so there are fewer places for outlaws to hide. Streetlamps shine a light on both the good and the bad.

And while civilians are no longer interested in going nose to nose with hardened criminals, they understand that the law needs their help. A description, a tip, a name, might be all the police need to close a case. The banker who spotted Ben Kilpatrick's forged banknotes was a genteel clerk who was alert enough and brave enough to bring down a fugitive who'd been on the run for years.

So there is hope after all. Not in vigilantes, because the vigilante deals in fear, not hope. In punishment, not justice. In violence, not salvation. And hope is only tangentially in good laws, brave cops, and stout prisons, because they are the last defense. Even a good upbringing in a good family isn't the ultimate hope; plenty of the worst criminals emerged from the best families, and plenty of good men like Red Galvin made themselves from the roughest of beginnings. The true hope was, and is, in the will of the human heart to do the right thing.

Maybe the book of Genesis is right, and there will always be evil people. So far we haven't evolved past greed, selfishness, envy, twisted minds, and hardened hearts. But the only real danger is in succumbing to that belief, and the only real hope is in pressing on. A little at a time, one kind act, one brave act, one self-sacrificing act at a time, people embrace life, and in so doing, make it better for those following.

Acknowledgments

My heartfelt thanks to the Missouri History Museum and Victoria Monks, who had the vision to make this historical trilogy a reality. Also, my deepest gratitude to Lauren Mitchell, editor, guide, and encourager. And to Keri McBride, who beckons the public to discover our books.

This book would not have been possible without the research and historical interpretation skills of Carole Goggin. She didn't know exactly where the project would lead, but she jumped in unafraid, and all along the way, her enthusiasm, resourcefulness, and creativity added to the adventure.

Also, thanks to Graham Lee Brewer, accomplished journalist and our Oklahoma City researcher. His resourcefulness and reporter's instincts were fuel for the forge. Thanks to my friend Russ Tallchief, whose vast community of friends led me to Graham. We also had help with Oklahoma City historical details and photos from Ron Owens and Steve Lackmeyer.

Sending thanks to Jason Stratman of the Missouri History Museum for wide-ranging research at home and afar. He repeatedly rose to the challenge of finding what no one else could find. Jan Jacobs and Bob Seago helped search the Creede Historical Society archives.

Finally, thanks to my beautiful wife, Becky, for her faithfulness and encouragement. She's an inspiration to everyone who knows her. And my gratitude to Luke, Will, Dedee, Eli, and Jessica, for reminding me every day how blessed we all are.

Notable Sources

Burton, Jeffrey. *The Deadliest Outlaws: The Ketchum Gang and the Wild Bunch*. Denton: University of North Texas Press, 2009.

Edwards, John N. *Noted Guerrillas*. New York: Morningside Bookshop, 1975.

Everybody's Magazine 14, 1906.

Friedman, Morris. *The Pinkerton's Labor Spy*. Chatsworth, CA: Wilshire Book Company, 1907.

Horan, James D. *Desperate Men: The James Gang and the Wild Bunch*. Rev. ed. Lincoln: University of Nebraska Press, 1997.

James, Jesse, Jr. *Jesse James, My Father*. Cleveland: Buckeye Publishing, 1899.

Love, Robertus. *The Rise and Fall of Jesse James*. Lincoln: University of Nebraska Press, 1990.

Missouri General Assembly, House of Representatives. *Journal of the House of Representatives of the State of Missouri at the 26th Session of the General Assembly*. 1883.

Owens, Ron. *Oklahoma Heroes: The Oklahoma Peace Officers Memorial*, Nashville: Turner Publishing Company, 2000.

———. *Oklahoma Justice: The Oklahoma City Police, a Century of Gunfighters, Gangsters and* Terrorists. Nashville: Turner Publishing Company, 1995.

Petersen, Paul R. *Quantrill of Missouri—The Making of a Guerrilla Warrior: The Man, the Myth, the Soldier*. Nashville: Cumberland House, 2003.

Petrone, Gerard S. *Judgment at Gallatin: The Trial of Frank James.* Lubbock: Texas Tech University Press, 1998.

Pinkerton, A. Frank. *Jim Cummings: Or, The Great Adams Express Robbery.* Chicago: Laird & Lee, 1887.

Piott, Steven L. *Holy Joe: Joseph W. Folk and the Missouri Idea.* Columbia: University of Missouri Press, 1997.

Ree, Dorothy. *Walsenburg: Crossroads Town,* Author, 2006.

Ries, Judith. *Ed O'Kelley: The Man Who Murdered Jesse James' Murderer.* St. Louis: Patches Publications, 1994.

Ross, Kirby, ed. *Autobiography of Samuel S. Hildebrand.* Fayetteville: University of Arkansas Press, 2005.

Southern Law Review and Chart of the Southern Law and Collection Union, Volume 8. Nashville: Roberts & Purvis, 1883.

Stewart, Roy. *Born Grown.* Nashville: Turner Publishing Company, 1995.

Stiles, T. J. *Jesse James: Last Rebel of the Civil War.* New York: Knopf, 2002.

The War of the Rebellion: A Compilation of the Official Records of the Union and Confederate Armies. Washington, DC: Government Printing Office, 1880.

Yeatman, Ted P. *Frank and Jesse James: The Story Behind the Legend.* Nashville: Cumberland House Publishing, 2003.

Newspapers
Canadian Free Press (Canadian, Texas)
Daily Oklahoman
Daily Times-Journal
Evening Gazette
Oklahoma City Times
St. Louis Globe-Democrat
St. Louis Post-Dispatch
St. Louis Republic

Index

About the Author

Missouri native Joe Johnston is the author of *The Mack Marsden Murder Mystery: Vigilantism or Justice?* and *Necessary Evil: Settling Missouri with a Rope and a Gun*, both award-winning books published by the Missouri History Museum as part of its Missouri Vigilantes series. He is a frequent contributor to such magazines as *Wild West*, *True West*, and *America's Civil War*. He's an accomplished writer, artist, and songwriter, who now lives in Tennessee.